Ready *to* HANG

Ready *to* HANG

Seven Famous New Orleans Murders

ROBERT TALLANT

PELICAN PUBLISHING COMPANY
GRETNA 2012

First edition, 1952
First Pelican edition, 2012

*The word "Pelican" and the depiction of a pelican
are trademarks of Pelican Publishing Company, Inc.,
and are registered in the U.S. Patent and Trademark Office.*

Library of Congress catalog card number: 52-5475

ISBN 9781455616664

Printed in the United States of America
Published by Pelican Publishing Company, Inc.
1000 Burmaster Street, Gretna, Louisiana 70053

CONTENTS

INTRODUCTION

One December afternoon a friend and I were sitting at the windows of a hotel suite in New York looking down into Central Park. It was a gloomy day, a light snow was falling, and the world outside was drawn with pen and ink. The only life visible to our view was the occasional appearance of a human being, fastened to a leash, and in the process of being dragged by a dog through one of the park lanes below. As we watched, a blonde in a fur coat was pulled into our range of vision by a poodle, and soon vanished into a curving path. Then, quite suddenly, the dog reappeared, its leash dragging, and, as we watched, departed the park, running across the street beneath us.

"That's nice," I said. "I wonder where the blonde is?"

"Oh, she's been murdered," my friend replied. "It happens all the time."

"Fine," I said. "That's why I like New York. Never dull. Of course it could happen in New Orleans too, but never while I'm watching."

For several seconds I reflected solemnly upon what might have occurred. Beyond that gentle curve in the lonely path there had awaited a dark Shape. Probably It had been crouching in some bushes, waiting and leering fiendishly. The blonde had come into the path, passing the bushes. There had been the flash of a glittering blade, a muffled shriek—or perhaps the deed had been done with a silk scarf and there had been no outcry at all. The terrified poodle had fled. Motive? A discarded lover, a jealous husband, an outraged wife, or perhaps the Shape had been a maniac on the loose. I had discarded both the knife and the scarf as weapons and replaced

vii

them with naked, insanely strong fingers against the windpipe, when the blonde reappeared, giving chase to her dog, and opening and closing her mouth in yells we couldn't hear.

"We've had some pretty good murders in New Orleans whether you saw them or not," said my friend, and not without indignation, for he was from New Orleans too. "There was the Annie Crawford case. Since that happened before you were born you couldn't have been there. I've always thought it compared very well to Lizzie Borden's affair."

"I ought to do a book about New Orleans murders," I said.

"It would be nice to be able to talk about something without you feeling you should do a book about it," he told me. "But, anyway, Annie Crawford was wonderful. She loved to go to lots of funerals."

"I've always wanted to do a story about Kate Townsend," I said.

"You would," he said. "No one mentions any subject—"

"And what about the Lamana case?" I asked. "People were still talking about it when I was small. Mean parents had a fine time frightening their children by talking about it."

"The Crawford case was the best of all," he insisted.

"What about the Axman?" I asked. "I can remember that excitement vaguely. Of course I never saw him."

"That was pretty wonderful," he admitted.

"I've always been interested in Dr. Deschamps," I said.

"Let me tell you about the Crawford affair," he said. "The Crawfords lived in what used to be called a 'camelback' house on Peters Avenue. One day Elise came home from the office where she was working feeling quite sick. . . ."

That is actually how this book began. As soon as I was back in New Orleans I began thinking about murder, so to speak.

In selecting the cases I waded in gore so deep that I am convinced New Orleans need never apologize for its murder history. The city did not earn its appellation of "Hell on earth" without good reason, a nickname it retained, at least among some types of visitors, from a period beginning some decades before the Civil War until a time within the memory of living persons. In 1849 a visitor from New England wrote his wife (let us hope with some exaggeration), "The corpse of a murdered man can lie in a New Orleans street for three days without the citizens paying it the slightest notice. Only the odor of decomposition stirs them into action."

No one can really believe that, yet on Christmas Day, 1859, a New Orleans newspaper, the *True Delta*, reported that "murder seems to be one of the daily recurring topics of the city papers; the record of one deed of blood has hardly dried upon the paper when another recital of crime has to follow it; each chapter a brutal and bloody continuation of the preceding." And in the years immediately following the Civil War homicide was so rampant that it was charged that the city government itself was in the hands of criminals, an accusation that seems to have been sometimes entirely and· often partially true. As late as 1883 someone wrote in the *Mascot*, a publication popular among the sporting fraternity, that "Nine-tenths of the criminals arrested are city employees." In 1885 the Orleans Parish Grand Jury called to the attention of the mayor the fact that it was a common practice of city employees to carry revolvers "and commit lawless acts."

However, the vast majority of the murders so frequent during those years were of the type described by Thomas De Quincy as that of "a knife, a purse, and a dark lane." Such ordinary homicide is seldom of much interest except to those persons immediately involved. The motive is always the same—robbery—the weapons, and usually the people, are ordinary. For one thing murder by a stranger, of a stranger, is almost invariably dull. Murder, like all climacterics, is an intimate and very personal affair, and if one is to be done in the service should be rendered by a lover, a friend, an enemy, or at least a relative. This does not deprive murder for gain of all interest. Profit may have been the motive behind the removal from this earth of the Crawfords, although, on the other hand, it may have been simply that someone liked to go to funerals. Troisville Sykes may have slain Miss Kate for an inheritance he was sure would be his; on the other hand he may have slashed her to slithers of festering fat simply to free himself from a bondage that had became unbearable. Kenneth Neu needed money, but there were other elements involved. It does seem that profit alone is not enough, insofar as an interesting murder motive is concerned.

I have endeavored to choose a variety of cases and also some that were in one way or another as typical of New Orleans as it is possible for murder to be typical of a city. Murder has, of course, no particular or preferable locale, for it is as international as love, so it was possible to find New Orleans characteristics only in some of the people involved, in the reactions and general behavior of the citizenry, and in the backgrounds against which the dramas were played. But those elements make a difference.

I wish to thank all those who told me what they could recall of these cases, the members of the New Orleans Police Department who assisted in the finding of material, the publishers of the *Times-Picayune*, the *New Orleans States*, and the *New Orleans Item*, and especially John Hall Jacobs, Miss Margaret Ruckert, and the staff of the New Orleans Public Library. I should also like to express my gratitude to the unknown blonde in Central Park, who was not murdered, at least not then, and to her poodle.

ROBERT TALLANT

New Orleans
1952

READY TO HANG

MURDER IN BASIN STREET

On Saturday morning, November 3, 1883, Mr. Troisville Sykes left the residence of Miss Kate Townsend at No. 40 Basin Street a few minutes after nine o'clock and set out, as was his daily custom, for a stroll before breakfast.

Few people were up and about in Basin Street at this hour, for it was the habit of the residents to sleep late, and Mr. Sykes passed doors and windows as closed against the morning sun as were the eyes of the "female boarders" beyond them. At the corner of Canal Street Officers Clarke and Hormle stood just outside the swinging doors of a saloon. Mr. Sykes bowed to these men, offered a comment on the fine weather which was persisting so late this year, and went his way, turning into Canal Street, the principal business thoroughfare of New Orleans, where there was more activity, with carriages and horsecars rumbling past and men of business going about their affairs.

As he vanished, one of the policemen remarked casually to the other that Mr. Sykes, in his dignified black suit and pearl gray waistcoat and hat, with his trim beard and waxed mustaches, and swinging his cane with such an air, had all the appearance of a gentleman, and that it was "a pity. . . ."

Basin Street was now enjoying one of its most tranquil hours, but the policemen knew there was little hope that it would remain so peaceful. They entered the saloon, ordered beers, and chatted with the bartender. Ahead lay a long day on a beat where almost anything might happen. They probably did not foresee murder.

One hour after he had started out, almost to the minute, for he was a man precise in his habits, Troisville Sykes, still bearing him-

1

self in his usual jaunty manner, retraced his steps to the mansion of Kate Townsend. He entered by the front door with his own key, then closed the door, of heavy oak, ornately carved and further embellished with a pane of thick cut glass, behind him. For a long time after that the silence of the street was disturbed only by the occasional clatter of horses' hoofs as a carriage or a wagon traversed the thoroughfare. Once there was the low sweet whistle of a colored boy carrying a basket of goceries down an alley between two of the houses.

It was nearly eleven o'clock when the elaborate door of the Townsend house opened and a colored woman, her head wrapped in a red *tignon*, and holding an empty water tumbler in her hand, ran down the steps to the banquette. From somewhere within the depths of the house came a high shrill scream. Then a white woman with rumpled hair and wearing a bright yellow satin kimono ran out and turned in at the house next door, where she beat upon the knocker with frantic haste.

The padded slippers of the colored woman sped toward the corner, and as she ran she wept. She pushed through the saloon doors. Of the gaping bartender she demanded fifteen cents of whisky, proffering her glass, still crying and shivering with terror. Officers Clarke and Hormle, recognizing her as Rosa Garcia, Kate Townsend's cook, were at her side in an instant. When she reached the street again, holding fast to her glass of bourbon, she was far behind the officers as they ran toward the house.

Basin Street came alive now. All along the block doors opened, and women, most of them in night dress and brilliant kimonos and wrappers, came out, chattering excitedly and fumbling with their hair. Most of their faces were streaked and smudged with last night's paint. Jewels glittered in their ears and upon their fingers and arms. They were full-bodied, plump women, whose large breasts quivered under the thin coverings of silk and lace. They held up their trailing garments as they crossed the cobble-stones to gather outside the Townsend house, or perched upon their stoops, some of them boldly smoking cigarettes. Here and there a man, who had dressed hastily and who wore trousers from which suspenders were hitched up over a collarless shirt, joined them for a few minutes, then vanished inside a house again, to reappear completely garbed, wearing hat and gloves, and sometimes in evening clothes, and did his best to appear to be a passerby attracted by the excitement. One gentleman held a small black mask over his eyes.

When Officers Clarke and Hormle reached their destination they had to force their way between the women who crowded the hall outside the ground floor room belonging to the mistress of the establishment. They glanced upon what lay upon the huge fourpost bed in that room. Officer Clarke turned quickly and strode out of the room. Officer Hormle remained to stare at Kate Townsend, stretched across her bed, clothed only in a chemise, now slashed and torn and crimson with blood, her monstrous breasts and abdomen stabbed and hacked, her feet resting in a pool of her blood on the carpet. Above the body, suspended from the center of the tester of the bed, a basket of fresh-cut flowers—roses as red as the gore beneath them and white bridal wreath—swayed slightly as the women in the room moved about. Rosa Garcia came in then with the whisky, and Mollie Johnson, one of the "boarders," snatched the glass from her hand, and, dropping to her knees, tried to rub life back into the body on the bed, by chafing the hands and the feet, the wrists and the ankles.

Officer Clarke found the street outside already crowded. Now people were hurrying toward the house from all over the neighborhood, even from Canal Street. A carriage appeared, and Clarke, recognizing Dr. Veasey, on his way to the Charity Hospital, a few blocks away, called to him, and the doctor drew up his horses, sprang from the vehicle, and followed the policeman into the house.

Dr. Veasey found it necessary to look only once at the body. He said, "She's been dead too long to talk about."

Mollie Johnson stopped her work upon the legs, now turning cold under her whisky-soaked hands, and told Dr. Veasey that she had already fetched Dr. Charles W. Lewis from next door. Dr. Lewis, she said, was now upstairs with Mr. Sykes, who was "cut and bleeding." Followed by Officer Clarke, Dr. Veasey left the room and climbed the stairs leading from the hall outside.

Then there came the sound of whining, and a diminutive black and tan dog crawled from beneath the bed. The animal was borne out of sight by one of the women. Only once in all the newspaper accounts of the murder of Kate Townsend is her pet mentioned. One wonders what became of it.

Upstairs, Dr. Veasey and Officer Clarke found Sykes waiting. Dr. Lewis had dressed his wounds, a deep gash on the inner right thigh and some scratches on his chest, and helped him into fresh clothing. In one corner of the small room off a gallery lay his black trousers, one leg slashed and stained with blood, a ripped and torn undershirt, and a pair of drawers, cut in half, also covered with blood.

Sykes turned to Clarke and said, "I'm going to give myself up. I had to do it." On the way downstairs he added, "She drew the knife on me and I took it away. Then she drew the scissors and I cut her."

A reporter from the *Daily Picayune*, arriving as Sykes reached the lower hall, attempted to question him, but "the man seemed incapable of speech. For a moment his eyes wandered restlessly, until they reached the door of the room wherein lay his slaughtered paramour, and then he said, 'Don't press me to answer; I'll tell you some other time.' "

The crowd outside numbered more than three thousand persons by now. Sykes, limping and in pain, was helped into a carriage and driven away with Officer Clarke. A Sergeant Grabert was assigned to keep the mob in order, and this he did "only with great difficulty," according to that *Daily Picayune* which appeared the next day. When the crowd was quieter the sergeant began a search for the weapon, and, with the aid of Mr. Charles Donneaud, a reporter for the *Times-Democrat*, he soon found not one weapon, but two. In a few minutes the policeman appeared on the steps before the house and held up a bowie knife with a nine-inch blade. "When the bloody weapon was produced and held up to the crowd, a cry of horror came from the females present," said the *Daily States* that afternoon. "Soon afterwards another bloodstained weapon was exhibited. It was a pair of pruning shears—doubtless the weapon referred to by Sykes when he spoke of the scissors."

Troisville Sykes (the papers sometimes spelled his given name "Tresville," and once even "Travail," but he was known as "Bill" Sykes to his friends of Basin Street, in a possible reference to the Charles Dickens character) had gone straight to his own room upon returning from his morning walk. Divesting himself of coat, shirt, and cravat, he proceeded downstairs in his trousers and undershirt. He found Marie Philomene, the mulatto housekeeper, in the dining room, asked her to bring him a cup of coffee and a cinnamon roll, and seated himself at one end of the polished mahogany table. When the housekeeper returned with his breakfast his face was buried in his hands, and Marie Philomene thought he looked very unhappy. She was about to ask him a discreet question when Kate Townsend rang her bell. Marie Philomene hurried to answer, for Miss Kate had been in a bad mood during the past few days, as she always was when she was drinking.

Miss Kate's room was across the hall from the dining room. Marie Philomene knocked lightly and, in an irritable tone of voice, Miss Kate bade her enter. The madam of the house was standing at a window, looking out, clad only in her chemise, her bare feet sinking into the carpet. Her face was bloated and her eyes were bloodshot, but it was something else that startled the mulatto woman. In one of her fat hands Miss Kate held a bowie knife, a vicious instrument, upon the surface of which reflected the glittering diamonds of the fingers that held it.

She snapped at Marie Philomene, ordering her to bring her coffee at once. Then noticing the housekeeper's eyes could not leave the knife, she added the information that she had been cutting her corns. As Marie Philomene turned to go, she called after her and asked her where was "that —— Sykes?" Later Marie Philomene reported that Miss Kate had used a horrid word she could not bring herself to repeat and that she had replied that Mr. Sykes was in the dining room having his coffee.

"Tell him I want to see him right away" had been Miss Kate's reply.

Marie Philomene delivered the message to Sykes, and, a few minutes later, returned to the room with the coffee. Miss Kate had seated herself at a small table; Sykes was standing. They both looked angry. The knife was not in view.

The housekeeper left them as quickly as possible and repaired to the kitchen, where she engaged in conversation with Rosa Garcia. Rosa volunteered the information that Miss Kate and Miss Mollie had been out late the evening before in the company of two gentlemen. A bit later both the housekeeper and the cook heard Miss Kate and Sykes quarreling, but, as this was far from unusual, neither paid much attention.

However, as the shouts grew louder, Marie Philomene said to Rosa that maybe "she ought to go see," left the kitchen, crossed the hall and put an ear to the door of her mistress's room. She was never able to remember a word that she heard, except that the argument "had something to do with money." Miss Kate then released a particularly loud cry, so Marie Philomene, though she had doubts as to the propriety of entering, pushed the door ajar. Both Miss Kate and Sykes stood in the middle of the room facing each other. Sykes swung around and said angrily, "Never mind, Philomene; go about your business. I can attend to this affair."

The housekeeper then backed out of the room. Sykes shut the door behind her and she heard the key turn in the lock. She paused in the hall a moment or two, but could not hear anything else. She was certain that at that time neither Sykes nor Miss Kate held any weapon in their hands. Neither was there any sign of blood.

Back in the kitchen she and Rosa discussed the quarrels between Miss Kate and her "fancy man," then she went out into the back yard to attend to some chore. Rosa was making hash for the "big" twelve o'clock breakfast.

A few minutes later there were loud screams from behind the door of Kate Townsend's room. Almost simultaneously Sykes called to Rosa from the hall.

He had "a wild look in his eyes" when Rosa reached him. He said, "She's gone, Rosa."

The colored woman cried, "What have you done, Mr. Sykes?"

Then the housekeeper joined them in the hall, and the women stared at Sykes. His undershirt and trousers were torn, and blood dripped from him as he moved away from them and went to the door of Mollie Johnson's room, which was down the hall just beyond the gleaming staircase. Mollie Johnson appeared at the door as he reached it. He said, "My God, I had to do it, Mollie. Don't call the police yet. I'm going to change my clothes and give myself up." He turned immediately and went up the stairs, staggering, and clutching the railing tightly.

Miss Mollie ran at once to the door of Miss Kate's room. She pushed it open. She screamed. The other "female boarders" began appearing, uttering shrieks as they saw within the room. Miss Mollie, composing herself, then ordered Rosa to take a glass and to go out and buy whisky (evidently only wines were kept in the house), and sent Marie Philomene to the kitchen for ice.

The residents of New Orleans were interested in many things that November in 1883. They were already discussing the forthcoming presidential election. President Arthur had visited the city not long before, and "What this country needs is a good five-cent cigar!" was the popular expression of the day. The newspapers that very day of the third had reported a race riot in Virginia, and that the Crees of South Dakota were on the warpath, plundering ranches and carrying off cattle. New Orleans, at last recovering from the long headache of Reconstruction, was enjoying a momentous theatrical season, with two operatic, three dramatic, and numerous other kinds of performances being presented nightly. It was even expected that the great Henry Irving, who had just arrived in New York from London, would honor the city with a presentation of his current success, *Louis XI.*

There was a rumor prevalent of a cholera epidemic breaking out in Europe, and New Orleanians, not unfamiliar with the dread disease, shuddered. The City Hall officials had ordered the repair of two garbage boats upon the river and taken other precautions. The new winter fashion for the ladies was "masher" hats. Gentlemen were reported to be wearing silk underwear and nightgowns, according to the advertisements, "of the most fine imported pongee, exquisitely embroidered in a variety of colored flower patterns at the wrists and collar and down the front." Professor Allen Curr was lecturing in the basement of the Felicity Street Methodist Church on the subject: "The Master Passion, or Wooing, Winning and Wedding," a lecture "adorned with poetical gems and frequent humorous sallies which were enjoyed by his auditors." Mrs. Curr also appeared on the program, declaiming the "Bugle Call" by Tennyson.

Yet all these events lost savor when the citizens learned of the violent death of Kate Townsend, and not only Orleanians but newspaper readers in St. Louis, San Francisco, New York, and Chicago became excited over the case.

Perhaps it is difficult now for some of us to realize the sensation the murder created. But then even those persons who had never heard of Kate Townsend knew that the New Orleans tenderloin was the most notorious in the country. Now they learned from their newspapers that Kate Townsend had been its reigning queen. Here was the end, appropriately frightful, of the most infamous madam in Basin Street. And in red-light districts in other cities her name was well known, for Miss Kate had traveled far and wide to secure her "female boarders," as they were listed in the New Orleans City Directory. Women of the profession throughout the United States looked forward to working in Kate Townsend's house almost as any American actress today looks forward to a season on Broadway. The Townsend mansion was the most sumptuous in Basin Street, and nowhere else in the country did more elaborate brothels exist than in that street, the name of which is not forgotten even now, although it may be best remembered as the birthplace of jazz.

In its earliest days Basin Street had been one of the finest residential thoroughfares in New Orleans. It was occupied by what old residents still called the "Americans," for it lay a little beyond the original Creole city. However, about a decade before the Civil War the prostitutes began to invade it, and the owners of the mansions lining the handsome street moved with a certain haste and no small amount of outraged indignation far away, to other parts of the city. The prostitutes remained in control until the outbreak of World War I, when their profession was declared illegal by city authorities. Later certain factions contrived to have the street's name changed. That portion north of Canal Street was renamed Crozat Street and Saratoga Street; that part extending south of Canal Street to Tulane Avenue was called Elk's Place. Recently the name has been restored to the "downtown" part.

In Kate Townsend's day Basin Street was inhabited entirely by brothels. Elsewhere in the city there were other houses of vice, but here were the most expensive and the most elegant, two- and three-storied mansions of brick and marble, furnished in the garish but costly taste of their occupants. The business was stripped of everything that was sordid. Beyond the handsome doors of carved and polished wood lay interiors lush with thick carpets and draperies of damask, silk, and lace, and containing elaborate furniture in black walnut and mahogany, huge oil paintings of doubtful taste, but lavish in design and color, a multitude of mirrors framed magnificently in gilt, nude statuary and glittering crystal chandeliers. Bedrooms were done in tufted satin in some of the houses. At least one boasted a chamber with walls and a ceiling composed entirely of mirrors.

The ladies received in evening dress in most of the houses. Champagne, lesser wines, and beer were sold. Music, sometimes provided by the inmates, sometimes by itinerant musicians who toured the district nightly, was often performed. Jugglers and other kinds of entertainers dropped in at the houses to amuse the women and their guests.

All business was done within certain unwritten rules and in accord with a code of etiquette as peculiar to the environment and as rigid in its application as any devised for any other stratum of society. When a man called he was received in one of the parlors, and he was expected first to buy drinks for all the women present. If he wished he might select a girl and go upstairs, but he was not openly solicited in the best of the houses. The "female boarders" would chat with the gentleman, drink wine with him, and sometimes there was dancing. They did not make any lewd suggestions. A man might remain all evening, and he could remain precisely as long as his money lasted. It was, however, by no means an inexpensive evening. Champagne and other wines sold for from fifteen to fifty dollars a bottle.

A brief visit upstairs cost from five to twenty dollars. If a gentleman desired to spend the night a hundred dollars was the average price. However, every attention was included. In the morning breakfast would be served. He would find his clothes pressed and his shoes polished.

Many of the houses were openly supported by politicians, city officials, and New Orleans gamblers, who drew heavy graft from the madams, to whom they offered police protection and complete assurance that indignant citizens could not pass any laws in their disfavor. Therefore, the murder of Kate Townsend must have been viewed with some satisfaction by many a resident, and in respectable circles the fate of the queen of the demimonde was without a doubt considered a veritable act of vengeance by a God of wrath.

Relatively speaking, the Townsend house was a new one. Built in 1866, it was from its opening until the death of its mistress the most lavish in the street. According to the *Times-Democrat* of September 22, 1870, it was erected "at the joint expense of a high police official, a Recorder, and several members of the Commission Council." This "joint expense" must have been in the nature of a loan for at Kate's death she owned the house.

There can be little doubt of Kate Townsend's influence with the city officials. It was known generally that her house had been a rendezvous for carpetbagger politicians, and that same article in the *Times-Democrat* described how the wife of an alderman, having heard that her husband frequented the house, resolved to see for herself if this was so. "She disguised herself and entered the house, where she found most of the city government, with the President of the Board of Aldermen, or the Mayor, we forget which, at the head of the table, and her husband at the foot."

Never modest, Miss Kate boasted that her house was the finest in the country and that her girls were the most desirable that could be obtained. Her furnishings, she often said, had cost her $40,000. She was proud of always offering a most "refined" atmosphere.

Only gentlemen were admitted to the Townsend establishment. It is said that upon a man's first visit to No. 40 Basin Street he had to present credentials of identification and of credit. Then he was taken into a private room by the madam herself for a thorough interrogation. If he passed this examination Miss Kate conducted him to the parlors and presented him to the ladies, who, always attired in evening gowns of the latest fashion, were trained to conduct themselves properly. No rough behavior or vulgar language was tolerated for an instant in Miss Kate's house.

The visitor would order drinks for everyone present, and would then indulge in conversation with the ladies and other gentlemen guests and enjoy whatever other entertainment was provided. He might remain as long as he liked now, for after Miss Kate's questioning he was established. In this house, if he spent all his money—and it went fast—he could even open a charge account, for had his credit not been worthy of such a risk he would have been asked to leave in the beginning. If he desired to go upstairs with a "boarder" of his choice, it was a rule of the house that he first communicate this wish to Miss Kate, who would then convey the suggestion to the chosen beauty, whereupon the young woman would retire and, after a decent period, the man would be escorted to the door of her bedchamber.

In the Townsend house prices were the highest in Basin Street—usually about fifteen dollars an hour, though an occasional inmate demanded more for her services. Miss Kate would accommodate very special guests herself, though her popularity in this respect must have been on the decline during the last years of her life, for at her death she weighed more than three hundred pounds. A reporter who described the madam in the *Daily States* that afternoon of the murder remarked that "her bust was one of the sights of the city."

Sykes and Miss Kate had met when she was the inmate of a house on Canal Street between Basin and Rampart streets. When she opened her own place he moved in with her. The newspapers, as they were fond of doing at that period, were inclined to romanticize the love affair after her death, and Sykes was described by the *Daily Picayune* as "the scion of an aristocratic family who became an outcast when he joined his fortunes with those of Kate Town-send."

Sykes was arraigned before Assistant Recorder R. C. Davey at the Central Station the afternoon of the murder. The *Daily Picayune* said next morning, "He came out of the dock limping and pale as a ghost." He pleaded "not guilty," to the astonishment of many persons, and named Messrs. Lionel Adams and A. D. Henriques as his attorneys. He was remanded to Parish Prison and held without bail. Here he was visited on the same day by a brother, and to him Sykes gave detailed instructions as to the funeral of the woman he had killed.

Coroner Y. R. LeMonnier arrived at No. 40 Basin Street just a few minutes after Sykes had been taken away. "The large hall and elegantly furnished apartments were crowded with spectators who wanted to witness the autopsy," said the *Daily States* on November 4. "Conversation was carried on in whispers and the tread of many feet were hushed by the soft velvet carpets on the floor. When the coroner arrived Police Sergeant Grabert, Corporals Andy Finn and Thomas Duffy had considerable trouble in clearing the room in which lay the gory corpse on the beautifully carved bed, with its costly hangings and trimmings now all stained with blood."

A sheet covered Miss Kate's face, but "it could not conceal the red stains on the white counterpanes, sheets, and mattress. The bare feet were yet standing on the floor, dipped in a pool of blood, which darkened the crimson hue which prevailed in the pattern of the carpet. When the sheet was lifted, however, the deed in all its shocking reality was revealed."

That morning the *Daily Picayune* had described the room thus:

In the left hand corner was a magnificent *etagère*, upon which were statuettes, the work of renowned artists, and small articles of verdu, betraying great taste both in selection and arrangement. A finely carved though small table stood next, while adjoining this was a splendid glass door armoire, on the shelves of which were stored a plethora of the finest linen wear and bed clothing. Next the armoire was a rep and damask sofa and over the mantel was a French mirror with a gilt frame. A large sideboard stood in the corner next a window on the other side of the chimney, and in this was stored a large quantity of silverware. Another armoire, similar to the one just described, a table and the bed completed the furnishings in the room, saving the armchairs, of which there were a number, covered with the finest rep and damask, with *tête-à-têtes* to match. The hangings of the bed, even the mosquito bar, were of lace, and an exquisite basket of flowers hung suspended from the tester of the bed. Around the walls were suspended chaste and costly oil paintings. The bloodstained carpet was of the finest velvet.

With Coroner LeMonnier at the autopsy was his assistant, a Dr. Archinard, a jury of five men, and reporters from the three leading New Orleans newspapers. The representative of the *Times-Democrat*, Charles Donneaud, who, with Sergeant Grabert, had found the bowie knife and pruning shears, was not allowed to print his story. The next day a small paragraph in his paper stated that "the editor feels the details of the slaying of the infamous Kate Townsend by her paramour, Sykes, are so nauseating as to preclude their presentation to the public." The other editors were less squeamish. Their accounts told all. It took eight men to lift the body and place it on a table in the room. There were eleven wounds, three of which were fatal. The jury decided upon a verdict of death from hemorrhage, the result of deep punctures of the left lung, the heart and large blood vessels. The doctors had to cut through six inches of fat during the autopsy. "It was a sight to make the strongest men shudder."

Public Administrator Wiltz ordered the effects of the dead woman sealed. An appraisal placed the value of her jewelry at $10,000; her silverware was valued at $5,000. An examination revealed that one of the armoires in the room held linen stained with blood and silverware that was bent and also bloodstained. Had Miss Kate, already cut and bleeding, gone into the armoire in search of something? Was it here she had kept her pruning shears?

Finally the last detail was attended to and Miss Kate's body was placed in charge of an undertaker, a Mr. F. Johnson. The date of the funeral was set for the following afternoon, Sunday.

The newspapers did much speculation in regard to the amount of Kate Townsend's wealth, the *Daily States* expressing the belief that "it is well over $200,000." It was always added that there were no heirs and that the victim had no relatives. The *Daily Picayune*, on Sunday morning, contributed the information that "it was only last year that the Townsend woman went before a notary and in order to avoid the law of concubinage, which says that but one-tenth of all the property left can be willed to a stranger, and sold part of her estate to Sykes, giving him the money to pay for it." The law mentioned had been in operation in Louisiana for many years.

The same *Daily Picayune* reporter had interviewed Mollie Johnson, and learned from her that the bowie knife used in the slaying had slaughtered its second, rather than its first, human being. In 1869 two men, James White and Gus Taney, had quarreled in the house over who was to pay for drinks to which they had jointly treated the "boarders." In the fight that ensued White had killed Taney on the stairway. The police, said Mollie, had given the knife to Miss Kate as a souvenir, and she had kept it all these years, often beneath her pillow as she slept.

Another woman, identified only as "a woman of the town," told the same reporter that Sykes had stolen three thousand dollars from Miss Kate the morning before the slaying, and that it was this that had precipitated the quarrel.

A romantic note was thrown into this account with the statement that "when Sykes met Kate Townsend she was only eighteen years old and very beautiful, and their love affair lasted for twenty-five years." There were, also, rumors that the pair were legally married. Mollie Johnson said that she had always believed so.

The death notice, also appearing in the Sunday papers, was simple:

TOWNSEND—On Saturday morning, November 3, 1883, at 11 o'clock, Miss Kate Townsend, aged 44 years.

Her funeral will take place from her late residence, No. 40 Basin Street, this [Sunday] evening, at half-past three o'clock. Her friends and acquaintances are respectfully invited to attend. Chicago, New York and St. Louis papers please copy.

The crowd that appeared as the hour of the funeral drew near was greater than that which had gathered the morning of the crime, but only those selected by Mollie Johnson, now in charge of the house, were admitted inside the parlors.

Only forty persons, all of them women, were allowed to view Miss Kate's body Saturday night. Mollie explained that Miss Kate had expressed definite wishes as to how her wake and funeral were to be conducted when she died. No man was to view her body. Champagne and other refreshments were to be served and everybody was to have a good time. At last, toward morning, Mollie did relent a bit and permitted "four sporting men" and two newspaper reporters to enter the parlors for brief periods. The reporters found the women present all attired in mourning or half-mourning. Mollie Johnson wore the deepest black. Wines, including champagne, and sandwiches were served. There was much weeping.

The corpse was laid out in appropriate elegance. On the day of the funeral the *Daily States* described the scene thus:

> The looking-glasses and pictures and ornaments were all covered with white silk, not with white linen, as is the custom. The room was literally covered with flowers and floral offerings. At the head of the coffin stood an enormous horseshoe of white roses and on each side was a dove made entirely of sweetpeas.
>
> At the foot stood a column four feet high made of everlastings.
>
> The corpse was clad in white silk, embroidered down the front and trimmed with lace, costing $50 a yard.

THIS ROBE COST $600

alone. She lay in a $400 metallic casket, on the corner of which was a silver cross with the inscription:

KATE TOWNSEND
Died November 3d, 1883
Aged 44 years

Mollie admitted many more women into the house on Sunday afternoon, but all men were barred. At three-thirty a Lutheran minister appeared and said some prayers. Then, in twenty carriages, not a man in any of them, except the colored drivers, the women followed the hearse to the Metairie Cemetery. Nearly every prostitute in Basin Street was there. That night the houses remained closed in honor of Miss Kate.

At the coroner's preliminary investigation, held on the following Wednesday, Drs. Lewis and Veasey, Officers Clarke and Hormle, Marie Philomene, Rosa Garcia, and Mollie Johnson appeared to describe their parts in the happenings of the previous Saturday morning. Lottie Lee, one of the "female boarders" of the house, was also questioned. She admitted looking through a keyhole while the lovers were fighting, but said that although she saw some blood she "thought nothing of it." Frankie Novell, a colored housemaid, vowed that she had not even heard the screams of her mistress. The verdict from this investigation was that "Kate Townsend came to her death from hemorrhage caused by punctured wounds' of the chest inflicted on the morning of November 3, 1883, with a bowie knife in the hands of Troisville Egbert Sykes, now in custody."

On the same day Troisville Sykes, acting through his attorneys from his cell in Parish Prison, mortgaged four pieces of property formerly belonging to Kate Townsend, but which he had bought with money she had given him, for $20,000. Lawyers Adams and Henriques received $10,000 of this and Attorney Andrew J. Murphy the other $10,000. The long fight had begun.

On Tuesday the will was read. It was quite clear that Kate Townsend, at the time the will was made, eleven years before, had intended that Sykes should have all she possessed when she died. On the 19th of September, 1872, she had appeared before A. E. Bienvenue, her attorney, and in the presence of Alexis Robert, Wilkemus Bienvenue, and Edward Fulton, dictated the following:

My name is Kate Townsend. I have no father or mother living, and no false heirs. I do hereby give and bequeath to Mr. Troisville Sykes, of this city, all the property, real and personal, which

I may die possessed of, hereby constituting him my sole and universal legatee, and in case of the death of said Troisville Sykes, I do hereby give and bequeath to Mrs. Stephenie Sykes, his mother, and to all her children all the property real and personal, which I may die possessed of. I do further constitute and appoint the said Troisville Sykes my testamentary executor; and, finally, I revoke all wills and codicils which I may have heretofore made.

On Friday, November 10, Sykes and his attorneys appeared in the Civil Court and filed an application for the probation of this will and the appointment of Sykes as testamentary executor. The accused was still limping. His wound broke open in the court and his trousers showed a red stain.

Judge W. T. Houston heard the arguments of Mr. Adams and Mr. Henriques, together with those of Mr. H. H. Hall, who represented the State and the Public Administrator, and Mr. Thomas R. Rozier, who represented the missing heirs. Mr. Rozier reminded the court that a person charged with murder could not be appointed testamentary executor for the estate of the individual whose death he was charged with causing until he was cleared of such charges. Judge Houston said he would have to investigate the law on the subject before reaching a decision and instructed Mr. Rozier to bring in witnesses to prove that missing heirs existed.

Who was Kate Townsend? None of her associates seemed to have any idea of her real identity. If she had ever confided her history to Sykes he never revealed it. Mollie Johnson told everyone that she had always thought Miss Kate was Irish because she had a slight Irish brogue, but she knew nothing else. At the autopsy the coroner had found the name "A. Pimm" tattooed upon Kate's left arm. Was this her real name, or was it the name of some lover in her past? Nothing was known of her beyond the fact that she had appeared in the tenderloin of New Orleans at the approximate age of eighteen, and that she had been unusually successful, opening her own house while she was still in her twenties.

Her relationship with the Sykes family now drew much comment from the gossips. The will had repudiated the legend started by the newspapers that the Sykes family had disowned "Bill" because of his relationship with Kate. She had made his mother her beneficiary in case Sykes would precede her in death. Had the two women been friendly? And wasn't the will indicative of a deeper affection between the lovers than usually existed in such cases? Many who had followed the case closely now began to give to what had at first seemed a licentious and scandalous relationship a rosy glow of Victorian sentimentalism and "true love."

Mr. Rozier did not have much success in locating missing heirs. He did produce Mary Ann Cullen, a washerwoman residing at 248 Rampart Street. Mary Ann was Irish and had been born in Queenstown, County of Cork. She told Judge Houston she had known Kate Townsend eight years before, when Miss Kate had called at her home about some laundry. At that time, said Mary Ann, Miss Kate had told her that she, too, was Irish, that she had married, when very young, a sailor on a man-of-war in Liverpool. Miss Kate had also confessed that she had two children, who resided with an aunt in England, and that each quarter of the year, when a certain ship's captain came to New Orleans, she sent money to her children. Mary Ann added that Miss Kate had claimed to have a sister in Australia, who was married to a British naval officer, and that Miss Kate's real name was Catherine Cunningham.

The *Mascot*, a sensational New Orleans tabloid of the period, published Mary Ann's story on November 18, embellishing it a bit here and there, apparently believing the tale.

But Mary Ann did not do well under cross-examination. She became very nervous and burst into tears, immediately after describing a locket Miss Kate had shown her, which held a picture of her supposed husband, "a nice-looking gentleman, with dark hair, blue eyes and a fair complexion." Then she admitted to Judge Houston that she had been paid to present this information by a Mr. John Chadwick. Who was Mr. Chadwick? Mary Ann didn't know. She had met him on the street. Mary Ann was warned as to the law on perjury and dismissed. Mr. Chadwick was never found.

One of the women residing at No. 40 Basin Street, who gave the name of Clara Fisher, stated that she had known Miss Kate since 1858, and that in all that time she had never known Miss Kate to write a letter to anyone, nor had she ever heard her mention relatives. Mollie Johnson said that during the fourteen years she had known Miss Kate she had never written a letter. At this time the fact that Kate Townsend was so illiterate that she could scarcely sign her own name does not seem to have occurred to anyone.

On November 22 Judge Houston confirmed Sykes as testamentary executor, and Andrew Hero, Jr., notary public; William Walsh and V. J. Lambert were ordered to make an inventory of the Townsend estate. Reuben B. Sykes, a brother of the accused, was granted permission to be present.

As might be expected, the value of the estate, placed at more than $200,000 by the newspapers, was found to have been somewhat exaggerated. The final appraisal placed it at $90,888.15. There were four pieces of property, valued at slightly more than $80,000. There was $1,500 in cash in the bank and another $1,500 in a safe in the house. Something strange had occurred in regard to Miss Kate's jewelry. Now its value was established as $4,000, instead of the $10,000 in the first estimate. Some of it seems to have vanished during the three weeks between the two appraisals. Many of the women who had lived in the house had also vanished, as had Marie Philomene, none of these persons ever to appear again. The balance of the estate was in silverware, of which the madam seems to have been inordinately fond, and in household furnishings, which apparently were not valued at anything near the $40,000 as Miss Kate had boasted.

There is a nice implication in the fact that among the jewelry found were seven silver pocket knives.

The Grand Jury met on December 8 and after a preliminary questioning of witnesses returned a true bill of murder against Troisville Sykes. He pleaded "not guilty." The trial was then scheduled to begin on January 29, 1884.

January has always been one of the gayest months in New Orleans and the year of 1884 was no exception. The carnival balls were well under way; the first of the season had been the Twelfth Night Revelers, "a masque of flowers, at the brilliant ball at the

French Opera House." *Martha* was being presented at the St. Charles Theatre, "with a strong company." The great tragedienne Clara Morris had just closed an engagement in the city; in an interview with a reporter of the *Daily States* she had explained how she was influenced by the costumes she wore for each role in her repertoire, and how sensitive she was to color and design. "In gray I am pensive, moody, saddened," she said. "In crimson I am a woman aflame!" Modjeska, too, had recently stirred theatergoing New Orleanians with her offerings of *Frou Frou* and *Camille*. Mr. Maurice Barrymore had been her Armand.

But as Sykes went on trial the case again eclipsed all other events in the interests of the citizens. The details were reviewed in the newspapers, which gave much space to the love affair of Kate Townsend and Sykes. As is usual in America, the accused murderer began to become a hero, the papers stressing how he had been abused and mistreated by his monstrous mistress during the past twenty-five years, for it was known that she had dominated him completely, and she had often beat him, cut him with knives, refused him money—sometimes, it was said, even food.

The day the trial opened Judge Roman's court was filled with the curious. They squeezed into every inch of seating space and crowded behind the railing at the rear. They lingered in the corridors outside and even in the street. The painted faces of Basin Street and the unadorned ones of respectable women were side by side, for more than three quarters of that first-day audience was female.

Surrounding Sykes at the defense's table were Lionel Adams, A. D. Henriques, Charles H. Luzenberg, and Arthur Gastinel, probably the most distinguished criminal lawyers in the city. Sykes was impeccably attired and appeared to be in excellent spirits. "His beard and mustache had been neatly trimmed and brushed. His appearance was that of a gentleman. He smiled quietly while conversing with his counsel," said the *Daily States* that afternoon.

The prosecution was represented by District Attorney Finney, his assistant, Branch K. Miller, and W. L. Evans.

By three o'clock that afternoon a jury had been impaneled. Of those selected a Mr. John U. Spengler alone had known Sykes previously. He had been his barber for the past sixteen years. Neither the State nor the defense seems to have objected to this acquaintanceship.

Dr. LeMonnier was the first witness summoned by the State. He described in detail the position of the body when he had first viewed it and the sort of weapon that in his opinion had been used to inflict the wounds. When he was shown the bowie knife found on the premises of the murdered woman and asked if such a weapon might have been used, he replied in the affirmative. He was then shown an ordinary kitchen knife and asked the same question. His answer to this was in the negative.

Police Sergeant Grabert, the next witness, told of being summoned to No. 40 Basin Street and of seeing Kate Townsend's body stretched across the bed, "with the small of the back on the edge of the bed and the feet on the carpet." He also described the "bloody linen" in the armoire, and asserted that a mirror in the room had been broken. He and Mr. Donneaud had searched together for a weapon and had found both the bowie knife and the pruning shears in an alley outside the window of Kate Townsend's bedroom. Both instruments had been bloodstained. Under cross-examination by Mr. Henriques, of the defense, Grabert admitted there had been no overturned furniture or any signs of a struggle. He did not recall seeing blood anywhere except on the linen in the armoire and upon the body.

Charles Donneaud, the *Times-Democrat* reporter, testified that he had first seen the bowie knife sticking in the board fence of the alley, looking as if it had been hurled from the window. He did not know if this was a feat requiring an expert in handling such a knife. The shears had been on the ground a few feet away. He had himself examined Kate Townsend's body, and the attack upon her had been ferocious in the extreme.

The next witness was Newland Holmes, who identified himself as a collector, who often worked in the neighborhood of No. 40 Basin Street. He had known Sykes for at least twenty-five years. He had been one of the men who had helped the coroner lift the body and place it on the table for the autopsy, which he had remained to witness. Chris Lindauer of the *Daily States* told of the same experience. He had noticed one other thing in the room. There had been the fragments of a smashed water goblet upon the floor.

The State now recalled Dr. LeMonnier and presented for his inspection a tattered chemise covered with red-brown stains. The coroner was "visibly affected, and covered his face with one hand, only stealing furtive glances at the gory relic." However, he identified it as the garment worn by the victim. The defense questioned him "regarding the case of a negro, who, shot through the heart, lived eighteen hours." To this he replied that he was familiar with the case, but that the deceased had received eleven wounds, three of them of so vital a nature that any one would have made instant death a certainty.

Now Mollie Johnson was called. It is too bad we don't know more about Mollie, for all through the case her role grows in importance, yet little exists that gives much information about her as a person. The *Mascot*, reporting on the trial, described her as a St. Louis woman, whose real name was Mary Buckley. She was "a handsome woman, a favorite in the sporting world," says the *Mascot* gaily. At the funeral she had been "in deepest black," but at the trial she was wearing "a costume of pale lavender silk, trimmed with black lace, and cut in the latest mode. Her hair, elaborately dressed and falling in thick curls, was further adorned with a small toque edged with the same lace as her dress. She carried a small parasol, which she clutched nervously throughout her examination. Unlike the others of the demimonde in the court, she was unpainted." The *Daily States* added the information that "Sykes did not take his eyes from her face."

Mollie told in detail of the "fatal morning," and how Sykes had come to her room and announced his intention of giving himself over to the police, after which she had gone "to the room where Miss Kate lay." Under cross-examination by Mr. Adams she said that she had resided at No. 40 Basin Street for fourteen years and that during that time Sykes had always lived in the house. He had attended to all Miss Kate's business affairs, as Miss Kate could neither read nor write. She then admitted, in reply to Mr. Adams' persistent questioning, that Miss Kate had threatened Sykes's life on many occasions and that she had repeated these threats to Sykes.

The district attorney objected, and the court sustained the State, on the grounds that the defense had entered no plea of self-defense and had taken no action to warrant the introduction of this type of testimony.

The defense attorneys then conferred with Sykes and a few minutes later announced that their client wished to change his plea from that of "not guilty" to one of "self-defense." The court assented, and Mr. Luzenberg rose and made a formal announcement to the jury that Troisville Sykes admitted to jusifiable homicide in self-defense.

The cross-examination of Mollie Johnson then continued. She stated that Miss Kate had made threats against the prisoner on many occasions, that the couple had quarreled frequently during the past few years, and that they had been arrested several times. Miss Kate was always the aggressor. On All Saints' Day, November 1, two days before the killing, Miss Kate went upstairs with the bowie knife in her hand, after telling Mollie that she intended to find Sykes and "cut that bastard's belly open." Mollie had repeated the threat of Miss Kate to Sykes the next day. Sykes had not been home the day Miss Kate had been looking for him.

The night before the slaying, Mollie said, she and Miss Kate, in the company of two men, had been in Pizini's Restaurant. Miss Kate was very drunk. That morning she had given Sykes twenty dollars to buy himself an overcoat, and now she kept saying she was sorry she had done so. She said as soon as she got home she was going to "open his belly." Mollie described Miss Kate as a dangerous woman, especially when she was drinking. Unusually strong, she had often beat not only Sykes, but men who misbehaved in her house and did not conduct themselves like "gentlemen." She always boasted that she did not need to employ a bouncer, but could handle anyone she wanted to evict from the place.

Mollie Johnson concluded her testimony by stating that she had supposed that Miss Kate and Sykes were legally married. He never worked and Miss Kate paid all his bills, although he might be said to have repaid her by his help in operating the business. Miss Kate, too, had always listened to his advice—when she was sober.

Rosa Garcia was called. She told of an occasion some weeks before when Miss Kate came into the kitchen and borrowed a knife, with which she told Rosa she intended to "cut Sykes up." Rosa had also once seen Miss Kate stab Sykes with a pair of scissors. Sometimes when Sykes went for a walk Miss Kate would send Rosa out to look for him and to bring him home because "she felt like fighting."

The police had to hold back the crowds that attempted to enter the courtroom the following day. When order was established District Attorney Finney offered as evidence the records of the succession of property of Kate Townsend and of the sales of property by Troisville Sykes to one Leon Lamothe. At this Mr. Henriques arose and objected on the grounds that these papers were irrelevant to the issue before the jury. Judge Roman, however, upheld the prosecution, stating that the obvious intention of the State was to establish a motive for the crime with which the accused was charged.

Assistant District Attorney Miller then read Sykes's petition to the Civil District Court. He also read the will and all the documents which had followed Sykes's original petition, and offered as additional evidence the following notarial sales before Andrew Hero, Jr.:

An act of donation by Troisville Sykes to his mother, Mrs. Stephenie Cecile Sykes.
An act of mortgage by same in favor of A. J. Murphy for the sum of $10,000.
An act of mortgage by same in favor of Lionel Adams and A. D. Henriques for the sum of $10,000.
An act by same creating Leon Lamothe his attorney in fact.
An act of sale by same and Mrs. Stephenie C. Sykes to Leon Lamothe of the lot and improvements known as No. 40 Basin Street.
An act of sale by same and Mrs. Stephenie C. Sykes to Leon

Lamothe for two lots and improvements known as 120 Carondelet Street.

An act of sale by same and Mrs. Stephenie C. Sykes to Widow Peter Morphy of one lot and improvements known as 191 Gravier Street.

Mr. Adams again objected, arguing that since these acts took place after the death of Kate Townsend they were wholly irrelevant. Again he was overruled.

After receiving brief testimony from Andrew Hero, Jr., to the effect that he was the notary public whose name was appended to all the acts read, the district attorney announced that the State had no further witnesses.

The first person summoned by the defense was a Dr. Kuhner, a practicing physician, who had treated Sykes at the Parish Prison for his wounds. He had found that the gash in the thigh of the accused was very close to the femoral artery, and that had the artery been severed death would have resulted within five minutes.

Thomas Duffy, the civil sheriff, admitted that Kate Townsend's reputation for bad temper had been notorious. He had known her fifteen years and could recall many instances when she had been guilty of violence. Sykes, on the other hand, was of an exceedingly mild disposition, and in the opinion of Mr. Duffy, was of a cowardly nature.

There was now a long line of witnesses who each reiterated the same opinion. M. J. Sheehan, former recorder of the First District, said Kate Townsend had a violent temper, while Sykes was quiet. James McCracken, Henry Heidenheim, and Theodore Bruning, all of whom had known the victim and the accused for many years, made similar statements. Judge T. J. Ford said that Sykes's reputation had been that of a man of a very mild and gentle nature. All these political and legal gentlemen were well acquainted with Miss Kate and Sykes.

Thomas N. Boylan, a former police chief, had known Sykes since boyhood. Sykes had always been "good natured," he said. The State chose to cross-examine Mr. Boylan. He had first heard that Sykes and Kate Townsend were living together in 1859. He said that when he was chief of police he had often visited them. To his certain knowledge Sykes had never been employed, nor did he have any private means. Apparently Kate Townsend had supported him during the years in which they had lived together.

Judge R. C. Davey of the First Recorder's Court, disagreed somewhat with the testimony of the others when he took the stand. He believed that "Miss Kate was violent only with Sykes. Otherwise she was a quiet woman." The defense tried, without success, to get a qualification of this statement from the witness. Judge Davey could not be swayed. He said that he thought the slain woman had used Sykes as a target for any ill humor from which she might be suffering, but with others she was different. He admitted that Sykes was the weaker of the pair, although he did not consider him a coward, but, indeed, under certain circumstances, a man "capable of acts of considerable bravery."

Lottie Lee was the last witness called. She vowed she knew nothing—nothing of the quarrels Miss Kate and Sykes had, nothing of the events of the morning Miss Kate had died. She knew Miss Kate had a bad temper, but Lottie said that she was a woman who minded her own business and what went on between Miss Kate and Sykes was none of her concern.

When the court adjourned for the day Sykes "in good spirits, picked up his overcoat and hat and left the room, walking with a jaunty air," said the *Daily States* of January 31.

The attorneys' arguments were scheduled to begin the following day. When the court opened at ten o'clock it was discovered by the crowds waiting outside that a thing almost without precedent in New Orleans had occurred. All ladies were barred from the room. The *Daily Picayune* thought it a good thing and that day remarked, "The trial has been fraught with indecencies. . . . " The women had to be content with standing in the halls and on the steps outside, hopeful that some male, departing, might give them some information.

Neither the State nor the defense had summoned Sykes to the

witness box. That morning Mr. Luzenberg announced that his client would like to make a statement directly to the jury, and, after instructing the jury that such a statement was not to be construed as evidence, Judge Roman granted permission.

Smoothing his hair lightly with "an aristocratic hand," Sykes rose, faced the jury, and began speaking "calmly and in a natural tone of voice."

On the Thursday before their last quarrel, he said, Kate Townsend had given him money to buy an overcoat. That night she went out, returning very late, very drunk, and in a quarrelsome mood. She continued to drink all day Friday, so he "kept out of her way." Saturday morning, as he set out for his walk, Mollie Johnson stopped him in the hall and warned him that Kate had again threatened his life and had, bowie knife in hand, been searching for him. He replied to Mollie, "That is all right," because he had never really believed that Kate would carry out her threats, as she made them so often. He returned from his walk, had his coffee in the dining room, and then went into Kate's room after Marie Philomene told him the deceased wanted to see him. Kate was seated at a table. He walked over to her, picked up a goblet of water, and began to drink from it, whereupon she sprang to her feet and hit him over the head with another goblet that had also been on the table. He was "astonished, and asked why she had done that." At that moment Marie Philomene re-entered the room with the coffee her mistress had ordered. As soon as the housekeeper was gone Kate sprang at him again, this time with the bowie knife in her hand. He twisted her arm and disarmed her. They struggled fiercely in the space between the bed and an armoire, as she tried to re-capture the knife he now held. Finally Kate broke away from him, pulled open the armoire doors and seized the pruning shears. She rushed at him with that in her hand. He begged her to stop, but she kept slashing at him. She screamed at him, "You French son-of-a-bitch, you knew I'd kill you one day! I have you this time and I'm going to do it!" After that, Sykes said, he could remember nothing. Everything went blank. When his brain cleared he was bending over the body of Kate Townsend with the bloody bowie knife in his hand. He went to the window, opened it, and threw both the knife and the shears into the alley. Then he called the cook and Mollie Johnson, and prepared to surrender himself to the police.

Sykes bowed slightly to the jury and resumed his seat. His expression was serious, even a little grim, but he seemed as calm as when he had begun his address.

Assistant District Attorney Miller opened the arguments for the State by reminding the jury that Sykes, by his own admission, had not taken the threats of the slain woman with any degree of seriousness. He had regarded them as the idle threats of "a woman of her class," perhaps indicating that he well knew her real feelings toward him and that she had no intention of harming him. Had not she willed him all her wealth? And had she not failed during all these years to change that will? She would certainly have changed it if her affection had turned to hatred so bitter that she wanted to kill him. This contradicted the charges of animosity on her part toward the man she had supported for twenty-five years. In any case, threats did not justify murder, unless the person making such threats attempted to put them into execution. Sykes knew of the threats, yet he chose to remain in Kate Townsend's house. He had willingly gone to her room that morning. It had been the screams of Kate Townsend, not any cries from Sykes that had attracted the servants. The multiplicity of the wounds attested to the savage nature of the attack. Would a man acting in self-defense slash to ribbons the body of the woman he loved? This was not self-defense, but the most ghastly crime in the history of Louisiana. As for motive, Sykes was Kate Townsend's heir. The indecent haste with which he had begun to dispose of the estate testified to his sentiments in that regard.

Arthur Gastinel was first to speak for the defense. Sykes, he said, had not feared losing the estate. Kate Townsend had allowed the will to stand for ten years. Sykes had considered whatever she possessed his also, for they had been together for twenty-five years. He had not taken her threats seriously because he had believed she loved him. She would beat him, it was true, but then she would

nurse the injuries she had inflicted upon him. It was not until the
morning of November 3 that he had realized his life was in danger.
Then he had fought back, as would any man. Mr. Gastinel closed
by referring to the bad taste of the State in parading the bloody
chemise before the jury.

W. L. Evans spoke briefly for the State. Either this was the most
foul of crimes or Sykes was innocent. If Sykes had brutally and
with malice murdered a woman in broad daylight in the midst of
250,000 civilized people he should receive the severest punishment.
If he were innocent he should be freed. At this point Mr. Finney,
the district attorney, interrupted Mr. Evans. An argument ensued
in which Mr. Finney implied that it was difficult to decide whether
Mr. Evans represented the State or the defense! Mr. Evans withdrew from the case, and left the courtroom in a rage.

When the excitement was quieted Mr. Henriques arose and
began his address for the defense. He first read from the law, defin-
ing murder, justifiable homicide and excusable homicide, or self-
defense. He reminded the jury that they must have proof of malice
before rendering a verdict of "guilty" on a charge of murder. Was
there any proof that Sykes had gone to the room of his paramour
with the intention of killing her? There was evidence that she had
awaited him with a weapon in her hand, while Sykes had been
unarmed. No one had seen the encounter in the room. The threats
of the deceased, together with her reputation for violence, particularly toward Sykes, left no doubt as to her character. He, on the
other hand, was a quiet and peace-loving man. Mr. Henriques then
reviewed the testimony of the witnesses. Sykes had borne the abuse
of this woman for a long time. Yet only when she had him cornered
in that room, between the bed and the armoire, had he fought back.
He had fought to save his own life. He had been blind with fear,
"engulfed in a passion beyond his control."

The newspapers called Mr. Henriques' argument "brilliant," and
remarked that Sykes had engaged the most notable counsel in the
state. When the court recessed at three-thirty in the afternoon
Sykes "chatted amiably with his attorneys, and smiled and bowed
to friends in the room, appearing optimistic about the outcome."

Mr. Lionel Adams began his address at six o'clock. The State, he said, took the absurd attitude that since Sykes had not broken through the walls of the room and run the risk of being stabbed in the back by a drunken, vicious woman he had no right to plead self-defense. A person convinced of the intention of another to take his life was justified even in making the first attack.

Kate Townsend's cries had not disturbed the household seriously because they were not unusual. She had been long given to screaming invectives at Sykes, and the women in the house were accustomed to the noise she made. The State had no right to assume what had emanated from that room were cries of pain. If they had been of that nature it was absurd to imagine they would have been ignored. As for the feeble attempt of the State to establish gain as a motive, that could be dismissed at once. If Sykes had planned a murder for profit he would have committed it under quite different circumstances and would have made some effort to conceal his crime. In such an establishment, frequented by many men, there would have been opportunities for doing this. Sykes had gone to the room without a weapon, but wearily, expecting only another argument. Kate Townsend had the weapon—both the weapons used in the encounter. The ferocity of the attack was due to fear so extreme that Sykes's mind had gone blank. Finally, Sykes had made no attempt to flee, but had at once announced his intention of surrendering to the police. He was not a criminal, just a man who lived on the bounty of a lewd woman. Nowhere in his record was there any evidence of violence in the past.

Mr. Luzenberg succeeded Mr. Adams. He opened by stating there was little remaining to be said. The jury now knew its verdict depended on the ability of the State to prove that a murder with malice had been committed. It was the State's duty to prove Sykes guilty, not the obligation of the defense to prove him innocent. Under the law a man was considered innocent until proven guilty. Sykes had merely defended his life.

District Attorney Finney closed the argument for the State. He had never known, he said, a case in which there was so little justification for a plea of self-defense. The deceased had been a

strong woman, but she was dead and "could not be exhibited" be-
for the jury. But had the gentlemen looked well at the accused?

Mr. Finney asked Sykes to rise. Here, he said, was a man in the
prime of life, above average in size, of large proportions and obviously of more than ordinary physical vigor. He had been strong
enough to take the knife from the hands of the deceased. Was it
necessary that he kill her? He had lived for twenty-five years "on
her lust." She had shown him every kindness. Was it not natural
that such a woman, in such a position, especially when inflamed
with drink, would sometimes quarrel with the man she kept? Perhaps she had threatened to rid herself of this parasite. Perhaps she
had made threats in the presence of Mollie Johnson. If Sykes had
believed those threats why had he not gone away? No. He knew if
he left that house he would lose the estate to which he was heir.
He had feared this, and when he had gone to Kate Townsend's
room that morning he had realized that she was through with him.
Then he had killed her, not in fear for his life, but in fear of losing
money and property. With that, Mr. Finney submitted the case to
the jury.

It was ten-twenty o'clock that night when Judge Roman completed his charge. He announced his intention of waiting upon the
jury's decision until eleven-fifteen, and at that time sent to inquire
as to whether or not a verdict had been reached. The reply being
negative, court was adjourned until ten-thirty the next morning.
Outside, even in the street, a great crowd waited.

At ten-forty the next morning the jury brought in a verdict of
"not guilty." Sykes departed at once with his attorneys. In the
corridors friends greeted him and shook his hand.

The decision of the jury had not come quickly. The first vote
had been eight for manslaughter, only four for acquittal. Yet during
the night the four had brought the eight to their way of thinking.
One of the jurymen is reported to have remarked, "A great many
people are going to be sore."

Some Orleanians applauded the release of Sykes, but others were
sore. Perhaps most of them did not believe that he had made the
first attack upon Kate Townsend, but the immoral characters of the

persons involved outraged many, and it seemed that Sykes, a disreputable person, was going to escape all punishment and to profit by what they referred to in 1884 as "his ill-gotten gain." The *Daily Picayune* was so indignant that on February 3 it editorialized at great length upon the outcome of the trial, saying in part:

> The pimp of an abandoned woman slays her, and opens her succession in his own favor before the court can try the charge against him. He is acquitted and enters upon the enjoyment of his ill-gotten gains, and there is no power in Christendom to say him nay. Cool, calm and collected, he says, "I slew this woman because I was obliged to, and I claim the accumulation of her lust."
>
> The case is so revolting that it is difficult, without indelicacy, to enter into its details. Only human nature surging toward its last residuum of degradation can realize the status in which Sykes was presented to his countrymen. He admits that he killed the woman. He acknowledges he took from her hands the knife with which the fatal deed was done. Was he, then, obliged to kill her? No; he only says that he forgot himself—and that he remembers no more until the fond supporter of his miserable existence lay dead and bleeding from eleven speechless wounds!
>
> Nobody remembers any more. The man is free and rich. Good men, brave men, pure men have said that is just. We leave him to the remnants of his conscience; but we lay our protest at the doors of society.
>
> In this case shall we blame the jury, the law, or the officers of the law? Sykes was tried by at least a jury of average intelligence and probity. It is supposed that some one or more of his friends were in the box, but the verdict was unanimous and that fact hushes cavil at the outset. The sad truth is that our people do not appreciate the sacredness of life, and we are not prepared to draw the deadline between self-defense and murder. Sooner or later they will get it written in the blood of their sons and in the desecration of their household altars!

Where was the terrible penalty of sin as promised from the pulpit? Where were the "just deserts" of the villain as every play of the era portrayed? What example was set for the young and the virtuous? Everyone knew that Mollie Johnson had reopened No. 40 Basin Street and was conducting business even as the trial of Sykes was proceeding. Now it became known that when Sykes departed the court where he had faced a trial for his life he had returned to his gallery room in the house where he had lived so long and where the mysterious struggle between him and his former mistress had resulted in her death.

However, events were not going so smoothly as was at first thought. Sykes had sold No. 40 to Leon Lamothe, who, in turn, had leased it to Mollie Johnson. Most of the public probably missed a small item that appeared in the *Daily States* on January 29, the very day the trial opened. On that day it was announced that Judge W. T. Houston of Division B, Civil District Court, ordered Mollie Johnson "and all women of lewd life" to vacate No. 40 Basin Street, "there residing and carrying on their commerce under a pretended lease from one Leon Lamothe, who sets up to be the owner of the premises." Judge Houston decreed that Sykes had no right to sell the property, that his role of testamentary executor precluded the privilege of disposing of any of the property of the succession. Mr. Francis Baker, counsel for Mollie Johnson, appeared before the Supreme Court that same afternoon and filed a motion for writs of mandamus and prohibition.

Mollie Johnson remained at No. 40 Basin Street. However, on February 2, Andrew Hero, Jr., the notary public who had acted at the sales, was sentenced to ten days in jail by Judge Houston for refusing to produce the diamonds and the jewelry belonging to Kate Townsend. His attorney, W. S. Benedict, obtained his release and posted a $5,000 bond. Tried on February 6 in the Supreme Court, Mr. Hero protested that the jewelry was not in his possession but in the keeping of Troisville Sykes. He was acquitted.

Judge Houston then ordered Sykes to produce the valuables, and, when he failed to appear, issued an order for his arrest. Sykes then chose to disappear. On February 18, an order was issued for his removal as testamentary executor, which read, "It is ordered, adjudged and decreed that Troisville Skyes, testamentary executor to the succession of Kate Townsend, has withdrawn sums of money from the bank without authority, that he failed to deposit $4,538.05, and that therefore he must pay interest at the rate of 20% per annum on the sum of $4,538.05 and on the $2,700.00 withdrawn without said authority, and be dismissed and deprived of all powers and functions as of this date."

On March 12, the *Daily Picayune* printed a small notice regarding the disappearance of Sykes, commenting with no little satisfaction upon the fact that it seemed that Sykes had lost the succession—"the ill-gotten gains."

It was April before Sykes reappeared, to begin a long fight to regain the estate. This continued for years, but in January, 1888, despite his persistence and the eminence of his counsel, the Supreme Court upheld the State and the Public Administrator. But so long and so expensive had been the struggle in the end the State received only slightly more than $34,000. Sykes, under the law of concubinage, was granted $340. The attorneys had pocketed the balance.

Now a new story was abroad about No. 40 Basin Street. The house was haunted.

It was said that Marie Philomene had first seen the fat ghost of Kate Townsend and had fled screaming into the street, never to be seen again. After that—all this even before the trial began—the portly wraith frightened away nearly all the "female boarders."

The Public Administrator had secured the house from Leon Lamothe in 1884. He promptly leased it to Mollie Johnson, a fact that somewhat shocked the respectable element of New Orleans, although, situated where it was, the mansion could not have served any but its original purpose.

However, Mollie had many difficulties in her attempt to supplant Miss Kate as the madam. The scene of two murders (the newspapers had refreshed the memory of the public in regard to the Taney-White affair), the house, for all its elegant trappings, did not seem to appeal now to its former clients, or to attract new ones. Dark and sordid memories smothered its former grandeur, and the ghost stories were told repeatedly by the women in the other Basin Street houses. Not only Miss Kate appeared, they said, but on certain nights Jim White and Gus Taney renewed their battle on the fine, curving stairway.

As soon as a month after the death of Kate Townsend only Mollie Johnson, Lottie Lee, and Rosa Garcia remained in the house. Rosa departed a few days after the trial, and Lottie Lee a few months later. It seems that as hard as she tried to mind her own business even Lottie Lee could not ignore the spooks.

During the years that followed Mollie coaxed other women to enlist under her command, but they declined in beauty and merit until they were at last only such ones as could not find locations in other Basin Street establishments.

Prices grew cheaper, and where champagne had flowed there was only beer. It became difficult to retain servants. Even the clientele spread gossip of queer phenomena. On occasion men fled the house and told strange stories in the neighboring parlors. Mollie is said to have confided to intimates of having found it impossible to occupy Miss Kate's bedchamber. She had moved into it, but had been unable to endure the things that sometimes occurred.

In 1889 she gave up the struggle, closed the house, and returned to St. Louis. The contents went under the hammer at public auction, which New Orleanians attended as if it were a circus. After that one of the most pretentious brothels in the United States remained untenanted for years. It was finally razed. In 1917 a clubhouse for the Benevolent Patriotic Order of Elks was erected on the site. Today the offices of the United States Employment Service occupy this building.

JULIETTE AND THE KIND DOCTOR

At about the time of the opening of the Cotton Exposition in New Orleans in 1884 there arrived in the city a French gentleman who after taking a room in a house at what is now 714 St. Peter Street, began to appear daily in nearby Jackson Square and on street corners, where he distributed cards that created a small stir among certain circles. The cards read:

> Let us look for the truth!
> Let us do good!
> Let us be magnetized!
> DR. EUGENE ETIENNE
> 68 Rue St. Pierre

During the last decades of the nineteenth century faith cures, hypnotic treatments for illness, and something called magnetic physiology were much the fashion, and the doctor had the disadvantages of competition and his inability to speak English. Nevertheless, since his fees were small and his establishment was in the Vieux Carré, where French was still perhaps the most frequently spoken tongue, he soon developed a clientele attracted by the cards and the shingle, written in French, which inquired: "Searching for truth? Doing it well? Dr. Etienne, professor of magnetic physiology of Paris. All maladies cured by magnetism. Treatment at domicile."

For several years the doctor, aside from his charlatanism, seems to have done no particular harm. His practices were curious, and it is said that dazed and sickish persons sometimes stumbled down the steps of his house and were seen being sick upon the banquette

36

outside. It was known that the doctor often administered small doses of chloroform and ether during his "treatments," rendering his patients unconscious so that they might be more easily subject to his magnetic will, but this was looked upon as more interesting than harmful, and the patients often returned for more.

Soon the doctor had quite a reputation. For one thing, he was a fine-looking man in his middle fifties, who dressed well, possessed the most polished manners and genuine charm. Tall for a Frenchman, he was burly-chested and strong, and richly caparisoned with a remarkable silver beard that reached the middle of his massive chest. His female patients found him most attractive and enjoyed his "treatments" with or without chloroform. To male patients he offered a special cure for impotence, and as the doctor was himself a splendid example of health and virility, due, as he explained, to self-magnetizing, his success was no less here.

But the doctor seems to have been lonely. His patients did not become his friends. They visited with him for an hour or so in his one little third floor room, then departed down the winding stairs to go about their lives. It seems to have been this loneliness that brought about his ruin.

In 1888 he at last found a friend in Jules Deitsch, a carpenter, who lived close by in the Rue Chartres. Deitsch, despite his humble trade, was a man of culture and education, a Parisian, who had been in the United States but a few years. He had come to the doctor as a patient and became a disciple, with a firm belief in magnetic physiology. In the evenings the doctor would call upon the carpenter, and, over a glass of wine, they would enjoy stimulating and cultured conversation, such, as each told the other, they had not enjoyed since their youthful days in Paris. Father Deitsch, as he was known in the neighborhood, was a lonely man, too, a widower with two young daughters, Laurence, aged nine, and Juliette, aged exactly twelve. Juliette was a large girl for her age.

To Father Deitsch the doctor confided the story of his life. Eugene Etienne, he admitted, was an alias. His real name was Etienne Deschamps, and he had been born in Rennes, France in 1830. The eldest child of a wealthy family, he had been well-educated and had graduated with honors from a dental college in Paris. Then there came a period of youthful excesses, which shocked his family and brought about a permanent alienation from them. When the Crimean War began young Etienne joined the cavalry, and in the Battle of Sevastopol was wounded by the lance of a charging Russian. The returned hero then entered French politics, and with such enthusiasm that, as he told Father Deitsch, his fight for the right caused him to be driven from his country in 1870. There had followed a brief career in Brazil, but here again his politics, the variety of which he never described, were unpopular and within a few years he returned to Paris to practice dentistry. It was at this time that he discovered his magnetic powers, realized what a gift he had to give to the world, and began to dabble extensively in the occult. His ill fate pursued him, however, and pressure of various sorts, some of it emanating from his own family, encouraged him to seek his fortune in the newer nation across the Atlantic Ocean. He chose New Orleans because he believed that its French culture and the prevalence of the French language might seem more like home.

Dr. Deschamps described many of his most secret plans to Father Deitsch. He did not intend by any means to confine his activities to healing the sick. He had developed a master scheme which would enrich him, and, if he were co-operative, his friend, M. Deitsch. The doctor said that his magnetic powers had now developed so that they could be used in extraordinary ways. One of these was that he intended to locate the buried treasure of Jean Lafitte, the famous pirate, who was known to have concealed great wealth among the swamps and islands of Barataria. Indeed the doctor had already made many trips to the locality and was well on the scent. There was one difficulty, however; he could not work alone. He needed a medium, through whom, with his powers of hypnotism and magnetism, he could work at finding the treasure. The best medium, of course, was a young girl, a virgin—a girl like Juliette.

Father Deitsch was more than impressed. He was honored that this great man should select a member of his family for such a role.

He knew Juliette would be willing. The children were already so fond of the good doctor.

From then on the doctor seems to have spent some time in increasing the affection of Juliette and Laurence, the latter perhaps because of the possibility that sometime in the future she might be useful. He took them for walks and rides to the lake. They became frequent visitors to his room, where candy and fresh fruit always awaited them. He bought them little trinkets at the French Market.

During that summer of 1888 Dr. Deschamps and Juliette made some trips alone, however. They visited Grand Isle and the Barataria country, at which places he introduced the plump little girl as his daughter. Upon their return he always explained to Father Deitsch that things were progressing nicely, that Juliette was a perfect medium and that it would not be long before she would, during one of her trances induced by hypnotism, reveal the gold of Lafitte. Then they would all be rich, and they would return to Paris and live in great style.

In October the doctor took a trip alone, and it was then that Juliette exhibited a precocious interest in boys and young men that distressed her father. There were young hoodlums in the neighborhood from whom the carpenter had determined that, when the time came—for he had until now considered it too early to worry— he would protect his girls. But Juliette seemed to be pursuing the hoodlums! On several occasions he discovered the twelve-year-old in the dark alleyways of the section in company with some youth a few years older and in circumstances that were no less than compromising. In one such case the boy was named Tony, and Juliette told her parent that she loved Tony.

"You must," chided Father Deitsch, "love no one but your papa and the doctor."

Father Deitsch was certain that nothing really disastrous had occurred between Tony and Juliette, so he soon forgot about it after Tony, frightened of the carpenter's ire, absented himself from the neighborhood. When the doctor returned, however, the father told him of his fright, and the hypnotist promised to aid him in guarding the purity of the little girl. Juliette must remain a virgin, explained

Dr. Deschamps. Otherwise she would be of no use to him as a medium, and they would never be rich. At this time Dr. Deschamps talked a great deal of winning at lottery.

From then on both the little girls spent more time with their bearded friend. They attended the private school of Miss Roux, located only two houses from the doctor's, and it became their habit to drop in after school each evening. Often the doctor would then walk home with them. On holidays the doctor was always with them. Later neighbors remembered how when they walked through the streets the doctor would always be in the center, the girls clinging each to an arm, and Juliette was said to have gripped the arm of her friend tightly and affectionately, sometimes with both hands. Many persons thought they were the children of Dr. Deschamps, which he never denied, and both of them were considered very pretty, Juliette in particular, for she had thick and curling brown hair and milk white skin and was so tall and plump that usually she was thought to be a year or two older than her twelve years.

At four-thirty on the afternoon of January 30, 1889, Jules Deitsch was at work in the courtyard behind the house in which he had an apartment when his aged mother, who kept house for the small family, called to him in so urgent a manner that the man ran quickly up to their second floor apartment. Laurence was sitting on a bed crying hysterically and the old lady had been unable to obtain a word from her as to why she wept. By her side was a heavy bundle she had dragged home, and Deitsch opened this immediately. It contained books that belonged to Dr. Deschamps. This was so strange that Father Deitsch knelt beside the child and shook her, and demanded to know what had happened. Where was Juliette?

"Juliette is asleep," Laurence sobbed at last. "The doctor told me that she is asleep and that he is going to die."

Deitsch seized his little girl's hand and half dragged her down the stairs and through the streets toward the house in St. Peter Street. They stumbled up those stairs, and Deitsch beat upon the door of the room, but could get no response. Then he tried the next room and aroused Charles Serra, a private night watchman. Serra attempted to open the door of the doctor's room, but without success. Later Serra said he thought he heard moans from within, but he was not positive.

Father Deitsch beseeched Serra to help him break down the door, but this the watchman refused to do. For some unknown reason they do not seem to have sought the landlady of the house who had a duplicate key. Instead the two men and the little girl set out for the Third Precinct Station some three blocks away. They returned with three policemen who obtained the duplicate key from the frightened landlady and raced up the stairs.

When they opened that door what confronted them was a curiously quiet scene. The shutters of the windows were drawn, and upon the mantelpiece a single candle flickered in a dirty glass. In the fireplace charred papers smoldered and sent out smoke into the room. All about was utter filth, for the room looked as if it had not been cleaned in months. There were stacks of yellowed newspapers and magazines, books piled and scattered everywhere and two open trunks from which hung articles of male clothing. Upon the bed, entirely nude, lay Juliette and the doctor, the pretty brown head of the girl resting upon the massive hairy chest of the hypnotist-dentist.

They moved Juliette gently. She was still warm, but she was quite dead. The doctor, however, moaned when they touched him. There were four wounds in his chest, from which blood had oozed but already coagulated. On the floor at the side of the bed was a sharp dental instrument. The doctor opened his eyes, and said in French, "I meant to die," then became unconscious once more. An ambulance was sent for. The police began an examination of the room. In an open trunk on top of some old clothes was a neat pile of letters. They were all addressed to Dr. Deschamps and were signed by, or seemed to be signed by, Juliette.

Coroner Y. R. LeMonnier held his inquest the next day. It was of course little Laurence whose testimony was the most important, and the detailed account she gave of the relationship between

Juliette and the doctor was so shocking that not even the news-papers would print all of it.

Laurence said that she and her sister had gone to Dr. Deschamps' room from school on the afternoon of January 30. They had eaten some candy and sat about talking. The doctor then went out to get some kindling wood to make a fire, and while he was gone Juliette told Laurence that he was going to "put her to sleep again."

When the doctor returned he closed in the shutters and lighted a candle. He built a fire in the fireplace. Then he told Juliette to strip off her clothes and get into bed, which she did at once. The doctor then also stripped naked, and crawled into bed beside her. Laurence said that she had not paid much attention to them. The doctor saturated a clean handkerchief with chloroform and laid it over Juliette's nose and mouth. He repeated this several times, then asked Juliette what she saw. She replied that she saw, "God, the Holy Virgin, and Jackson Square.*"

Then the doctor gave Juliette the bottle of chloroform to hold to her nose. Juliette "went to sleep," and the doctor climbed out of bed. He began gathering together a lot of papers and letters and these he burned in the fireplace, while Laurence watched curiously, but without alarm for her sister. The doctor then dressed, and told Laurence to watch her sister, but not to touch or arouse her, and that he would return in a few minutes. When he left the room he locked the door behind him. Laurence walked over to the bed, but obeyed the instructions and did not attempt to awaken Juliette.

The doctor returned with two bottles of chloroform, and again stripped to the nude and got into bed. He began once more to apply saturated cloths to the nose and mouth of the little girl. Laurence sat upon a footstool at the end of the bed, and, once or twice, when she asked questions, the doctor replied that this was going to be "our most successful experiment."

Laurence did not know just how much later it was, but all at once the doctor leaped from the bed and fell to his knees, his head clasped in his hands, and cried, "*Mon Dieu! Mon Dieu! Qu' ai-je fait?*" (My God! My God! What have I done?)

* A square in the French Quarter of New Orleans.

This frightened Laurence. She began to cry. The doctor seized her in his huge arms and clasped her to his naked body. "Go to your father," he said. "Tell him that I am going to die!"

But before she was allowed to go the doctor made a bundle of some heavy books, and made her take the package with her. This, Laurence said, made the trip home much slower than usual, for she could not run, but even had to stop and put the books down to rest several times.

Laurence said that she had frequently seen the doctor and Juliette naked in bed together. Juliette did not seem to mind and whatever they did was, according to the doctor, a part of their experiments. At least twice, Laurence testified, she had taken off her clothes and joined them, but the doctor had not "done anything" to her. She could not take the chloroform the doctor administered. It always made her ill and she vomited. He had more success with Juliette, who frequently had visions while under its influence, and usually saw religious visions, such as angels and the Holy Virgin. The doctor talked all the time of finding buried treasure, and said that Juliette would one day see where it was hidden while in one of her trances induced by chloroform.

Juliette had loved the doctor, and so did she, said Laurence. He had always been good and kind to them, and had never hurt them in any way. They enjoyed his company. A few times Juliette had gone to see the doctor alone, but almost always Laurence had accompanied her.

That morning Coroner LeMonnier performed an autopsy upon Juliette's body. The lips were burned from the chloroform, and the brain and heart showed that death had resulted from an overdose of the anesthetic. Coroner LeMonnier reported that the child had been misused many times and apparently over a long period of time. She had also been abused in an unnatural way, and upon her body were old and new marks of nails and teeth.

Poor Jules Deitsch had no money with which to bury his little girl, so a subscription was raised. A crowd of more than forty thousand persons attempted to view the body at the simple funeral on the afternoon of January 31.

Dr. Deschamps' wounds were superficial. Apparently he had lacked the courage to plunge the dental instrument he had used as a weapon deep enough into his chest, and so slight were the punctures that he was removed from the Charity Hospital to Parish Prison within forty-eight hours.

His only statements were wild and almost incoherent. He said that he had discovered some months before that Juliette was not a virgin, that she was already "no better than a common prostitute." He said that he and Juliette had loved each other and, because of the difference in their ages, had decided to die together, for they knew their affair could not remain concealed from Father Deitsch much longer. In the next breath he insisted that Juliette's death was an accident, that, with the assistance of chloroform, he had often mesmerized her. The use of chloroform as an aid in hypnotism was a common practice, he insisted, and had been developed by hypnotists in Germany.

He told police officials that he had, during his travels among the islands below New Orleans, found some old coins buried in the sand, and that he knew that he could find the concealed wealth of Lafitte's Baratarians if they would only not insist upon keeping him locked up, unjustly and cruelly, in the prison. He had committed no crime, he told everyone. He was a French gentleman. He was a scientist—a great man.

A few days later Deschamps was found hanging by the neck from his own belt, which he had attached to the bars of his cell. Most of the strain of the belt was upon his chin, which was uncomfortable and brought forth loud moans that attracted the guards. Cut down he roared, "They won't even let me die!"

The letters in the open trunk found in his room were examined. All of them purported to be from Juliette, and bore such signatures as, "from your little mistress," "Your love forever, Juliette Deitsch," and "Your mistress, J.D." Handwriting experts were doubtful that the girl had written them, and believed at least some had been written by the doctor himself. Miss Roux said that Juliette had been quite backward in school and could not have composed them, although she might have copied them from letters written by someone else.

In the letters were references to "Charlie," implying that he was a former lover of the little girl's. "Charlie" was identified as a young jeweler in the neighborhood, who was happily married and had not, beyond a doubt, had any such relationship with the child. It was apparent that Dr. Deschamps had wanted to create the impression that he was not the first to seduce Juliette, if, as it was believed, he was the author of the letters.

Deschamps was arraigned before Judge R. H. Marr on February 18. He made a scene, was extremely noisy, and had to be almost dragged from court. It was a "crime" he said to bring him to trial, and it was worse that he would be tried in an English-speaking court, since he understood only French. He was a gentleman. He was not a murderer, and he would not be thought one. The whole thing was nothing less than a plot to besmirch the fair name of France. From this Judge Marr deduced that the plea was "not guilty," and set the date of trial for April 29.

On that day, however, it was discovered that Deschamps had employed no counsel and had refused to even discuss the employment of any. Judge Marr then appointed James Dowling to represent the accused. Mr. Dowling asked for thirty days in which to prepare his case. Judge Marr granted him only two, and announced that the trial would begin on May 1.

That night Deschamps climbed to the upper bunk in his cell and jumped off head first. He had a headache for days, but was not seriously injured.

The trial was brief, and little of the evidence presented was new to the authorities or to the public. The court was filled, about seventy-five people standing all day. Perhaps a dozen ladies were present. Deschamps had shaved off his bushy beard, wore only a mustache, but looked unkempt and dirty. He had to use Deputy Sheriff Jacques Villeré as an interpreter so that he could converse with his attorney, who spoke no French.

Jules Deitsch was the first witness called. He looked worn and thin, and, like the accused, knew no English, so that all his testimony was through an interpreter. In answers to questions put to him by District Attorney Charles H. Luzenberg, Deitsch described the homecoming of Laurence on the afternoon of the tragedy, and his discovery of the body of Juliette after the police had unlocked the door of Deschamps' room.

He had known Deschamps for nearly a year. The doctor often took the little girls out and they saw him every day. Deitsch admitted he knew of the experiments being conducted, and he had given his approval, for he had believed in the doctor's mesmeric powers. He had not, of course, guessed at the other relationship between Juliette and the doctor. She was and had always been a good little girl. Deschamps had often tried to put the witness to sleep with hypnotism, but without success. Juliette had been tall for her age and plump, but she had not been mature or well-developed; she was not yet a woman.

Mr. Luzenberg now exhibited a small piece of ebony in the center of which was a small disk that glittered like glass but was not a mirror. The witness had seen this many times. It was used for hypnotic purposes, the medium concentrating upon it until a trance was induced. The witness had tried it himself. Luzenberg explained to the court that the instrument had been found in the bed with the victim and the accused.

The cross-examination by Mr. Dowling was brief. He made Father Deitsch admit that he could not state of his own knowledge what had caused Juliette's death. He had been told it was due to the chloroform. Yes, he had known of the use of chloroform. He had tried it himself six or seven times.

Captain John Journee, of the Third Precinct, and Officers Fernand De Rance and George Legendre all testified that they had entered the room with Jules Deitsch and Charles Serra, and had seen the bodies in the bed. Both the man and the little girl were naked and covered to the waist with a blanket. Her head was upon his chest and his arm around her, as if he had pulled her to him.

They all described the handkerchiefs, the almost empty bottles, the fumes of chloroform that permeated everything in the room.

Charles Serra, after describing the arrival of Deitsch and Laurence and their frantic trip to the police station, admitted that he had touched the arm of the girl. It had still been warm. He told Mr. Dowling that he had seen the children in the house many times. He often heard the girls singing while they were in Deschamps' rooms. Mrs. Elizabeth Hilroy, the landlady of the house where the doctor roomed, said that she knew her tenant only slightly although he had been there for some years. He had little to say, and always locked his room when he left it. He did whatever cleaning was done himself, and insisted upon doing this. She had become used to seeing the children almost every day.

The next witness presented, and the most important of the trial, was little Laurence. She was dressed all in black, and looked somewhat pale, but showed no other signs of nervousness. James Dowling at once objected to the acceptance of testimony from so young a child, but he was overruled by Judge Marr. In a gentle tone Judge Marr asked Laurence if she understood the meaning of her oath, to which she replied she went to Mass every Sunday and she knew it was wrong to tell a lie. She then repeated to Mr. Luzenberg and the jury the details she had related at the inquest. Mr. Dowling kept objecting to all questions relative to the sexual relationship between Juliette and Deschamps, but Judge Marr ruled that such testimony was relevant to the case.

"How many times would you say," asked Luzenberg, "that you saw your sister take off her clothes and go to bed with the doctor?"

"Your Honor!" cried the defense attorney. "The prisoner is being tried for murder, not seduction!"

Luzenberg then dismissed the small witness without pressing the question, and summoned Coroner LeMonnier, who for the rest of the day described the findings of the autopsy, which had revealed conclusively that Juliette Deitsch had died from the overadministration of chloroform.

On the second and last day the defense asked Laurence to take the stand. The child's answers to Mr. Dowling's questions were prompt. She had not paid too much attention to Juliette and the doctor. They had talked some while in bed, but in low tones that she could not hear, except once when her sister had said that she could see, "God, the Holy Virgin, and Jackson Square." No, she had never thought that Dr. Deschamps would ever hurt Juliette on purpose. He had looked "scared" when he got out of the bed the second time. He had fallen to his knees, saying, "My God! My God! What have I done?" in French. Later, weeping, he had hugged Laurence, and said, "Dear God, let me die! I want to die!"

Recalled to the stand Dr. LeMonnier testified that Juliette was not, as had been reported, pregnant, that she had not yet reached sufficient maturity to be in danger of pregnancy, although it might have soon happened.

At two-fifty in the afternoon the case was submitted to the jury, without testimony from the accused and without argument by counsel. The jury was out only eighteen minutes. The verdict was "guilty as charged."

This was only the beginning, however.

Deschamps employed John G. McMahon as his attorney. Mr. McMahon appealed to the Supreme Court, and they reversed the decision on the grounds that the defense had not had sufficient time to prepare its evidence. A new trial was ordered for March 28, 1890.

During the ten months between the trials Deschamps became the most unruly and most uncontrollable of prisoners. He would speak to no one. Whenever released from his cell he would make foolish sprints for freedom, racing down corridors, until overcome by guards. If a newspaperman attempted to interview him he would go to a corner of his cell, turn his back, bend over, and assume what the reporters would later describe as "an insulting position." He was scornful of other prisoners, calling them "criminals," and telling them they were not fit associates for a fine French gentleman. It is doubtful that any inmate of the Parish Prison was ever so disliked by both the other prisoners and the personnel. One of the doctor's favorite statements, which he reiterated again and again was, "I was tried in a language I did not understand, then led to a stall to be fattened, now they would like to slaughter me like a beef in the abattoirs of Paris!"

But he never believed he would be "slaughtered," for he was certain his second trial would set him free. Then, he said, he would return to France and see that war was declared upon the United States at once.

The new trial began with a somewhat remarkable occurrence. Judge Alfred Roman appeared and announced that he was going to represent the defendant. Attorney John G. McMahon then sprang forward and declared that he had been paid a fee by the prisoner as his attorney, and that certainly he would defend the case. Roman said that McMahon had never visited the prisoner, and that Dr. Deschamps had employed him. Judge Marr suggested that both the gentlemen consult with the prisoner for fifteen minutes, so that a decision as to which one was his attorney might be reached. McMahon objected to this, and he and Roman were only prevented from engaging in a fist fight in the court by Judge Marr's threats of contempt charges. McMahon then withdrew and left the courtroom.

The second trial, like the first, lasted but two days. The first witnesses summoned were Jules Deitsch, the policemen who had opened the door to the doctor's room, and Charles Serra. Their testimony was the same. Alfed Roman, in his cross-examination, concentrated upon the fact that Father Deitsch had known that Deschamps was using both hypnotism and chloroform upon his daughters and had permitted such practices. Roman exhibited the pink cards Dr. Deschamps used to advertise his business. What sort of a father allowed his daughters to form a close friendship with a charlatan of this caliber?

Once more the letters were read aloud. It was obvious, said Mr. Luzenberg, that they had not been written by a girl of twelve. Deschamps had written them, and this was evidence that his crime had been planned.

Two druggists living in the neighborhood of St. Peter Street admitted that they had sold Deschamps chloroform on at least several occasions, and in unlabeled bottles.

Laurence once more took the stand. The doctor had always been kind to her and to Juliette. Again she repeated that she had seen Juliette and the doctor in bed together naked many times. Juliette had told her never to tell her father. Yes, so had the doctor. She had never done so because she thought it was a part of the way they would find the buried treasure of the pirate.

Judge Roman addressed the jury for three and a half hours when the testimony was complete. The defense admitted that the accused was a fakir and was guilty of carelessness in his administration of the chloroform, but he was not on trial for that. Neither was he on trial for seduction. He was being tried for murder, and only murder, and the only question for the jury to decide at this time was whether Etienne Deschamps was or was not guilty of a premeditated murder. The State had failed to prove this. The case was obviously one containing such ingredients as a negligent father, a perhaps wayward daughter, and a mentally deranged charlatan of the worst type. But the accused was not guilty of murder. It had been a stupid, even a cruel accident, yet Deschamps had not intended to kill his little friend. When he had found that she was beyond resuscitation he had been frantic, and he had called upon God for help. He had begged God to let him die, too, and then he had tried to take his own life. If premeditation had been a factor, if he had planned to murder Juliette, would he have committed his deed in such a way, and in his own room? There were other ways. The girl had already been with him on trips to the country. It would be reasonable to assume that he might have found a better opportunity on such a journey. No, Juliette's death was an accident. Etienne Deschamps might be guilty of other crimes, but he was not guilty of murder. Judge Roman then read from the law on murder, pleading with the jury to remember that their duty was to decide only upon the crime for which the accused was now on trial.

Mr. Luzenberg denied all of this. Fear, he reasoned, had driven the prisoner—this monster!—at last to the most heinous crime a human being can commit against another. Perhaps Deschamps had

intended to commit suicide, but that did not matter. He had slain
Juliette in cold blood. Little Laurence had described how he had
continued to apply the chloroform-saturated handkerchief. When
his bottle was empty, he had dressed and gone out to buy more. He
wanted to be sure that she was dead. It was an act of fear—fear that
his first crime would be discovered. He had seduced and misused
this girl, a child not yet mature. He had abused her in ways too
horrible even to be described in court. He well knew discovery was
close at hand, so he had decided to murder her, then either to kill
himself, or to pretend to do so. Mr. Luzenberg spoke for a bit more
than an hour.

Hangman Taylor, seated in the courtroom, watched the progress
of the trial with much interest. Several times he was heard to ask
Sheriff Frank LeBlanc, who sat near him, "Boss, do you think we'll
win this time?"

The jury was out only thirteen minutes. The verdict was the same
as in the first trial: "Guilty as charged."

"*Mon Dieu! Mon Dieu!*" cried Deschamps loudly. He had
learned that much English.

From then on the behavior of the prisoner became more ec-
centric than ever. Many persons were convinced that he was insane, and his performances now indicated that either such was the
case, or else he was an actor of talent. His insults to everyone who
approached him were more gross than ever. He would talk to
Juliette for hours at a time, and he also conversed with Jean
Lafitte.

Letters of protest came to the police and to the newspapers from
all over the nation. Judge Marr was persecuted by individuals who
disagreed with the outcome of the second trial and who believed
Dr. Deschamps was not only insane, but that the death of Juliette
Deitsch had been due to an accident and was not premeditated
murder. The overwhelming majority of Orleanians approved of the
verdict, but this, it must be admitted, was more the result of their
outrage over the rape of Juliette than a belief that "the mad doctor," as he was now often called, had intended to kill her.

Many prominent citizens did not believe Deschamps should go to the gallows, and from these came a self-appointed board of physicians and mental experts who besieged the police, Judge Marr, and Governor Francis T. Nicholls of Louisiana with their opinion that Deschamps was a lunatic. This commission was composed of some of the best and most highly regarded medical men in the city, including Dr. J. G. Hava, Dr. E. J. Mioton, Dr. F. Fiomento, Dr. D. Borneo, Dr. E. D. Beach, Dr. George Lewis, Dr. John Dell'Orto and Dr. P. Fourzelle.

None of this swayed Judge Marr from his opinion that the accused was both sane and guilty of murder in the first degree. He therefore sentenced Deschamps to be hanged on January 18, 1891. Supporting him was Coroner LeMonnier, who stated that he was in complete disagreement with his fellows and that Deschamps was perfectly sane. Dr. LeMonnier said that he would prove this by performing an autopsy upon the brain of the condemned man after the execution.

But Deschamps did not die on January 18, 1891. The commission of doctors who sincerely believed the man insane prevailed upon Governor Nicholls to postpone sentence so that they might have more time to prove their diagnosis. This was fought with determination by Dr. LeMonnier, who even published a paper upon the subject of Deschamps' sanity, which was read before the American Medical Association, and by the New Orleans newspapers, who were equally determined this monster should not escape the gallows.

In August, 1890, Judge Roman had applied to the Board of Pardons for a commutation of sentence. There was long debate. A year passed. At last Governor Nicholls set the date for the hanging once more. It was to be January 3, 1892. Eighteen months had already gone by since the second trial. Juliette Deitsch had been dead for three years.

Never for a moment had Deschamps ceased to play the lunatic. He would sometimes talk to the moon and to spirits all day long. He complained that his food was made of stewed cigars. He continued to attempt to escape, but always in such a foolish and senseless way that it did not seriously annoy the guards of the prison.

His cell was now filled with his favorite books and magazines, and he would frequently read aloud from Voltaire or Anatole France, to the mixed annoyance and amusement of the police. "I will educate you," he would tell them, which some of them doubtless considered further evidence of insanity.

As January, 1892, neared Judge Roman sent another plea for commutation of sentence to the Board of Pardons. There was a further delay. The month passed and Deschamps still jabbered and read aloud in his cell, still assumed his "insulting" posture in the corner, still conversed with Jean Lafitte.

There were now two other men in condemned row. Henry Johnson had been so careless as to shoot a policeman to death. The other man, Philip Baker, had cut the throat of a woman proprietor of the grocery store where he had been employed as a clerk. To these neighbors Deschamps had little to say, although on occasion he would taunt them with such remarks as "I'll live to see you both swing from the gallows! Murderers!"

He turned his most vindictive hatred upon Coroner LeMonnier, for he knew the coroner had vigorously opposed the medical commission who believed him insane.

"Assassin LeMonnier!" he often cried. "Assassin LeMonnier!"

In February he was one day taken out upon a gallery overlooking the courtyard of Parish Prison for an airing. His guards were careless enough to leave him alone for a moment. He at once dived head foremost to the pavement below. His head must have been unusually hard. Nothing resulted but a recurrence of his headaches.

By now only two persons could talk to him, and one of these was Dr. Hava, who came now and then to see him and to study his behavior. Whether or not he realized that the physician thought him insane is difficult to decide, but he welcomed Dr. Hava's company, although he often released upon him a tirade of abuse regarding Dr. LeMonnier, which was probably acutely embarrassing to Dr. Hava. The other man he trusted was Sheriff Edgar White, who would discuss his French authors with him and listen with infinite patience to his arguments on the subject of his entire innocence of the crime of which he was accused.

Governor Nicholls now set the date for his execution as April. 22, the same date that Philip Baker would climb the gallows.

"They want to slaughter me with a murderer!" protested Dr. Deschamps.

In March he requested that he be allowed to write his will. Judge Theodule Buisson drew up the document for him. To Sheriff White he left the contents of his cell, which consisted of his beloved books, written, said the New Orleans newspapers, "by the French infidel writers," his magazines and his newspaper clippings, all of which he considered very valuable. He left his body to Dr. Hava. He had nothing else.

But the French Consul at New Orleans went to Baton Rouge on April 12, and called first upon Lieutenant Governor Jeffries and then upon Governor Nicholls. The State officials appear to have been greatly confused by now, and they must have been exhausted by this long and ever changing affair. They thanked the consul for his interest in a citizen of his country, but expressed their regrets. Deschamps must die with Philip Baker on the date of April 22.

Then there came the most mysterious occurrence of the entire case, if it were relevant to the case, a matter about which Orleanians, particularly in legal circles, still argue. On the morning of the nineteenth of April, Judge Robert H. Marr, who had presided over both the trials of Deschamps, went to the polls to vote in the then current election. He was seen by several people about an hour later walking along the levee edging the Mississippi River near Carrollton Avenue. Then he was never seen again. He vanished as completely and as permanently as if, as Mr. Charles Fort would have put it, he had been fished for from the sky!

However, no such occult and romantic theories were held by the authorities. Neither was there much consideration given to the possibility that any human agency had removed the judge from the scene. There was little talk of suicide. The aging and frail man was eminently successful, beloved in the community, and without known enemies. It was at last decided that in some way he had fallen into the river, despite the fact that the waters of the Mississippi were lapping away a good hundred feet from the levee upon which Judge Marr was last seen. On the other hand he may have left the levee and walked closer in. No body was ever found.

His connection with the Deschamps trial could not be overlooked at the moment. He had been one of the most persistent leaders of that side of the argument that wished to place the rope about the doctor's neck with as much speed as possible. He had opposed those factions whose desire it was to declare the doctor insane. Seldom in the papers but often in the street the question was asked: Was there any connection between the disappearance of the judge and the case of Deschamps?

As for the condemned man he received the news with elation. He had, he said, arranged it with the moon. Dr. LeMonnier would be next. He, Etienne Deschamps, would never hang.

Three days remained before the date scheduled for the dual hanging of the doctor and Philip Baker.

On the morning of April 22 a gasp of astonishment and no little disappointment fluttered from the lips of those who had come to witness the executions.

Someone called out, "Only one rope!"

Early that morning Deschamps awoke from a night of sound slumber and dressed himself for the execution. He ate a good breakfast and attended chapel, although he refused to confess to the priest who visited him in his cell. Baker, who seems to have been a courageous young man, attempted to talk to him, but Deschamps rejected both conversation and the proffered hand. After chapel he sat on the edge of his bunk, staring into space morosely. His behavior was more normal than usual, and it was apparent that he had resigned himself, and no longer had hope of escaping what was to take place shortly after noon. Sheriff Edgar White visited him, and he asked White to take good care of his books.

At eleven-thirty came a telegram from Lieutenant Governor Joseph Jeffries. Governor Nicholls had once more reprieved him. Deschamps put his face in his hands and remained in that position for more than an hour.

Baker went to the gallows at twelve-fifty. Deschamps said to Sheriff White, who was again with him, "Don't you see that I am not a murderer?"

What had happened is not quite clear. The self-appointed sanity commission had presented the governor with another report on the mental condition of Deschamps. The disappearance of Judge Marr played a not inconsiderable part. The newspapers hinted that sinister forces were at work, and speculated anew upon a connection between the vanished judge and the reprieve. A rumor spread through Roman Catholic New Orleans that Deschamps was a Mason and that "Masons never hang." Masonic dignitaries, outraged, replied that Deschamps was not a Mason but a Catholic, which he was.

Within a few days, and no doubt besieged by disputers from both sides, Governor Nicholls set a new date.

And Deschamps did hang. On May 12, 1892, he again dressed himself for death, and again attended chapel. He still refused to give confession to the priest. "You want me to confess to murder," he said. "I did not commit murder."

Walking through the corridor leading from the condemned row to the courtyard where the gallows waited he denounced Dr. LeMonnier loudly, but he walked as a strong man walks, and there was no indication of fear, only rage.

He came face to face with the man he most hated as he neared the gallows. "Assassin LeMonnier!" he cried. "You could have saved me. You, even you, of all others. But no! You preferred to disgrace me and France."

There was comment among those who watched the hanging as to Deschamps' altered appearance. He was thin almost to the stage of emaciation. With the beard gone his chin was weak, his mouth sensual, thick-lipped, and red.

Hangman Taylor adjusted the rope about his neck, but before he tightened it Deschamps turned burning eyes upon the figure in the black domino and mask. Yet he said only, and quietly, "Adieu." He looked down upon the witnesses below, and said, "I am innocent. LeMonnier is the criminal." Then he added once more, "Adieu."

The trap was sprung at one-ten in the afternoon. Twenty minutes later the body was cut down. Dr. LeMonnier opened the skull and removed the brain. It was a healthy brain with no indication of degeneration.

Henry C. Castellanos, who mentioned the case of Deschamps in his *New Orleans As It Was*, asks, "Was he a criminal, or was he insane?" and answers his own questions thus, "Though his reasoning faculties were no doubt defective, he certainly deserved that degrading punishment which he underwent, for offenses *other* than that of which he was found guilty. But he was a victim of prejudice. That his conviction on the charge of *murder* was a judicial error, a blot upon the administration of criminal justice, a fatal mistake, is an opinion to which I have firmly clung, and my reasons therefor are very clear." Castellanos was living and writing at the time of the crime and its consequences. The italics are his.

There is no doubt but that the punishment meted out to Deschamps was more the result of public rage in regard to the rape of little Juliette, a heinous offense according to both law and public opinion, than it was because it was proven satisfactorily that murder, as it is legally defined, had been committed.

Yet was not perhaps murder, even according to that strict definition, done? Deschamps had been using chloroform for some time, and he must have had some slight knowledge of the amount of it that could be inhaled without endangering life. If Laurence told the truth, and there is no reason to believe she did not, Deschamps applied the anesthetic again and again, and was not even satisfied when the child first slept, but went out to buy more, which he continued to apply. It is at least possible that he did, as the prosecution insisted, fear exposure of his relationship with a child of twelve years of age, and he must have known that such exposure was inevitable. Is it not possible that he sought then to create the impression that her death was at worst due to his bungling, that it was perhaps manslaughter, but not murder, planned and premeditated?

Or perhaps he was insane. There are types of insanity that Dr. LeMonnier could not have discovered during his autopsy upon the brain. Surely he was not normal.

There are many unanswered questions. Did Juliette actually fancy herself so in love with this old Romeo that she had plotted a suicide-murder pact with him? It is possible. Did he, in his abnormal lust, think himself in love with the child?

The letters were dismissed much too lightly. And what was in the other letters and papers the doctor burned? Was it true that Juliette was incapable of composing such letters?

There is no doubt that Deschamps did want to die after he knew Juliette was dead. Why else should he have cried out his wish to do so with no one in the room but Laurence?

And, of course, there is a final question, perhaps the most interesting of all, yet perhaps without any bearing upon the case. What happened to Judge Marr?

A PROBLEM IN GOOD AND EVIL

Young Robert Robinson liked his job. In 1903 the gangsters of the Prohibition era, the motion pictures, and Dick Tracy had not yet increased the interest of the young in the position held by Robert's boss, yet, even then, there were few dull moments for the district attorney's office boy. Daily association with crime might become dull for an older person, but not for one of sixteen. The carelessly unclosed door, the raised voice from within Mr. Gurley's private office, and the inclination of mysterious callers to confide their innermost secrets while awaiting an interview all gave to the position the sensual qualities of the wince, the quiver, and the thrill, the rise of the blood to events of violence and excitement, all second hand, of course, but yet newer and in more detail than the outside world would ever know. Still the office itself was serene and quiet, and it is doubtful that Robert ever expected to witness murder.

On the morning of July 20 the lad was tardy in arriving at the office. He unlocked the door at a few minutes past nine o'clock, and at once began eradicating evidence of the lost minutes with an increase in speed, opening windows, the mail, placing the somewhat melted ice that had awaited him in the hall into the water cooler, and performing whatever other tasks were usual in the mornings. He had just settled down to peruse the newspaper at nine-thirty when the door opened and there was the intrusion of a tall gentleman in his middle years, who had under his stiff straw hat a bald and bony head and who wore a droopy white mustache. Robert recognized him as Lewis W. Lyons, who had often called at the office and whom he had seen many times lingering outside the Macheca Building, where the office was located.

Lyons asked if Mr. Gurley had come in yet, and Robert replied he had not, and would Mr. Lyons wait? Mr. Lyons said he would return in a quarter of an hour. Robert added that the district attorney always arrived at exactly nine-fifty, and then resumed his reading as Lyons exited through the door by which he had entered. Even Robert, who had a nose for gore, did not guess that in one of the visitor's pockets was a revolver, that in another pocket was enough cyanide of potassium to have eliminated every lawyer and policeman in the city of New Orleans, and that, apparently by way of extra precaution, there were additional lozenges of cyanide of potassium stuck into the gay band which adorned Mr. Lyon's straw caddie.

In the meantime, at about nine-twenty, J. Ward Gurley and Mrs. Gurley had boarded a Tulane Belt streetcar at the corner of St. Charles and Henry Clay avenues. They took a car going, naturally, in a downtown direction, and just before they stepped aboard they sighted Assistant District Attorney S. J. Montgomery, who was in the act of entering a trolley bound in the uptown direction. A tipping of derbies and bows were exchanged, and then the Gurleys settled down in their car to a discussion of Mrs. Gurley's plans for the day, which included a visit to the dentist, some shopping for their two daughters, and a luncheon with friends. It was quite an ordinary Monday morning.

Gurley left his wife at a downtown intersection, proceeded to the Macheca Building, and emerged from the elevator on the fourth floor at precisely nine-fifty. Entering his outer office, he greeted Robert, placed his hat on a tall stand near the door, and entered his sanctum. He had, according to the statement of his office boy, given later in the day, nothing unusual about his appearance.

The door of his private office had scarcely closed when a lady and Lyons entered the reception room almost simultaneously. The lady was Mrs. Rivero, who must have had a first name or at least an initial, but for some curious reason (perhaps it was a desire to shield her from as much publicity as possible on the part of the authorities) remains simply "Mrs. Rivero" in all reports of what followed. Robert knew the lady, so he rapped on the district attorney's door. Gurley appeared, bowed to the lady, but said, "I'll take you first, Mr. Lyons."

"No hurry," replied Mr. Lyons, gallantly. "I will wait awhile for you."

Mrs. Rivero entered the office, the door closed, and Lyons sat on the sill of a window, holding his hat containing the cyanide lozenges in his lap.

While the lady was in conference with Gurley several things happened. Delos C. Mellen, who had long been Gurley's law partner, entered, and passed into his own private office without speaking to Lyons. A moment later Dr. C. C. Buck, a dentist who had offices in the building, came in. He bowed to Lyons and entered Mellen's office. Then Frank Doran also entered and took a seat to await Gurley.

Mrs. Rivero emerged within a few minutes and Gurley escorted her to the door. Then he turned, said, "Lyons," and held open the door to his private office while his visitor entered it.

The door closed and everything was peaceful for a few minutes. Neither Robert nor Doran heard any loud talking until Lyon's voice came roaring through the stained-glass door in one uncompleted sentence.

"I'll show you I'm not one of your God-damned North Rampart Street—!" cried Lyons.

If the sentence was finished no one heard the last word, and for a splendid reason. It was drowned beneath the thrice repeated reports of a revolver. Then there was, according to all reports, a pause, during which, as was afterward deduced from the fact that three empty cartridges and two bullets were found upon Mr. Gurley's floor, Lyons broke the combination cylinder of his long-barreled pistol and reloaded it. Then he sent a fourth bullet into the bleeding district attorney upon the floor.

During this interval, presumably brief, Robert and Doran were momentarily paralyzed by shock. At that moment W. L. Shepard, a real estate agent, entered the anteroom and joined the other two in staring at the tall and stooped silhouette of Lyons that showed against the glass door. Dr. Buck and Mellen came bounding out of the latter's office as the fourth shot exploded, and Dr. V. K. Irion, another dentist with offices on the floor, his assistant, a young lady named Alice Wattingly, and George Terriberry, an attorney, also joined them.

They were all just about to go into action when the little door of the district attorney's office opened, and Lyons came out. Under one arm he had thin, small Mr. Gurley tucked up as if he intended to carry him away. "He stood Mr. Gurley on his feet," said Dr. Irion later, "and the two men looked into each other's eyes for a moment. Then he let my poor friend go, and Mr. Gurley stood swaying and staggering in an effort to keep his balance."

Dr. Irion saw no more of the immediate scene, for Lyons raised his right hand pointed the pistol at the dentist, and Dr. Irion sensibly ducked into the hall. The others quickly moved out of line, but Lyons lowered his gun, re-entered the inner office and closed the door behind him. Gurley fell forward into the arms of Lawyer Terriberry.

"My God! He's murdering me!" cried the district attorney.

It was afterward remarked that Terriberry was in danger. His back was to the door behind which the murderer still waited, but he remained beside the district attorney, trying to comfort him, as the little man kept moaning, "Murder! Murder! He murdered me for nothing!" Terriberry remembered later that while this was going on he heard Lyons snap the latch of the door.

A few seconds later there was another report of pistol fire from within the office.

By this time there was, as the newspapers said the next day, "a wild time in the Macheca Building." Robert had run down the hall screaming "Help! Murder!" in the very best tradition. Miss Wattingly stooped beside the district attorney weeping and repeating over and over, "O Mr. Gurley! O Mr. Gurley!" People were running up and down the stairs, elevator bells were jangling, the corridor outside the office was filling, and Mr. Doran and Mr. Mellen were endeavoring to keep the curious from entering the room where lay the dying man. "Lady shoppers in the streets outside dashed into stores, not knowing from whence the shooting was coming, nor whether or not it would be continued in the thoroughfare."

Dr. Buck met Private Detective Chris C. Cain and a policeman named Gessell in the hall outside and brought them into the office. Dr. Irion had by now telephoned for an ambulance and to police headquarters, and a few minutes later a wagon load of policemen, armed with clubs and drawn revolvers, forced their way through the excited mob in the hallways. As they entered the office George Terriberry announced sadly that Mr. Gurley was dead.

"Expecting a ferocious attack from within the locked office, for they were not at all sure what the final pistol report had meant . . ." the police, aided by Private Detective Cain and the building engineer, who had picked the lock on the door for them, rushed into the other room. Lyons lay on the floor with blood gushing from his self-inflicted head wound. Detective Cain stooped beside him and asked his name and his reason for killing Mr. Gurley, but the wounded man could only mutter incoherently. Robert and Mr. Mellen entered the room then and identified him. The stretcher-bearers arrived and bore the murderer away to the Charity Hospital, from which came an announcement that afternoon that he would live to stand trial for his crime. He had pointed the barrel at his forehead and meant to send the bullet straight through the cranium at a point just above the nose, but having held the pistol awkwardly, and no doubt pulled the trigger with his thumb, the bullet had careened and deflected, so that instead of going into the head and straight through the brain, it had passed through only his forehead and emerged above the temple. He might be blind, perhaps also deaf, it was said, but he would live.

This was much to the public satisfaction. J. Ward Gurley had been a popular figure in New Orleans—the word "beloved" was used—and, besides, there was widespread curiosity as to the motive. From then on each detail of the case was followed avidly. There was a murder in New Orleans nearly every day, but seldom was the district attorney the victim.

One of the most interesting angles was the cyanide of potassium, some of which was unloaded from Lyons' pocket after he was taken to the hospital, and more of which was found in his hat picked up from the floor of Gurley's office. Another was that despite the fact that the men outside had heard nothing that indicated a struggle, there was evidence that some sort of fight, conducted in spooky silence, must have taken place behind the closed door. A revolving bookcase was smashed, a pile of books that had been stacked against one wall had been knocked down and the books scattered in disorder about the floor, and a chair had been overturned. Since no one knew what had taken place within that closed room the conjectures were endless and varied. However, the most persistent question was—why?

Delos C. Mellen, who had been Mr. Gurley's law partner, supplied an answer.

"This is an old case," Mr. Mellen told the police. "It dates back to 1895. In that year Lyons was out drinking one night with a man named Dan S. Carroll, who was an auditor for the telephone exchange, and a man named McGrath and another, whose name I have forgotten. They were drinking in the Smile Saloon. Lyons left and took a car for his home in Carrollton about twelve o'clock. The others drifted to the Little Diamond Saloon, on Burgundy and Customhouse streets, and at three in the morning Carroll found that his diamond stickpin was gone. He reported the matter to the police, and gave the names of those who had been with him. Carroll was so drunk that he did not know what he was doing.

"The next day Detectives De Rance and Kerwin saw Lyons at Baronne and Canal streets, and De Rance asked if he knew McGrath and where he lived. Lyons said that he did and offered to go to the place with the detectives. McGrath was not home, so they returned to Canal Street, and in front of the Grand Opera House met Carroll. One of the detectives asked Carroll if Lyons had been with him the night before, and Carroll answered, 'Yes.'

"Lyons said, 'You know that I was not with you when the pin was stolen.' Carroll said, 'Never mind, I will fix you tomorrow!'

Then the detectives arrested Lyons and locked him up, charged with stealing the pin. He was kept in jail all that night, but was released the next day under a $500 bond. He was tried two weeks later, and at that time Carroll said Lyons had nothing to do with the stealing of the pin, so he was discharged."

It was then, Mellen said, that he and Mr. Gurley had met Lyons, who sought them out and engaged them to represent him in a suit against Carroll and Detectives De Rance and Kerwin for damages of $5,040.

"Lyons was particularly outraged," added Mellen, "because he had spent a night in the bull pen with Negroes and filthy white men who had been arrested during the night for vagrancy and similar charges. He never seemed able to forget that night."

It was Mellen who conducted the case in the Civil District Court. An adverse decision was given. Lyons then accused Mellen of negligence, to which the attorney had replied that if he were not satisfied he might hire another attorney. Lyons called on Gurley and complained, and Gurley, after many importunities, consented to take the case to the Supreme Court. This was done, but the lower court was sustained, and Lyons had no further recourse.

Lyons' ire now turned upon Gurley. He called to see him nearly every day, so last, to satisfy him, Gurley, according to Mellen, appointed a committee of three attorneys, who reviewed all the evidence, the judgment of the lower court and the ruling of the Supreme Court, and came up with the decision that Lyons' attorneys had been without blame and that everything possible had been done.

However, Lyons still refused to be amicable. One day in 1901 he dispatched a second to Gurley's office and challenged the attorney to a duel. Duels were about out of fashion even in New Orleans at that time, but Gurley was irritated and could not decide what to do, so he called together four of his friends, a Mr. Montgomery, then one of his assistants, H. Gibbs Morgan, Theodore Wilkinson, and Mellen, and asked their opinion as to his proper and manly course of action. All agreed that a gentleman was no longer required to comply with such a challenge and that, particularly since

Gurley was of diminutive size and without experience with either pistol or rapier, the wisest procedure would be to ignore it.

Mr. Montgomery told of the next meeting between Lyons and Gurley. Lyons did not come to the office for some months after the challenge, but he wrote letters which Gurley did not answer. Then one day he arrived when Montgomery was in the outer room. Montgomery informed Gurley, in a jocular manner, "Your friend, Lyons, is outside."

"All right," replied the district attorney, "show him in, but you stay in the room."

"Why don't you answer my letters?" asked Lyons.

"I have said everything to you there is to say," replied Gurley.

"Why didn't you give me satisfaction?" was Lyons' next question. "I demanded satisfaction." He was referring to the duel.

"I owe you no satisfaction," said Gurley. "I have never harmed you, and why should I seek to harm you, or you me?"

To this Lyons replied in a long and eventually abusive tirade, asking, among other things, if Gurley "thought he was working for a N. Rampart Street pimp" (which seems to connect with the one phrase overheard the morning of the slaying) and ending with the statement that Gurley and Mellen had "ruined" him. Gurley then told him to get the hell out of his office, which he did.

After that Lyons was often seen hanging around outside the Macheca Building and in front of the courthouse when Gurley was prosecuting a case. Montgomery had not seen him in Gurley's office before the day he arrived loaded down with a pistol and lozenges of cyanide of potassium.

Lewis W. Lyons was an unfortunate man. Now he was fifty-four years of age, and he was not without reason for bitterness. His background was what was called then even more frequently than now one of "good family." He had prominent and wealthy relatives and connections, but he had somehow never been able to live up to the tradition. As a young man he had worked as a clerk in a warehouse, leaving after ten years of service to horrify his family by opening a saloon. This failed, however, and he obtained another clerical position in the cotton seed oil cake business. Later he had worked at Chalmette as a clerk, and was eventually discharged.

Other things had befallen him. His wife had taken her five children and separated from him, and he lived alone in a rooming house in Gravier near Dryades Street, a seedy establishment adjoining a laundry. He was not on very good terms, either, with his own family. At least one of his brothers had not spoken to him for years. Lately he had begun to drink, although his landlady testified that she had never seen him drunk. Much was made of his addiction to the demon bourbon and the fact that he was often seen playing dominoes in the saloons. "He was free with his money," wrote one reporter. "Only last Saturday night he was noted cashing a check for ten dollars in a barroom."

His appearance, too, came in for much comment. He was described as "tall and thin, with blue eyes, a drooping mustache, a retreating forehead and an aquiline nose. He was very dressy, in fact sporty in his attire, with which he took great pains." Of his personality it was said that he was "morose and moody, of an exceedingly quiet disposition, and had but little to say except when in his cups."

In direct contrast was J. Ward Gurley. About the same age, he had led a life of more than ordinary success, and the newspapers were filled the day after his murder with long eulogies on the career of "the lamented patriot, lawyer and public official." His family was a prominent one, too, and he had identified himself with public affairs even as a very young man. Particularly that time, some thirty years before, "when the manhood and courage of New Orleans was called upon to free the community of carpetbagger rule and to restore our fair city to Democratic principles," was recalled. In this J. Ward Gurley was said to have played an active role. He had held three public offices, that of assistant city attorney, that of United States district attorney, and, beginning in 1900, the one of which he was the incumbent at the time of his death. He was president of the Audubon Park Commission, and a member of such clubs as the Boston Club, the Pickwick Club and the Louisiana Club, and was otherwise connected with the municipal and social life of the city.

Mr. Gurley had been married twice, his first wife having died, and he had two daughters, the Misses Aurora and Helen, the former having made her debut during the season prior to her father's death, the latter being still a student at Newcomb College. He was a man below average height and of frail physique, with a squarish graying beard and mild blue eyes, but, said a reporter for the *Daily Picayune*, "beneath the calm exterior there dwelt a leonine and absolutely fearless soul. Duty was ever paramount with him, and although very kind and sympathetic by nature, he did not permit his feelings to swerve him from the path the law pointed out."

Statements from his friends bore out the esteem of those associated with him. "He was the gentlest man I ever knew," said Mr. Montgomery. "No man ever knew him that did not love him." Said the Reverend Dr. W. H. La Prade, of the Methodist Episcopal Church, South, "I regard Mr. Gurley's death as a public calamity. He was thoroughly above corruption." Added City Attorney Gilmore, "It is beyond my comprehension that Mr. Gurley should have incurred the deadly malice of any reasonably thinking man. He had a duty to perform for the people, and he religiously performed that."

The assassination of the district attorney thus aroused much public indignation, which was not decreased by the editorializing of the newspapers, who called attention to the lack of regard for law and order in the city, as evidenced by the fact that a prominent citizen such as Mr. Gurley could, as the *Daily Picayune* put it, "be done to death by a dissipated and worthless fellow named Lyons."

This crime is all the more startling [continued the editor] because it comes at a moment when respect for law and the operation for the machinery for the enforcement of law and the protection of public order are held on the lowest esteem. Violent and bloody crimes have been numerous and of the most audacious and defiant character. Gambling houses are run wide open on every prominent street, and public order and the protection of society are virtually at the mercy of the lawless classes. It should well become the people of this city to pause in the midst of the absorbing cares of their business and to arouse themselves from their usual indifference to public affairs, to consider what is to be the end of this reign of lawlessness. As to the wretched being who has startled the community by the atrocity of his deed, little need be said. His crime in the eyes of the law is neither greater nor less in seriousness than those of numerous other murderers who have gone through the courts before him and have escaped all punishment or have enjoyed official clemency in the form of a more or less brief detention in custody. It would not be profitable to the peace and safety of the community to attempt to forecast his case. Pleas of insanity or of self-defense are efficacious to cover every variety and degree of violent bloodshed in Louisiana.

Thus the two men, the murderer, the murdered, the evil, the good, the defeated, the successful.

Day after day the progress of Lyons' recovery was reported to the public as regularly and in as much detail as the public could wish, and it wished for all it could get. It was announced at the end of a week that Lyons was well out of danger, that he could soon be removed from Charity Hospital to the Parish Prison, and that he would retain the sight in his right eye and the hearing in his right ear, although the organs on the other side of his head were probably damaged beyond repair.

On July 23, three days after the killing, Coroner M. V. Richards, police officials, and some reporters were allowed to visit the wounded man. Dr. Richards by a curious coincidence was already acquainted with Lyons. Early in the morning of the shooting he had met the murderer in a saloon, where, Dr. Richards explained, he had gone with some friends to have a drink. Dr. Richards found some keys upon the floor and upon one of them was the name H. Conrad. He was inquiring of the bartender as to who H. Conrad might be, when Lyons stepped up and offered the information that the name was not that of the owner of the keys but that of a locksmith of his acquaintance who had made them. "I thought this was so nice of him," said Dr. Richards, generously, "that I offered to buy him a drink, which he accepted."

Lyons, however, did not recall the incident at the hospital. Furthermore, he was not inclined to talk to anyone, particularly the coroner. After some encouragement, however, he made several brief statements.

Still shocked by the tragedy that had befallen his friend, Dr. Richards asked, "What possessed you to shoot a man like Mr. Gurley?"

"I demanded satisfaction from him and he refused it to me," replied Lyons. "Mr. Mellen did not conduct my case properly, and I went to Mr. Gurley. I told him that Mellen was a crook, and I wanted him to take up my case and expose Mellen. When he refused I asked him to make Mellen reimburse me all the money I had lost through Mellen's practices and his own neglect, and he refused that, too. If he had given me the money I would have walked out and never spoken to him of the matter again. I repeatedly wrote Mr. Gurley, but he would not even answer my letters. Mr. Mellen had them on file and can show them if he wants to do so."

"You could hardly expect an attorney to refund a fee for a case he had already handled," said Dr. Richards.

"I was broke," said Lyons, "and I needed the money."

"You were seen," chided a reporter present, "cashing a check for ten dollars in a saloon last Saturday night."

"I spent it," confessed Lyons, humbly.

He then added the further information that he had known Gurley since boyhood. They had gone to school together for a time, but had never been close friends. He had never employed Gurley as an attorney until after Mellen had lost his damage suit against Carroll and the detectives. Then he had placed his trust in Gurley, and he had failed him, too.

"What were you going to do with the cyanide of potassium?" asked Dr. Richards. "Did you intend to use it for the purpose of suicide?"

"I don't know what you are talking about," said Lyons.

"There were lozenges of cyanide in your pocket and enough more in your hatband to have killed a regiment," replied the coroner.

"That," said Lyons, "is ridiculous, Dr. Richards."

Further questioning failed to change this denial of having the poison in his possession.

"Do you think," asked Dr. Richards, pursuing another course at last, "that every man who has a case lost by his attorney should kill him?"

The answer to the silly question was direct, complete, and classical.

"Yes," said Lyons, "I certainly do."

That ended the interview.

The arraignment before Judge Frank D. Chretien took place on August 6. Lyons was still feeble and his left eye was still bandaged. The usual curious mob awaited him outside the courthouse and followed inside, as he entered leaning on the shoulder of a deputy sheriff, even running up the stairs to catch another glimpse of him as he emerged from the elevator on the second floor.

Present in the courtroom was the new district attorney, Chandler C. Luzenberg and his assistant, St. Clair Adams.

"Are you guilty or not guilty?" asked Judge Chretien.

"Not guilty," replied the prisoner.

There was a little pause and then Judge Chretien asked if the prisoner had the means to employ counsel.

"No, Your Honor," was the reply. "I have not."

"Shall the court arrange counsel for you?"

"No, Your Honor," said Lyons. "I expect to arrange to be represented."

Reporters waited outside as the prisoner left the building, but Lyons requested of the deputy that he not be interviewed by them.

On August 9 he announced from his cell that he would talk to no one of his case except his attorneys. It was noted that he was still quite ill. Even the sight of the right eye was far from normal and pus ran from his ears.

A ghost story came on September 13. Lyons' cellmate, it was said, awoke at night to find a ghost standing beside his bunk. Lyons laughingly said it was foolishness. About this time he named his attorneys as Joseph E. Generelly and Warren Doyle.

The trial opened early in November, and the first five days were consumed by the selection of a jury. It was said that never had a jury been so difficult to obtain. So many of the men called for duty asserted that they did not believe in capital punishment that the newspapers were aroused to new and scorching indictments regarding the moral tone of the community.

Yesterday [said the *Daily Picayune* on November 12], the securing of a jury in the District Criminal Court to try Lewis W. Lyons for the murder of District Attorney J. Ward Gurley was concluded. The difficulty of securing this jury was extreme, not because men had formed prejudices for or against the accused, but because of the great number of male citizens of New Orleans who declared themselves absolutely incompetent to sit upon a jury in any capital case.

The number of talesmen summoned for jury duty in this case was 311. Of these 110 declared upon oath that they would not take part in a verdict that would condemn a man to death for any crime or under any circumstances whatever. Then there were, in addition, 56 who would not convict upon circumstantial evidence; that is to say, they would not convict in any capital case, such as murder or rape, unless witnesses would testify that they saw the criminal in the act of perpetrating the crime.

If these 166 talesmen out of a total of 311 are to be held as a test of the public conscience in this city, then, taking it for granted that there are in New Orleans, as was stated by the census of 1900, 65,000 literate males competent to sit upon a jury, in the proportion of the 166 constitutionally disqualified jurors to the 311 summoned, there would be in this city 34,371 male citizens who would be constitutionally unable or unwilling to punish with death a murderer or a ravisher. . . . Some persons have expressed the belief that the remarkable exhibition of opposition to inflicting capital punishment is merely a pretext to avoid jury duty, but since the talesmen in the premises answered under oath, and some of them in their eagerness to show their conscientious scruples on the subject, swore that they would not desire the death by judicial decree even of the murderer or ravisher of those nearest and dearest to them, it must be accepted that they are sincerely honest in their tenderness for such criminals.

Some persons, however, who have seen fit to comment on the remarkable exhibition mentioned, have averred that some of these same conscientious individuals who so declared their determination to take no part in rendering a legal verdict that would consign a criminal to a sentence of death, were actively engaged in the celebrated lynching of Italians in the Parish Prison here some years ago,* but if so it must be remembered that in moments of excitement conscientious scruples are cast to the winds and only operate when there is no temptation to discard them.

The great danger under such extreme conditions of tender conscience towards criminals is that the people of this and of every other community where such a state of feeling exists will despair more than ever of securing the punishment of murderers and ravishers, and will take matters into their own violent hands. There is no question that the growing prevalence of lynching arises from the increasing lack of confidence in the efficacy of judicial methods to punish criminals. The blame cannot be laid upon the judges or on the police, but it falls upon the people's representatives who make the laws, and upon the juries of the people who try the cases. The people alone are responsible.

It is true that in the early 1900's it was popular and fashionable to state that one did not believe in capital punishment, as it was popular to believe in socialism—of the palest and most delicate pink variety of course. There was great concern regarding this modish thinking on the part of the press. In New Orleans the people were daily informed that they were drifting into moral apathy, if not downright decadence, here there being a minimum of truth, but by no means a new truth as far as Orleanians were concerned. It was also true that there had been epidemics of lynchings in many parts of the country (while Lyons was on trial six Negroes were burned at the stake in Delaware for crimes ranging from rape and murder to impudence to a policeman) and, although all editors condemned such practices, it was pointed out that there could be times when the good citizens of a community were forced by the

* A reference to the conclusion of the Hennessy case.

laxity of other citizens and of the authorities to mete out their own justice. "Lynching will continue," said *Harper's Weekly* on July 11, 1903, "even increase in frequency and horror, wherever the people have reason to apprehend a failure of the law. The practice can be eradicated, but not by rebuking outraged human nature. It can be eradicated by recognizing the just demands and securing the implicit confidence of the people. And in no other way imaginable." This reprinted in a New Orleans newspaper may have been a solemn warning to those upon whom the fate of Lewis W. Lyons depended.

It was Wednesday, November 11, before the jury was at last complete and the testimony of witnesses began. The State's first questions were concerned with descriptions of the wounds of which Mr. Gurley had died, two of which were fatal, the other two having pierced only the right forearm. Dr. Richards was then called upon to describe the statements of Lyons while he was still in the hospital, to which the defense, represented by Mr. Generelly, argued that while Lyons was in durance he was suffering from his wound and not of sound mind.

The appearance of Lyons in court impressed all concerned deeply. The months in prison had so altered him that a number of witnesses called upon to identify him could scarcely recognize him as the same man. He looked, it was said, to have aged twenty years and had the appearance of an old man, broken in health and spirit. The lid of his left eye was nearly closed and his hearing was obviously affected, for he leaned forward frequently in an effort to hear the testimony of witnesses. His shoulders stooped and his cheeks were sunken and gaunt. Contributing to the appearance of great age was the fact that he had allowed his beard to grow while in jail, and it was snowy white. Regarding this latter fact the State several times hinted that it was a deliberate attempt to increase his pathetic appearance and arouse sympathy. Pity was also aroused by the sight of his mother, who was very old, and of his sisters, who attended the trial nearly every day.

Robert Robinson was one of the first witnesses called. "The little fellow was badly shaken up by the assassination of Mr. Gurley, to whom he was deeply attached," commented a reporter. "His grief was obvious as he took the witness chair." Robert described the occurrences of the morning in detail. When asked to identify Mr. Lyons, he looked at the bearded man and admitted that he hardly knew him now.

The other witnesses of the excitement that took place on the morning of July 20, including George Terriberry, Dr. Irion, Mr. Shepard, and Mr. Doran, corroborated Robert's description. A Mrs. Rivero was called and contributed one slightly interesting statement. She said she had heard some shooting as she left the Macheca Building, but she continued toward her destination, for she had an appointment with her dressmaker and was in a hurry.

Delos C. Mellen testified that he had known Gurley many years, and had been his law partner from 1889 until 1902. He also knew the accused. He had never worn a beard, remarked Mellen, such as he wore at the present time. He also appeared much weaker now than when he last saw him. Formerly, he had been robust and strong. Mellen said that he had brought a suit for damages for him against Dan R. Carroll and Detectives Kerwin and De Rance for false imprisonment. In the fall of 1898 the suit, for $5,040, was decided against Lyons. Lyons had paid him only $25 or $30 for the costs of citations and other fees. Mellen said he had been forced to pay about $70 out of his pocket. The case was then appealed to the Supreme Court and the witness believed he had paid another $20 of his own money for the clerk's fees for appeal. After the decision of the higher court was rendered against Lyons the latter had intimated to him that he had not tried to win his case, and he had told Lyons "in vigorous language" to find another attorney. From that day he had never "heard the sound of Lyons' voice."

District Attorney Luzenberg then produced the Annual Report of the Supreme Court and read the decision upon the case of L. W. Lyons vs. Daniel R. Carroll.

In the cross-examination Warren Doyle presented Mellen with three slips of paper, receipts for amounts of money paid to Mellen by Lyons, the last one for $100, which was in Mellen's handwriting.

The witness acknowledged that he must have received this money, but that he did not remember it.

Doyle then asked the witness if he had not remarked to a number of newspaper reporters that he thought Lyons was insane. Mellen replied that he may have used the word "crazy," but that he had meant it in a loose sense, not to say that Lyons was mentally defective in the definition of the law, and that he had never thought that he could be interdicted. He often used the word "crazy," meaning erratic and peculiar.

From about this point the defense concentrated upon an effort to prove Lewis W. Lyons insane.

Oliver P. Nobles testified that he had known the accused for twenty years. Lyons had been of good character and good habits until arrested on the charge of stealing the diamond stickpin. After that he became "morose, melancholy and utterly the reverse of what he had been before." He had frequently talked to the witness about his damage suit and he had blamed everyone connected with it, the lawyers, the judge, and even the stenographers. Nobles said he came to consider him insane. He had once asked Lyons to go into the furniture business with him, but the accused had refused, and seemed unable to discuss anything but his lost suit against Carroll and the detectives. He often described the night he had spent in jail with low and criminal characters, and said that the arrest had ruined him in the eyes of all except his closest friends, for he could not find work. Yet when the witness had offered him a means of earning his livelihood he had not been interested. The witness believed that anyone so obsessed by one subject must not be mentally balanced.

Dr. Marion Souchon said he had but a limited acquaintance with the defendant. Lyons had called on him a few times for treatment. The doctor did consider him a very peculiar man, although at the time he had known Lyons he had not questioned his mental condition. Lyons had not acted like an ordinary man. He would not classify him as insane. There were numerous persons with such oddities of behavior, who were not insane.

James Mott said that until the incident of the false arrest Lyons had been a pleasant companion, an intelligent and well-read man, always genial and sociable. After the arrest, however, he became a monomaniac on the subject of the injustice that had been committed upon him and the shame he had suffered. The witness said that Lyons had talked so incessantly upon the one subject that he had at last avoided him whenever possible, and had believed that Lyons was losing his mind. Once he had even told Lyons that he was "going crazy" on the subject of the suit. Mr. Mott ended his testimony by remarking that he had never heard that Lyons beat his wife.

At about this point there was an interruption in the day's proceedings. Judge Chretien ordered the court cleared of all persons but the accused and the attorneys for the State and the defense. He then announced that he had been informed by a note that one of the jurors had a statement to make. Mr. Faust, the first juror sworn, acted as spokesman and arose to say that one of the gentlemen, Mr. Gehbauer, had said that if the State could not produce better evidence than they had until now, that he had already formed his opinion. Mr. Faust was worried lest Mr. Gehbauer would not give the State a fair trial. Then Mr. Gehbauer arose and asserted that he had been misunderstood, and that all he had said was that the way things were going they should all be home by Saturday, and thank God, and this was the first time he had ever served on a jury and he didn't know anything about it, and, besides, he didn't like it very much. Judge Chretien expressed the hope that no remarks of that sort would be made in the future.

The defense now produced Miss Chatty Lyons, a sister of the accused, who said that until the incident of the stickpin her brother had been of a lively and cheerful disposition. He had been good to his wife and children and had provided for them to the best of his ability. The witness was shown a bundle of letters, which she identified as being in her brother's handwriting. Miss Lyons said that her brother was very domestic and devoted to his family. Mr. Luzenberg gallantly forbore a cross-examination of the lady. Mr. Generelly produced a long letter written by Lyons to Gurley and dated December 10, 1901. The first part of the letter was lucid, but it ended in incoherent phrases and wordage. District Attorney Luzenberg scrutinized the letter.

Lyons' mother impressed everyone in the court by "her age and great dignity" when she took the stand. Her son, she said, had changed lately. He would come to her home and sit in a corner and mope and cry. Once when she had scolded him for neglecting his children, he had written her a very disrespectful letter, which she had burned, reflecting that of late his mind had seemed affected.

There followed a number of witnesses, all friends and acquaintances of Lyons, who were of the opinion that the accused was either entirely insane, or at least so obsessed upon the one subject of his false arrest as not to be normal. Mrs. Mary O'Connor, the matron of the Parish Prison, said that Lyons would sometimes ask for his breakfast early, but that other mornings when his food was brought to him he would insist he had already had his breakfast. Mrs. O'Connor added that although the doctor had ordered him to walk about his cell for exercise he would not obey, and that he was odd in many other ways. He was not very talkative and became angry because he could not make cream cheese in his cell.

"Do you think his actions were for your benefit, knowing that you were around and could see him all the time?" asked Mr. Luzenberg.

"Poor me!" replied Mrs. O'Connor. "What effect could I have upon him?"

Dr. W. E. Jones, an eye specialist at the Charity Hospital, said that Lyons' left eye was entirely blinded. The right eye pupil was dilated and the optic nerve choked. In his right eye, explained the doctor, there was a choked disc. This had no connection with the bullet that he had fired into his own forehead. It was the result of violent and prolonged mental irritation.

"Whenever you see a man with a choked disc in his optic nerve," said the doctor, "there is going to be an explosion some time, and he is likely to become a dangerous person at any time, and I would not want to be near him."

On November 13 the defense summoned Dr. Y. R. LeMonnier. Dr. LeMonnier stated that he had specialized in mental illness for forty-five years, and had often been called upon to give expert testimony. He had been coroner in the city three times, and had long been connected with the Charity Hospital and the New Orleans Board of Health.

"That man is insane," said Dr. LeMonnier, pointing a finger at the accused. "I have studied his case thoroughly. He is a maniac. He possesses a reasoning mania, accompanied by delusions of persecution. He has been in this condition for from three to five years and I doubt very much that he will recover."

"What is an insane man?" asked Mr. Generelly.

"He is a man who has lost his free will. Lyons is a monomaniac. He has lost his free will and cannot reason rationally. He is suffering from the worst form of insanity, and that is delirium of persecution. It makes him a dangerous man, because he imagines everyone around him is persecuting him. He makes accusations against others because he imagines others are trying to harm him."

Dr. LeMonnier further stated that it was impossible to say where insanity commenced. He had studied Lyons' case and had traced his family for generations. There was no inherited insanity. The accused had enjoyed splendid physical and mental health until he began to brood over his false arrest. Until then he had been a good father, husband, and friend. Then he had begun to change until his disposition and personality were utterly different.

"Look at this man now," said Dr. LeMonnier. "He cannot hold himself erect. He is nothing but skin and bones, is weak, decrepit, and broken down. One eye and one ear have been destroyed. There has been a severe injury to the brain. Two conditions brought him where he is now. One is the bullet that pierced his temple last July, and the other is prolonged mental worry. His right eye is suffering from a serious affliction that impedes the circulation of the brain, and when it is so impeded there is bound to be a disorder of the mind. Had this case been called six months from now instead of today, you would not have had this trouble; he would be dead. He can hardly live that long."

Dr. LeMonnier now described at great length the probable re-

actions of Lyons to his arrest for stealing a stickpin and toward
Mellen and Gurley when they lost his damage suit.

"There was nothing left to satisfy him, but to kill," concluded
the expert. "Then he would commit suicide."

Mr. Luzenberg demanded to know if Dr. LeMonnier could be
sure that Lyons was insane on July 20, and the doctor cited in
reply the finding of the cyanide of potassium on the person of the
accused. Lyons, he said, had doubtless intended to take it, but had
then ·shot himself, a wholly illogical action because death by
cyanide would have been instantaneous. After further cross-
examination Dr. LeMonnier was allowed to leave the stand for the
day.

The State kept Dr. LeMonnier in the witness box nearly all the
next day, but none of District Attorney Luzenberg's skillful cross-
examination could bring from the doctor any doubt as to his sturdy
conviction that Lyons was now insane and had been insane at the
time of his attack upon Gurley.

Perhaps one of Luzenberg's best points was drawn up into the
form of the following question:

"Does it not seem peculiar that the accused, being insane,
should have waited until he needed money to commit the deed?"
asked the district atorney. "Lyons spoke often of money and it
was upon that angle that much of his grievance against the victim
seems to have depended. Would an insane man worry so about
money?"

"Not at all," replied the doctor, "in most cases. But it is not at
all peculiar that he wait for an indefinite period before committing
the act over which he had long brooded."

Mr. Luzenberg now produced letters, stenographers' notes, and a
manuscript entitled *Why Crime Thrives,* written by Lyons. Hand-
ing the essay to the doctor he inquired, "Does that show unsound-
ness of mind?"

"I'll admit what you ask," replied the doctor, "but you cannot
get me away from the idea that the man considered himself as
being wrongfully persecuted."

Dr. LeMonnier was given a letter to read that had been written to Gurley by Lyons. It read:

> You permitted many errors and caused me great injustice, because of the way my case was handled by you. I engaged you to represent my interest, and the case was almost wholly in the hands of your partner, Mellen. You are certainly not blind to Mellen's fault. If you are, I am not.

Mr. Luzenberg asked if that letter sounded like the product of a diseased brain. Dr. LeMonnier replied that it certainly indicated a delusion of persecution, and again stated that Lyons had held such a belief in regard to everyone connected with his damage suit, even the stenographers who took the notes. He then referred to two letters written by Lyons to his sister, one an affectionate note, the other unkind and rude in character.

"Might not one have been written while he was in a drunken condition?" asked Luzenberg.

"No, I seriously doubt that the severe one was written by a drunkard," replied the doctor. "It came from a diseased mind, because the tenor of it shows the trend of all his thoughts, for he even turned upon his mother and sister for being among his persecutors."

"Doctor, you seem to be guessing!" cried the prosecutor.

"No, I am not, but you are," said the witness.

When at last the doctor was released the defense called Mr. Mellen to the stand. Mr. Generelly showed him another receipt, this one for $42 paid to Mr. Lester Bobb by Lyons for transcribing some notes taken during the damage suit. Generelly referred once more to Mellen's statement that he had paid such fees from his own pocket.

"I am somewhat careless about such matters," said the witness, "but I am certain I paid such fees."

The defense now closed its case.

Now the prosecution, perhaps worried over the defense's insistence upon Lyons' insanity, particularly the three-day testimony of

Dr. LeMonnier, and maybe a little afraid of Juror Gehbauer's assertion, produced thirty-seven witnesses in rebuttal.

Dr. Danna, Dr. Salter, and Dr. Maylie expressed beliefs that Lyons was sane. Dr. Robin and Dr. Fish, oculists, contended that a choked disc did not have any relation to insanity and might occur from a number of causes. Mr. John Fitzsimmons, a bartender, said he had known the accused a year and a half and had always considered him a very sensible man. He said that the defendant often came to his saloon to play dominoes, that he sometimes stayed until the place closed at night, and that he had never heard Lyons mention the damage suit or Gurley. Lyons was looked upon as being so wise by the gentlemen who patronized his saloon, said Mr. Fitzsimmons, that he was always called upon to settle any argument or bet that arose between his customers.

There followed numerous acquaintances of the accused who reported that they had always thought him sane in every way, and that they had never heard him mention the man he killed.

Lyons' landlady, Mrs. Lena Heffner, of No. 1018 Gravier Street, asserted that he had roomed with her for about ten months before the murder and had occupied the front room upstairs, while she occupied the back one. He was a very quiet man, neat in his person and dress. On July 19, a Sunday, he had remained home all day reading the newspapers. They had held several conversations and he seemed perfectly rational. Never had he said anything to make her think he was insane. She had gone to see him in Parish Prison and had asked him how dare he get into trouble while he lived in her house. "I have children, you know," Mrs. Heffner explained to the court, "and he should not have done that." According to Mrs. Heffner, Lyons had replied, "I am a man who, when I may up my mind to do a thing, I do it, and it is all right."

At the close of the day of November 17 it was discovered that Mr. Gehbauer was ill, and Coroner Richards attended him. The other jurors, said a reporter, "were having a good time. They were playing the phonograph and singing in accompaniment, while Mr. Gehbauer was suffering from illness and extreme nervousness."

Dr. Maylie was kept busy nearly all the morning of November

18. He continued to assert that in his opinion Lyons was and had always been sane. Among other witnesses called that day was Mrs. Margaret Wallace, who had rented a house belonging to Lyons and next door to where he and his family resided before he left his wife. Mrs. Wallace asserted that he was a "mean man," but not crazy. She had seen him beat his wife several times and once saw him knock her down. She added that she "did not owe Lyons one nickel."

By six that evening it was made known that all witnesses had now been heard, and that the arguments would commence on the following morning.

Throughout the trial Lyons had sat with his head down, scarcely moving except for a nervous twitching of the shoulders. It was certain that he could scarcely see at all and doubtful that he could hear very well. He was a quivering wreck, who staggered and trembled each time he rose to leave the courtroom. He looked like a white-bearded, emaciated patriarch, apparently unconscious of all that transpired about him, or that he was the central figure of this drama.

The first arguments of counsel were brief. Assistant District Attorney S. J. Montgomery opened for the State with a review of the crime. He emphasized the sharp contrast between the natures of the victim and the accused. Gurley had been a gentle, patient man, Lyons was vicious and cruel, even to his wife. Gurley had borne the persecutions of the man who was to be his murderer for years, striving to reason with him and to help him. Lyons was certainly sane and had been so at the moment he had entered the office of his victim. The crime had been premeditated and brutal. Even when the man who had only tried to aid him in his difficulties had been mortally wounded Lyons had paused to reload his revolver and had again fired into the bleeding form of the victim.

Warren Doyle followed for the defense. The very fact that the accused had brooded so long over the real or imaginary wrong that had been committed against him was proof that he was not a sane man. And had the wrong been so imaginary? Receipts of money paid to the attorneys he had employed were evidence that his money had been accepted. The shock of that false arrest had been extreme to a man as sensitive as Lewis Lyons. Then when he discovered, or thought he discovered, for it did not matter which, that his suit for damages had been handled dishonestly and with negligence, he had brooded over the matter, which, together with his extreme financial troubles, had unbalanced his mind. The jury need only look upon that quivering specimen of humanity to see for themselves that he was not a normal man and not responsible for his actions.

Joseph E. Generelly completed the argument for the defense in much the same vein. Such an expert as Dr. LeMonnier, he reminded the jury, had spent three days in the witness chair reiterating his firm conviction that Lyons was insane. Letters and other documents had also offered evidence that the accused was not normal. Eye specialists had testified that a choked disc in the optic nerve would produce insanity. Lyons was no more to blame for this tragedy than if the poor victim had been slain by a stranger. The accused had not long to live. The defense asked only that his illness be recognized and that he be permitted to spend his last days in a proper institution. His aged mother and his fine, good sister did not deserve to suffer further. They knew their son and brother was afflicted with the most terrible of human ailments—a diseased brain. The accused asked for nothing, which was further proof of his mental condition. He had tried to commit suicide, and cared not if he lived or died.

Closing for the State, the district attorney spoke for three hours and a quarter. He reviewed the case with infinite care, opening his argument with a touching and eloquent account of the murder and of the noble and good man who had been killed. Witnesses, he said, had considered Lyons "a mean and vindictive man" for years before the murder.

Luzenberg took up the documentary evidence piece by piece and commented that the letters and documents did not in any way resemble those written by an insane man. Lyons had known right from wrong. When a man said, "Give me money or I'll kill you," that was no speech of a lunatic; it was the threat of a highwayman, a robber. Lyons had come armed to kill J. Ward Gurley. Locked in that office, he had committed that dreadful deed. When Gurley had said, "He's murdering me," he had well known what he meant, for he was a trained lawyer and knew the legal definition of murder in the fullest sense of the word. Let the jury remember that the Lyons who had come to Gurley's office was not in the physical condition of the accused today. His present state was the result of his attempt at suicide, an attempt, incidentally, that did not indicate insanity, for suicides were not necessarily insane.

In his charge to the jury Judge Chretien defined murder and manslaughter, and what constituted murder and manslaughter, in the usual tradition of judges addressing juries in murder cases. Then he spoke at great length on insanity as a defense. The gentlemen of the jury retired. It was noted that Mr. Gehbauer was still not well. Mr. Gehbauer was still managing to attract nearly as much attention as the man on trial.

"Come on, Mr. Lyons," said a deputy, as the jury vanished. Lyons rose unsteadily to his feet and followed to the sheriff's office. There his wife, mother, and sister awaited him. What they said to each other, remarked a reporter the next day, "shall be forever buried in a potter's field of pain." After this interview the Lyons family departed. It was remarked that the accused did not want them to hear the verdict.

The jury was out only thirty-five minutes. Judge Chretien had hardly had time to snatch a bite of lunch when a deputy informed him that the gentlemen were ready. Lyons was hustled back into court. He sat down and "opened his eyes for perhaps the first time to look upon the jurors as they filed into their places."

Foreman Faust spoke in a low tone: "Guilty as charged."

District Attorney Luzenberg rose and asked that both Mr. Generelly and Mr. Doyle be extended the thanks of the court for the manner in which they had conducted their case during the long two weeks it had consumed. Judge Chretien conplied and then extended his congratulations to the jury.

Mr. Faust willingly told a states reporter how he and his companions in the box had reached a verdict. The first vote had revealed that not one of them entertained any doubt as to Lyons' sanity. Ten had voted "guilty as charged," the other two "guilty without capital punishment." The second ballot had found only one who still held forth for a sentence of life imprisonment. He was quickly found and, after a consultation with him, a third ballot demonstrated that he had agreed with the others. One wonders if the dissenter was Mr. Gebhauer.

Lyons did not seem at all displeased with the verdict. Those receipts for the fees he had paid Mr. Mellen, he said, and which Mr. Mellen had denied receiving, had proven that Mellen was either a dishonest or a careless man, which he had been telling everybody all along. They were evidence, too, that Mellen had not handled his damage suit properly. "Both Mellen and Gurley made mistakes," he said, "and this was made plain to everybody at the trial. I was right. They did not handle my case the way they ought to have."

Lyons had only the highest praise for Mr. Generelly and Mr. Doyle, and said, "The boys were honest and conscientious, and I do not blame them for having lost."

The defense attorneys said they were "stunned" by the outcome. They announced that they would file a motion for a new trial at once.

"I was confident of an acquittal," said Generelly, "at least until the incident when Mr. Gehbauer is reported to have said that he had already made up his mind. Then I became a little discouraged, but still not to the extent to where I thought it was possible that an unqualified verdict of guilty would be brought in."

Mr. Gehbauer was interviewed by reporters at his home. He was found lying in bed and complained of feeling ill and of lack of sleep. "With regard to what took place in the jury room," said one reporter the next day, "he would not speak. All had taken the oath of secrecy as to what transpired and his lips were sealed upon the subject. He served faithfully and well. He is a solicitor by profession and has lost two weeks' work and perhaps his position. Mr. Gehbauer is an intelligent man."

A motion for a new trial was granted, and February 6, 1904, was fixed as the date for argument on the motion. This was, however, continued, and Lyons' counsel filed a plea of present insanity. A commission *de lunatico inquirendo*, composed of Drs. George A. B. Hays, J. D. Bloom, and Quitman Kohnke, was duly appointed. Lyons was declared sane, and Judge Chretien overruled both the plea entered and the bill of exception to his ruling. On May 18 the judge passed sentence on the accused, and sentenced Lyons to be hanged. His attorneys then filed a motion for suspensive appeal to the Supreme Court, which was granted. The case remained there all summer while the justices took their vacations. Arguments were heard in the fall, and the ruling of the lower court was affirmed. Messrs. Generelly and Doyle then filed another plea of insanity and requested the appointment of another commission, which Judge Chretien refused. Finally the Lyons family applied to the Board of Pardons, but commutation of sentence was denied. Governor N. C. Blanchard fixed the date of execution as March 24, 1905.

Lyons spent the long months in the condemned row of Parish Prison with four other men who were also to die at the end of a rope. He was morose and melancholy, but displayed no resentment toward anyone for the sentence that had been passed upon him. At first it was feared he might attempt suicide, and even his shoe laces were taken from him, but he made no such attempts. When he referred to his case at all, it was usually to remark that his trial had proven he had been right about the handling of his damage suit by Mellen and Gurley.

He had never been less than courageous, and he was not so now. The day before, the first of the five condemned men was taken to the gallows. He was Moses Louis, a Negro, who had raped and murdered a white girl. Johnston, the hangman, a notorious sadist, visited the condemned row and regaled the men with tales of previous hangings he had performed, describing the agonies of men who had strangled to death and the case of a murderer of unusual weight whose head had been severed from his body when the trap was sprung. The others were ill with fear after Johnston's visit, but Lyons seemed unaffected and talked quietly with the Negro who was to be the first to die, in an attempt to comfort him.

Through his attorneys Lyons purchased a plain mahogany coffin with a silver plaque, on which was inscribed simply "Rest in Peace," and a plot in the Carrollton Cemetery. A few days before March 24 he asked to speak with Sheriff Matt Long, and of him requested only that as few people as possible witness his end and that religious attendance be dispensed with. However, on the morning he was hanged a minister called upon him and Lyons permitted him to remain.

He slept little the night before, and complained that the conversation of the four sheriffs composing the death watch kept him awake. He refused breakfast, but drank a cup of warm milk and a large drink of rye whisky. He dressed himself with care in the clothes in which he was to be buried. Sam Sparo, the only one left of the condemned murderers, talked with him before they led him out of the row.

"Be brave now," said Sparo.

"There's no dunghill in me," said Lyons, "I'll walk to the gallows as easily as I'll walk through that door."

He did. With his long white beard and the fringe of white hair that fell over the collar of his black alpaca coat, he looked eighty-five instead of fifty-five, but his step was firm and steady now and there was none of the feebleness that had been so noticeable during the trial.

Johnston did not perform the necessary details, for he had been angered by newspaper accounts of his brutality and had resigned. The new executioner wore a black robe and hood with slits for his eyes and carried a gleaming meat cleaver which was used to sever the trap cord. Lyons said to him, "I have no grudge against you."

They bound his hands behind his back and then his legs.

"Have you anything to say?" asked Matt Long.

"No. Nothing at all," said Lyons.

He bowed his head so that the short executioner could place the noose about his neck. He could see his coffin waiting near the wall a little to the left. The minister said a prayer as the hood was placed over his head. The meat cleaver gleamed for an instant in the sunlight.

It was an expert, perfect job. The body dropped nine feet, and the neck and spine were neatly broken. Death was instantaneous.

The *Daily Picayune* remarked the next day, March 25:

> The successful prosecution of five murderers within the past year or two does not seem to have had the desired effect. Four of these men have been hanged and but one remains to pay his debt to society. Yet there have been seven murders in New Orleans within the past two months, and six men and one woman await their trials at the present time. There seems little hope that the condemned row at the Parish Prison will ever be unoccupied.

THE LAST OF THE MAFIA

The little boy was playing alone beneath the arches that led into the courtyard of his father's undertaking establishment at 624 St. Philip Street in New Orleans. It was that hour when the Vieux Carré glows in pink gold tones for a few minutes, just before the Mississippi River seems to swallow the day.

Oscar Antoine, one of the drivers, returning late from a funeral, spoke to the child, as he drove his horses into the yard. After that he paid no attention. He was tired and very anxious to go home.

While Antoine was busy in the stables another man entered the arches. He, too, spoke to Walter. The boy knew the man, and thought he was nice, although he hesitated when the man extended an invitation. It was almost time for supper, and Walter knew his father would soon be looking for him. But he was only seven years old, and what the man offered was more tempting than any supper. Ice cream!

Walter gave this man a small, trusting hand, and the two went away together.

Did anyone see them go? If so, they tried to forget it quickly.

When one of his other children told Peter Lamana that Walter was not about it failed to disturb the father at first. In the courtyard and stables there were many places where his children played at hiding. Sometimes Walter climbed into a wagon and went to sleep. So Peter Lamana looked here and there, calling the child's name.

At last Mr. Lamana went out to the banquette in front of his place. Now it was getting dark. Yellow light from the corner lamps streaked the old cobblestones, and the Italian men and women sat out on their stoops and in chairs placed on the banquette itself. They greeted Mr. Lamana respectfully, for he was an important man in the neighborhood. No one could recall seeing Walter.

Some of the Lamana children joined their father. He gave directions. "You go this way. You that way."

The long search had begun.

This was June 8, 1907. The neighborhood where the Lamanas lived is still largely inhabited by a poor Sicilian population. It is still dark at night and filled with tenements and gaping alleyways. But in 1907 no part of the French Quarter was as it is today, for the period of restoration, when the Quarter was to again become fashionable, had not yet arrived. Then there were streets where only the brave would walk after dusk, and deep ditches and gullies where stagnant water filled the air with an unwholesome stench. Piles of trash and barrels of oyster shells stood at the curbs, and the neglected courtyards were often filled by heaps of refuse and horse manure. The entrances of alleys and carriageways were black mouths opening to devour the timid passerby. Sinister windows, high in the walls, seemed to watch.

Mr. Lamana questioned everyone. No, they had not seen his *bambino*. Even then he did not worry. He knew these people. They were poor, good, God-fearing, priest-fearing. They would harm no one, least of all a child. They made much over Walter and his twin sister Octavia, who were such beautiful children. Five years ago both had taken prizes as the most beautiful babies in New Orleans.

It is true there were bad people in the section. There were men who lurked along the river front, not far away, who had evil faces and mysterious occupations. Some of them still wore their glittering hoop earrings as they had in Sicily, fierce mustachios and bandannas about their sweaty brows. The good people avoided them, and whispered of Mafia and Black Hand. According to the police, Mafia and Black Hand no longer existed in New Orleans, but the Italians, in intimate groups of relatives and friends, still gossiped of these organizations, and there was a fear—a terrible fear. One never knew. Things happened, and when they happened one did not go to the police. That was the worst thing to do.

As Mr. Lamana searched the neighborhood there was one memory he must have tried to prevent from intruding into his thoughts. But the hours passed. At home the mother wept, and supper grew cold. At last the recollection could no longer be barred.

Two years before, just before the yellow fever epidemic of 1905, Mr. Lamana had been summoned to the entrance of his home. Under the arches stood a Negro, who put a note into the undertaker's hand and then fled. Mr. Lamana could still hear the feet moving swiftly over the cobblestones. The note contained a threat. "We want money or your children will not be safe." The signature was a childish skull and crossbones. He had ignored it. Nothing had happened.

Toward midnight the police were notified, despite the advice of the neighbors. Now real terror unfolded like the cold petals of an evil flower in the hearts of the parents. The neighborhood had been scoured, and the search spread throughout the city. The river front and the wharves were searched. Detectives went under the old wharves with lanterns. Only rats scurried before the light, their red eyes vanishing into recesses too small to hold even a child's body. At dawn Mr. Lamana went with the police to the shores of Lake Pontchartrain. This he felt a little absurd. A child of seven could not have gone this far, and he refused to believe Walter was drowned. The child had always feared water.

Now it was morning. The mother had prayed and wept all through the night. The other children—John, aged fifteen, Stella, twelve, Charles, ten, and little Octavia—awoke from troubled sleep and stirred about, tying to help. The father came home, white-faced, filled with heinous fear, and attempted to comfort the others, although he could not comfort himself. The police had scoffed at any mention of Black Hand, but Mr. Lamana remembered all the rumors he had heard. It had been whispered that a new leader had lately arrived in the city. There had been ceremonies. Members had kissed the face and hands of this new leader and pledged allegiance and loyalty.

This day, a Sunday, was a day made dreadful by the fact that nothing happened at all. All day and again that night the police searched in vain. Mr. Lamana sometimes joined them, sometimes went out on expeditions of his own. His neighbors helped him. There was gossip and now and then a lead that led nowhere. The whole neighborhood throbbed with fear.

A letter came in the mail Monday morning, and then Mr. Lamana knew the terror of the past thirty-six hours was justified. The letter bore the postmark of Bogalusa, Louisiana, a small town not far from New Orleans, and it was written in Italian, in a scrawling, almost illegible handwriting. The signature was a skull and crossbones. It began: "Your boy is comfortably housed, clothed and fed. He is well and no harm will be done him, but we will not be responsible for the consequences should you fail to comply with our demands." That much was published in the *Daily Picayune* of June 11, 1907. The rest Mr. Lamana insisted on keeping secret, except that he admitted that the amount of ransom demanded was $6,000, and the newspaper account said, "There followed a statement as to how Mr. Lamana should proceed in turning over the ransom money to the kidnapers. Mr. Lamana claims that the place for payment of the money is somewhere in New Orleans, but others, who have seen the letter, claim it stipulated that Mr. Lamana should travel on horseback, alone, to Bogalusa. While passing through the woods en route he would be met by men, who would trade the money for his son." Some of the neighbors told reporters and others that the place of meeting was to be somewhere on the other side of the river from New Orleans. All this seems to have been without any proof. Mr. Lamana firmly refused to reveal the details of the instructions. He made only one statement. "Too much," he said, "has already been written about the kidnaping of my boy, and hereafter we want to keep everything as secret as possible." He admitted he would have a difficult time raising $6,000 in cash, but that he would do it.

Now rumor followed rumor in the newspapers. It was said the owner of a small candy shop near the Lamana residence was suspected and was being watched by the police. Italian tenants of the

Lamanas were mentioned. They, it was reported, had been angered because the undertaker had raised their rent. This was denied. Mr. Lamana said he had not raised the rent, and that they were all good friends. The Lamana home was crowded with visitors, reporters, and the police.

The horror and fear the Lamana case invoked in Orleanians was almost without precedent in the city's history. People still talk about it, and many an adult can remember how as a child he lay awake and trembling at night after thoughtless parents had discussed in his presence what happened to little Walter Lamana. For adults of that period it brought back memories of the terrifying history of the New Orleans Mafia, especially of the Chief Hennessy killing, and its bloody aftermath, when the whole city vibrated with cries of "Who killa da Chief?" And they wondered if all that was going to happen again, if the city would again be a scene of riot and massacre and slaughter. The Italian population bolted doors and windows at night now, and lay awake in their beds. Nearly all of this portion of Orleanians had worked ceaselessly to regain their respectable reputations, which had suffered so after the Hennessy affair, when the innocent had suffered with the guilty. Now they saw all this in danger once more.

The Mafia had a long history in New Orleans. Sicilian criminals poured into the city during the years following the War between the States when there was a large influx of immigrants from lower European countries. As early as March 19, 1869, the *Times* complained that the Second District of the city was infested with cutthroats and murderers. This was the Stoppagherra Society, a branch of the Mafia, a well-organized criminal group, led by four men driven from Palermo by Italian authorities. In 1880 Giuseppe Esposito, who had been second in command to the notorious Leoni, Sicilian Mafia leader, arrived in the country, and subsequently in New Orleans, where he began a new career under the name of Radzo. He managed the assassination of Tony Labruzzo, head of the New Orleans Mafia, and established himself as head of the band. Esposito was at last arrested in Jackson Square. He was returned to Italy in irons. But the New Orleans detectives, Mike and Dave Hennessy, who had arrested him were not forgotten. Five years later Mike was killed by a Mafia bullet in Houston, Texas.

By 1890 there had been at least ninety-five Mafia murders in New Orleans, and there were probably more, the guilt for which could not be traced to the society. In not one of these cases was a conviction ever effected. No Italian who cared for his life would dare to testify against a member of the dreaded organization. The balance of the New Orleans population was extremely callous about it. The Sicilians killed only other Sicilians, they argued. Let them kill themselves off. They were a disgrace to the city anyway and a most undesirable element.

However, Dave Hennessy was not content with this view of affairs. He was now chief of police, and, besides, he wanted to avenge his brother's death. He patiently collected evidence, and it has been said that he discovered the identity of a hundred murderers, all Sicilian and attached to the Mafia, all at large in the city.

In 1890 open war broke out between the Mafia and an organization headed by the Provenzano brothers. The Provenzanos had long held a monopoly over river-front labor employed in unloading fruit boats. They were not members of the Mafia, but were powerful politically and friends of Hennessy. In the late eighties the Mafia, headed by Tony and Charles Matranga now, and consisting of a membership of more than three hundred, turned labor racketeers, drove the Provenzano workers from the docks and seized the monopoly, reduced the wages of the stevedores from sixty cents an hour to fifteen cents, and pocketed the difference. The Provenzanos took it quietly for a time. They even opened a grocery store. The Mafia put them out of business again. Then came war. The Provenzanos organized a group of men and challenged the Mafia. A number of men died in the gun battles that followed. In May, 1890, Tony Matranga and several of his bodyguards were wounded. The Provenzanos were arrested.

In October, the month for which the trial was scheduled, Chief Hennessy publicly announced that he would appear at the trial and give evidence against the Mafia. Two days later, on the fifteenth, he was shot from ambush on Girod Street near Rampart.

"The Dagos got me" were his last words, spoken to Police Captain W. J. O'Connor, who was the first to reach him as he fell.

Now, almost for the first time, Orleanians were aroused against the Mafia. They had gone outside their own nationality. They had dared to assassinate a prominent public figure—the chief of police!

A $15,000 reward was announced by Mayor Shakespeare. The police began the arrest of every suspicious Sicilian in the city. Finally eleven were indicted for murder, eight others as accessories before the fact.

The trial of nine of the accused men began on February 6, 1891. On March 13 it was over. Five of the accused were declared not guilty, and mistrials were then announced in the cases of the others. It was commonly known that the jury had been tampered with. The Mafia had employed every device of threat and bribery with jury and attorneys, and had won.

That night the defendants celebrated in their prison cells with wine and spaghetti. Sicilian shops and markets were decorated with flags and banners. An American flag was flown upside down beneath the flag of Italy on one building. Anglo-Saxons, daring to enter the neighborhood, were spat upon and taunted. The Mafia sent forth a verbal message that it would soon take over the city. The State witnesses during the trial left the city or went into hiding, for the Mafia promised that they would not be forgotten.

But that very afternoon a group of twenty-eight prominent New Orleans men met, and, after a consultation, announced a mass meeting for ten o'clock the next morning, to which all "good citizens" were invited, to be held in Canal Street near the Clay statue.

The next day Canal Street was jammed with outraged Orleanians carrying shotguns, and, after some speeches by the committee, the march on the Parish Prison began.

It was over in an hour. Shouting, "Who killa da Chief?" the mob overcame the prison guards and found the Sicilians in their various hiding places, which they had sought when given the freedom of the jail by the authorities. One by one, they fell under a rain of bullets and rifle butts. Two were dragged forth alive and hanged outside the prison, one to a lamp post, the other from a tree.

Italians all over New Orleans feared a general massacre would follow, and many went into hiding. Even the life of the Italian consul was threatened. There was no more killing, but for a long time even innocent Italians had to endure much because of the actions of the Sicilian Mafia. "Who killa da Chief?" became a commonplace taunt to fling at any "Dago" at any time citizens of other nationalities chose. Even Italian children found school attendance difficult because other children, with the sadism of youth, tormented them with the phrase.

There were even more important repercussions. Italy withdrew her ambassador at Washington. For a short time a prospect of war threatened. In the end this of course all subsided.

Soon the New Orleans newspapers were announcing, and Orleanians were telling each other, that the Mafia in the city was either eradicated or at least demolished as an organization. The Italians began slowly to work their way back to favor with their fellows. Most of them were at last glad that it had all happened for they had gained the greatest boon of all. They had been the ones to most suffer from the Mafia. Now they resumed their places. Many rose to prominence in the city.

Yet in a few years a new menace came. This time it was called the Black Hand, a new name, but its object and methods were the same as the Mafia. And the attitude of Orleanians and the police was the same as it had been before the murder of Chief Hennessy, although the Black Hand's crimes had not yet reached nearly the number the Mafia was known to have committed before the city was aroused. There was, too, the same condition of fear among the victims themselves, who refused to report threats and extortions to the authorities.

But with the kidnaping of Walter Lamana the Italians themselves resolved to put an end to the Black Hand. Peter Lamana was a well-known and respected businessman, and his friends and associates came quickly to his assistance, although he probably feared the effect of such aid upon the fate of his small son.

On Wednesday, June 12, 1907, outraged Italian citizens gathered in the Union Française Hall. L. Federico, a prominent businessman, was named chairman of the committee formed. Judge Philip J. Patorno spoke, saying that he did not believe the Black Hand·in New Orleans included more than fifty persons, out of an Italian population of nearly thirty thousand. After his address non-Italians took the roster, among them Acting Mayor McRacken, Frank Echezebal, Louis P. Bryant, Edgar H. Farrar and, finally, Colonel John C. Wickliffe, who had been one of the leaders of the mass meeting held before the lynching of the Hennessy assassins. Colonel Wickliffe was greeted with a tumultuous ovation by the audience, composed largely of Italians.

An Italian committee was formed, which included, besides Mr. Federico, S. Messina, A. D. Piaggio, Joseph Vaccaro, Joseph Di Carlo, S. L. Nasa, Paul Peretto, Joseph Cangelosi, Peter Torre, A. Cusimano, J. Cusimano, P. J. Patorno, A. Patorno, A. Dell'Orto, A. D'Anna, Louis Tortorich, Fillipo Lombardo, B. Macalusa, S. Segari, A. Di Maggio, A. Monteleone, C. Testa, A. Peretti, Joseph Loyacano, and Frank Cabibi. Titling themselves the Italian Vigilance Committee, they pledged the apprehension of the kidnaper of Walter Lamana and the eradication of the Black Hand from New Orleans.

Meanwhile, on Tuesday night Peter Lamana had ridden on horseback from New Orleans to the town of Kenner, some twenty miles from the city, secretly followed at a discreet distance by a posse of detectives, also on horseback. Another letter had come to the grieved father that morning, instructing him to take such a ride. Whether or not the captors of his child had learned of his police protection is not known, but he met only one lone rider just outside Kenner, who satisfied the detectives as to his good character, and that he had no connection with the criminals they sought.

After the mass meeting Wednesday night the city police had to be reinforced. Crowds filled the streets of the Vieux Carré. Men gathered on street corners and in saloons, threatening to hunt down

"Dagos." At Congo Square, scene of many important events in New Orleans during the past, a riot was threatened. An angry mob of men there, some of them armed, began to shout:

"Let's make more history for Congo Square!"

Dispersed by the police, the men moved on, crying: "On to Treme Market!" Treme Market had long been a gathering place. There were mutterings of lynchings, of "decorating the lampposts."

Near midnight St. Philip Street outside the Lamana residence was crowded with angry Orleanians. By this time they were quite beyond police control.

Rumors came fast. It was said that other people in the vicinity had been Black Hand victims. One man had received an extortion letter and, when he failed to comply, had found his mules disemboweled in his own stables. Another had been instructed to leave money in a graveyard or die. Still another, a successful merchant on Decatur Street, had been told to give $500 to his best friend. He said he was trying to decide who was his best friend.

Gossip and false alarms never stopped for an instant. Word spread through the crowd that Mrs. Lamana was seriously ill and would not survive the night. Once it was reported that the boy had been found in a house at Dauphine and St. Philip streets. A stranger, it was said, had recently purchased a wagon from a dealer in the neighborhood—the type of wagon that had side curtains and a top. Strangely, this last story was the one item of truth amid all the falsification.

At last the crowd began to shout: "Lamana! Lamana!"

Someone stepped out upon the upper gallery of the house and informed the men below that Mr. Lamana was ill and could not appear at this time.

"Mrs. Lamana!" they cried. "We want to talk to Mrs. Lamana!"

This unconscious brutality was dismissed with a statement that Mrs. Lamana was also ill. The mob demanded to see the letters Mr. Lamana had received. They were told the letters were in the hands of the police department.

Inside the house the family tried not to listen to the noise outside, which must have added to their torture, and to comfort each other as best they could.

Another kind of shout went up. "We're going to search every house in this neighborhood! Let's go through the block."

They began with an ice-cream parlor, behind which were the living quarters of the owner and his family. The building was in darkness and all doors and windows were locked. A man came running with a crow bar to pry open the door.

Sturgis Adams, then clerk of the Criminal District Court, mounted a box and appealed to the men not to resort to violence, warning them that they might injure innocent persons. Then A. M. Campbell climbed on the box and added his plea.

Lights went on in the ice-cream parlor and the proprietor opened the door. Somehow this quieted the crowd. Two men only entered the establishment and searched it.

Several other houses were searched after that. No harm was done to anyone. There were no results. The men began to grow pessimistic.

Then, in a rooming house, they found two schoolboys. They offered what sounded like startling information. Both boys, whose names were Tony Voldini and Salvatore Conchilia, said they had seen Walter go off that Saturday evening with a man known in the neighborhood as Tony Costa. Costa, they said, roomed at a house on the corner of St. Philip and Chartres streets.

A few moments later the crowd reached the address where Costa was said to live. The house was ransacked. A woman there told them that Costa had been missing since Saturday. Tony Costa, she said, had no employment, but he always had money and was very well dressed. He claimed to be a gambler. Once he had been arrested on a charge of robbing a streetcar motorman, but he had been released because of insufficient identification.

Now the men began to drift homeward, promising to renew the search on the following night, and listening to and spreading more rumors. It was said that Mr. Lamana had been notified that he would receive the head of his small son the following day. And all their hatred was flung against a name they now believed to be at least one of the guilty ones. Costa.

By the following evening the Italian Vigilance Committee had the situation under control. Again a crowd gathered in St. Philip Street, but this time Mr. Campbell and several leaders of the Committee took charge. The police, they said, were searching for Costa, and there would be no further forced entries to the houses in the neighborhood. Men hung around for hours gossiping, but no buildings were entered and there were no demands for the appearance of the Lamana family.

That morning, June 13, the *Daily Picayune* announced that every organization, political and business, had pledged support to the Italian Vigilance Committee and to the finding of the missing child.

Every Orleanian was repeating two phrases now: "Get Costa!" and "The Black Hand must go!"

On Thursday morning another letter had come to Lamana. Written in Italian, its contents read:

> With tears in my eyes, I send you these few lines for your comfort, therefore be a man and accept my confidence. I do so for the love of your son. You will have this letter read by the Inspector of Police or the Italian Committee.
>
> Go to Harvey's Canal and call on a man named Marcorio Morti. He knows all. When you get him, ask him about the barber who was living at Harvey's Canal, and he will tell you all. The barber is from the village of Valle Lunga.
>
> This barber is the chief of all. I have no doubt that he has your son; moreover, he has served eight years in the penitentiary for counterfeiting, but keep this quiet, because the cat adores the mouse, and will disappear. But if you take this barber, sweat him. He is all. He has about twenty-four partners, their names are all of other nationalities, and big fellows, and also Americans. Enough if the Italians know how to work it, they will find out all. Moreover, I know those that have done wrong to Mr. Christina of Kennerville are Italians; the others are Americans. Christina knows who the parties are, but he is afraid to say so.
>
> But the barber is enough.
>
> The barber is a short, stout, but good-looking man. I do not know his name. No more for the present, and if I find out any

more I will let you know, because I am a man that works for you and for the honor of the noble Italian flag. Adieu, pray God that he will send you your son, so that you will have peace.

The letter was unsigned.

So New Orleans detectives, Mr. Lamana accompanying them, went across the river in search of a man whose last name was Morti—Death.

He was not difficult to find. Every Italian living at Harvey's Canal knew him. There had been Black Hand activity in the village for several years. Houses had been burned and cattle slaughtered during the night. There had been a murder or two that had gone unpunished.

Morti's real name, or at least another name he used, was Cimo. He denied everything, and said he had no connection with any secret Italian society. When asked why he was called "Morti" he shrugged his shoulders, then grew sullen. He was held as a dangerous and suspicious character.

Other arrests in Jefferson Parish took place the same day. Searching for a man named Ignazio Campisciano, the detectives rode into the farm of Ignacio Caravello. It was a mistake, but what seemed to be a fortunate one. Caravello lived with his mother and brothers and had a good reputation, but he seemed to know a great deal about Campisciano, who had long had an unsavory record. Too, he told the New Orleans police that a wagon, closed with heavy side and back curtains, had also driven into his yard in error on Sunday. Police recalled the story of the purchase in New Orleans of such a wagon. Had the wagon been new? Yes, it was brand new. Caravello told, too, of seeing Campisciano on horseback Sunday morning, riding toward New Orleans. He had never seen Campisciano ride a horse before. Caravello was taken into custody for further questioning.

Campisciano was arrested. Italians in the region had feared him for a long time. Mysterious strangers often stopped at his farm late at night. Three months ago his brother had been murdered. The man, it was generally believed, knew the identity of his brother's assassins, but he had refused to testify against them.

Following leads that were now coming fast, the police soon made other arrests. Sam Charimonte and Lorenzo Giambelluca, the first a barber, the other having no known occupation, were picked up. These men were held under suspicion as being members of a secret society.

President Federico of the Italian Vigilance Committee then insisted upon the arrest of Francisco Genova. This was perhaps the most astonishing of all the arrests, for Genova was a successful importer, who had been in business in the city for some time, and a wealthy man. Mr. Federico stated that all Italians in the city feared him, and the newspapers speculated on the possibility that Genova was actually Francisco Martisi, once a leader of the dread Camorra, a powerful and murderous society which the Italian government had tried to suppress some years before. This was, of course, vigorously denied by Genova.

Genova, held without formal charges, and denied bail, at once instituted proceedings for his release through his attorneys. A writ of *habeas corpus* was refused by Assistant City Attorney Adams and by Chandler C. Luzenberg, the attorney for the Italian Vigilance Committee. Genova threatened to take the matter to the Federal Court.

Cimo, or Morti, was, as requested in the anonymous letter Lamana had received, sweated by the police. At last he mentioned the name of a man he thought might have something to do with the crime—Bacelona. This Bacelona, said Cimo, might know something. He had not seen Bacelona for some time, for the latter lived in New Orleans. As to his own connection with the kidnaping, Cimo denied everything.

Now there came a story from a young street waif, known only as Pito in St. Philip Street. Pito, it seems, who was apparently about eight years of age, had been driven from his home by his cruel father some months before the disappearance of Walter. He slept in the neighborhood school basement and he was fed and clothed by the neighbors of the Lamanas. On that Saturday afternoon he had been playing marbles with the Lamana child. He had seen a man come along and talk to Walter. Walter had gone down the block a bit with the stranger, and had then been picked up bodily and thrown into the back of a closely curtained wagon. The stranger had hurriedly climbed into the driver's seat and the horse at the head of the wagon had sped away over the cobblestones.

The police did not know whether to believe Pito's story or whether it was childish imagination, yet there again was the suspicious wagon with its curtains and its unknown driver.

"How did you get mixed up in this?" Judge Patorno asked Caravello, when the youth appeared before him.

"God dragged me into it," replied the boy, then lowered his head, as if that statement had slipped past his lips involuntarily. It was for a time considered very suspicious.

Until now Tony Costa had been at large. On Friday, June 14, however, he was captured in a house in Clouet Street. He did not go willingly. Judge Patorno and a police officer were admitted to the house by Costa's young daughter, and they found the man in bed. Costa made quite a rumpus. According to the *Daily Picayune* of June 15, "he had a fit." He howled in Italian and gesticulated wildly. Judge Patorno put a pistol to his breast. Then Costa fell to his knees, shaped his fingers into a cross, kissed them, and swore by all the saints that he was innocent.

From this time on there was a strict censorship of news, particularly as far as the newspapers were concerned. Only occasional bits slipped into the pages of the press. It was known that an ice-cream, cake, and candy merchant in the Lamanas' neighborhood who was known to be a friend of Costa's was arrested on Friday also. There was gossip that Costa had been seen taking the Lamana boy into the ice-cream parlor, and that he had emerged alone.

Judge Patorno made one statement for the press, to the effect that secrecy was necessary for the present, and that there had already been too much publicity.

The police were beginning to worry about the men in jail. Most were held without charges and their retention was becoming increasingly difficult. The Italian Consul in the city appealed to Governor Blanchard, demanding immediate release of the men— in the name of King Victor Emmanuel.

Friday night, June 14, all but Costa and Genova were released. Saturday morning Genova, through his attorney, who was St. Clair Adams, obtained a writ of *habeas corpus*, and he also walked out of the Parish Prison.

There was wild joy in the Italian section when the men rejoined their families and friends. The streets and homes were scenes of embraces and kisses and tears. Several of the men who had been held gave out indignant statements. They were not bad ones, no, they protested. They were good men who had been persecuted. On Sunday it was discovered that Charimonte, the barber, who had been the most enraged of all, was out on bond under a charge of arson for setting fire to a house at Harvey's Canal. He was re-arrested. His assistant, Gus Girardot, was also picked up, on a charge of burglary.

On Saturday Peter Lamana, accompanied by a detective, visited Tony Costa in his cell. Costa greeted him with even more melodramatic behavior than he had upon his arrest. Falling to his knees before the father of the missing boy, he covered the man's hands with kisses and wept. "Oh, Mr. Lamana," he is reported as pleading, "I never harmed you or yours. I don't know where your little boy is, God and *Maria Mádre* bear me witness."

He then sprang to his feet, put on his hat and coat, and walked around his cell in circles, chattering and waving his arms in the air, explaining that this was the way he walked down the streets and minded his own business. He denied taking Walter into the ice-cream parlor. He admitted going into the place that day, but it was to get some ice cream for "a big fat woman who was sick." Then he sat down on the edge of his cot, his hat still on his head, and ate imaginary icecream from an imaginary saucer in his lap.

Later Mr. Lamana told a reporter for the *Daily Picayune* that he did not believe Costa was guilty. "The man wept," said Lamana. "No man who could commit such a crime would be capable of shedding tears."

A week had passed since Walter had vanished. Hope of finding him alive was ebbing, but the search was becoming more intense each day, and it had spread to every part of the New Orleans area.

Special trains went out daily to Kenner, St. Rose, Pecan Grove, McDonoghville, and many other towns scattered throughout that part of Louisiana.

Mr. Lamana now received a letter with a Black Hand signature ordering him to bring the money to a McDonoghville cemetery. The grieved father, accompanied by Judge Patorno, went there at once. Nothing happened.

At St. Rose police still watched Campisciano, who had returned home and worked his farm daily, and who avoided questions sullenly. The Campisciano home was a one-room shack, with a small closet attached to the rear. It had been searched before. In this hovel lived the man with his wife and children. Behind the farm stretched some of the densest swamps in Louisiana. The stories of the curtained wagon that had stopped at the Campisciano home persisted. Two youths, John Weaver and Leroy Behrens, told of seeing such a wagon on the day after Walter had disappeared. They said it had drawn up before the Campisciano Farm.

The search spread to Tangipahoa Parish, even as far away as Baton Rouge. On Sunday, June 16, there was a rumor that the child was in a house on Bayou Road in New Orleans, another that he was still in the Vieux Carré. Sixteen houses were searched that day.

On Monday, the seventeenth, Captain Thomas Capo was placed in charge of the police working on the Lamana case. The Italian Vigilance Committee announced that they had raised $5,000, most of it to be used for the hiring of special trains required by the various scouting parties going out from New Orleans to other parts of the state. Such trains were going out daily now.

Peter Lamana never rested. That week it was said he had had only ten hours' sleep, that he had scarcely eaten any food. He personally followed every clue, every rumor, and himself interrogated Italians in St. Rose, Harvey's Canal, Gretna, Sarpy's Station, Kenner, and other villages with large populations of his nationality. The rest of the family was at last allowed a little quiet. Mrs. Lamana, somewhat recovered, went each day to pray at the shrine of the Sisters of the Sacred Heart Chapel in St. Philip Street. The other Lamana children, it was announced, were being closely guarded.

In his cell, Costa still protested his innocence.

Wednesday twenty-five men with bloodhounds from Angola, the Louisiana State Penitentiary, set out into the swamps behind Campisciano's farm. The newspapers now stated that it was believed that a band of Black Hand members had the child hidden somewhere in that vicinity, and that Campisciano, though the truth could not be dragged from his lips, was working with them as a go-between, and that he supplied them with food.

The task of searching this swamp was tremendous. The men followed winding, zigzag trails that led to nowhere. They waded to their waists in swamps, ditches, and ponds for more than five miles. The jungle was sliced by bayous and ditches. At some spots it was dark as night. Mosquitos tormented them, and snakes lay in waiting.

Nothing was found. The tired men and the tired dogs had at last returned exhausted. Campisciano, working his land, looked at them as they emerged upon his property. He said nothing.

There were many trails, so many that it looked as if the right one could never be picked out of the maze. Yet it was there.

The New Orleans Italians, supported by the Italian Vigilance Committee, had become braver in reporting Black Hand activities than at any time in the city's history. To Judge Patorno came letter after letter, telling of attempts at extortion by the sinister society. Now it was revealed that for years the organization had attempted to bleed these people, and many had paid Black Hand money.

A prosperous Italian merchant was among others who came to Patorno. This was on Monday, June 10, just two days after the disappearance of Walter Lamana. The merchant had received a letter demanding $2,000, and he said he knew who had sent the letter, although it was not signed. He took Judge Patorno to a window of the latter's office, and pointed to a main loitering at the street corner.

"That is the man who wrote it," he said. "Tony Gendusa!"

It was just one of many clues, meaning little more than any of the others. But when he had gone Judge Patorno looked again at the first letter Peter Lamana had received, which had been given to Patorno by the police. The handwriting was very similar.

Judge Patorno went to the Gendusa home at the corner of Decatur and St. Philip streets. Tony Gendusa's mother and sister said they had not seen Tony for several days. He had a brother, Collagero, usually known as Frank, who lived in McDonoghville.

A few days later Frank was arrested and held on a charge of suspicion in a Gretna jail. Where was Tony? He did not know. Tony had a mistress, Crusiffissa Altamore, a beautiful woman. She lived at Pecan Grove. That was not far from the home of Campisciano. When the detectives reached her home it was in darkness. Neighbors said she had gone to visit relatives either at Kenner or Shrewsbury. No one had seen Tony Gendusa.

Days passed. In the meantime it was learned that Costa and Tony Gendusa had been seen together on several occasions just before the kidnaping, usually in the company of another man, Francisco Luchesi. Luchesi had disappeared from his old haunts, too. About that time came the arrest of Costa, who denied all knowledge of the crime. He knew Gendusa and Luchesi, yes, but he had not seen them for a long time.

Sheriff Marrero of Jefferson Parish now rearrested Cimo, or Morti, and held him in solitary confinement. Each day the sheriff went to visit Cimo and to grill him, but no one else was allowed to speak with the man. Marrero reported that Cimo was becoming more and more nervous, and that he expected to get a statement from him at any time. On Saturday, June 22, Tony Costa was taken from the Parish Prison to the Gretna jail and placed in the cell with Cimo. The results were not very satisfactory. The men at least pretended to scarcely know each other.

In the meantime other things were learned. It was discovered that the sister of Tony and Frank Gendusa was the sweetheart of Leonardo Gebbia, who lived at 613 St. Philip Street, in the same block with the Lamanas, and that Francisco Luchesi had been the suitor of Nicolina Gebbia, Leonardo's sister.

Frank Gendusa was visited by Peter Lamana and Judge Patorno. Lamana begged him to tell what he knew.

At last Frank Gendusa, probably in hope of saving himself, consented to help. He still claimed to know little about the crime, but he admitted his bother and Leonardo Gebbia had been involved in the kidnaping of Walter Lamana.

Now Judge Patorno and the police resorted to cunning. Frank Gendusa was brought to the New Orleans side of the river and instructed to go to 613 St. Philip Street and ask Gebbia for money to help his brother, Tony. Judge Patorno, Captain Capo, Sheriff Marrero, Mr. Federico of the Italian Vigilance Committee, and two policemen hid themselves on the other side of the street.

When Gendusa emerged he told the waiting men that Leonardo Gebbia was not home, but that his father had promised to have Leonardo meet Gendusa at the landing of the Canal Street ferry that evening at eight-thirty o'clock with some money. Gendusa had asked if the boy was well, and the elder Gebbia had said Walter Lamana was still alive and safe.

The police waited until the next morning to raid the house. It was an early hour. They caught Leonardo Gebbia in bed.

He confessed at once. He said he had seen Tony Costa take the child and turn him over to Francisco Luchesi and a man named Stefano Monfre. Gebbia insisted that the child was alive the last time he had heard from any of the persons involved. Costa, he said, had been the man who had entered the arches of the Lamana residence and had offered the boy two nickels to buy ice cream. He had walked with the child to the corner of Bourbon and St. Philip streets. Here Monfre and Luchesi had been waiting with the curtained wagon. The child had been thrown into the rear of the vehicle, and the men drove off in the direction of St. Rose. He said that Tony Gendusa had written the letter to Mr. Lamana.

Gebbia and Frank Gendusa pretended to know no more than that, but when they were jailed and subjected to what the newspapers described as a "vigorous examination," an art in which New Orleans police have long been expert, much more was extracted from them. The child, they confessed, had been taken to the home of Ignazio Campisciano, and had been held there by Luchesi, Campisciano, and a man named Angelo Incaratera.

Nicolina Gebbia, Luchesi's sweetheart, and, also, it was rumored, sought after by Tony Gendusa, was arrested and confined to the Gretna jail. She admitted knowledge of the entire plot and added some details. Other arrests followed quickly. The rest of the Gebbia and Gendusa families were locked up, as well as Angelo Monteleone and his wife, who were related to the Gebbias, and with them operated the rooming house at 613 St. Philip Street, and Mrs. Stefano Monfre.

On Saturday, June 22, a large group of men boarded a special train, from New Orleans, and arrived at St. Rose just after midnight. Among the many irate men on that train were Judge Philip J. Patorno, Captain Capo, Mr. Federico, Officers T. P. Simoni and J. W. Lucas, and Sheriff Marrero of Jefferson Parish. Train master Frank T. Mooney of the Illinois Central Railroad Company, who provided the special engine and one coach, also went along. It was Mr. Mooney who was the first to describe the details of what took place after the arrival of the posse at Campisciano's house to a *Daily Picayune* reporter. The story appeared Monday, June 24, in that newspaper.

"Four men were picketed about his house for fear he might attempt to escape," said Mr. Mooney. "The remainder of the party then walked up to Campisciano's door and knocked loudly. Minutes seemed like hours there in the inky night. The moon had set and it was black. Then, after five or six minutes, Campisciano came to the door and opened it. He was in his underclothes.

"The party pushed the door open and stepped inside. Judge Patorno spoke out sharply, 'Give us that boy. We came for the child.'

"Campisciano stood without a word.

" 'Where is the Lamana boy?' demanded the Judge.

"The Italian shrugged his shoulders, pleading ignorance. He declared he knew nothing of the matter and maintained his position."

It was the most awful moment since the beginning of the long search. Captive and captors must have felt the terrible tautness of the silver thread that was just about to break. The beating of their hearts must have sounded like drums in the swamp night. "Where is the Lamana boy?" Did any of the posse hope that he might still be alive? Did Campisciano imagine he could lie and shrug his way out of this? Behind him in the dim light of a coal oil lamp his wife crouched on the edge of the bed, their baby in her arms. The baby began to cry.

"Where is the Lamana boy?" The question came again and again, to be met with shrugs, denials, and gesticulations.

What followed should perhaps be described in Mr. Mooney's own words.

"Campisciano was quickly seized and bound hand and foot. His hands were pinioned behind his back and his legs bound with ropes. He was carried outside and a rope was fastened about his neck and drawn tight, and the crowd began to carry him off, when he extended his tongue and indicated that he wanted to say something. Then he told us that the boy was brought to his house and divulged the names of those who had planned the kidnaping. We brought him back into the house and made him sit down in the light so he could talk better.

"Then Campisciano suddenly became silent and not another word could be extracted from him. He refused to answer any questions.

"Quick as a flash he was again bound hand and foot, and the noose again adjusted about his neck, but a little tighter than before. He was half carried and half pulled toward a tree. At that very instant, his own baby, inside the house, broke out in a loud cry. He heard the voice.

" 'If you do not tell us where this boy is you will never again see your child or hear its voice,' was the command."

This was the end. "Campisciano shuddered." He turned toward Judge Patorno, and spoke "as best he could."

He said, "The boy is dead."

Then fear overcame him again. He said he was afraid to talk. The noose was tightened about his throat, and he tried to scream. He nodded his head that he would tell more. The noose was loosened.

He took the men to a small shack not far from his living quarters. It was here the child had been imprisoned on that Saturday night Costa and his henchmen had brought him. Angelo Incaratero and his wife had remained there a few nights. The child had cried continually and was a nuisance. Besides, they were all afraid of discovery if they held him too long.

Walter kept crying for his mother. Incaratero said, "I can stop him." He put his hands around the boy's small throat and throttled him. The boy lay crumpled on the floor. Incaratero took a length of iron pipe and struck him on the head.

Some of the posse had been questioning Mrs. Campisciano back at the house while the others worked on her husband. She could not be made to talk. Even when told of the confessions of the Gendusas and the Gebbias, she denied all knowledge of the crime. This woman was one of the most callous of the entire group of murderers.

Neighbors of Campisciano were questioned. Stories that should have long ago been told the police came freely now that Campisciano, whom they all had feared, was under arrest. Several neighbors had seen the child. Once he tried to run away. Campisciano had caught him and dragged him back into the house with his hand over his mouth. A number of these people—Georgio Guzzardo, Tony Oshello, Joseph Gariffo, Jennie Gariffo, Simo Lardonio, Joseph Pomello and Arty Fontano—were taken to the jail at Hahnville by one of the sheriffs and locked up that very night.

The men were not yet through with Campisciano. He was trying to deny that he knew where the body had been hid. He was "put through every degree known to the police." At last he could stand no more. He consented to lead the way to where the remains of the murdered child had been concealed.

A week before men and bloodhounds had hunted in vain in the almost impenetrable swamp behind Campisciano's property. Now he led them, almost with ease, through black trails for two miles. Much of the way they waded through water. Sometimes they even suspected that the Sicilian was deliberately leading them astray. On several occasions they threatened him with more punishment if he tried to trick them in any way. Yet on they went, a man holding each of his arms, another the rope that was still about his neck.

They reached some willow bows. He said, "There."

Under the branches was a gray-covered bundle, resting on some wild cane reeds.

Campisciano was made to lift the body and place it in a box brought along for the purpose. Water streamed from what had been a little boy, for the bundle had lain in a filthy pool. The men returned to the Campisciano house slowly. Sometimes they had to crawl on their hands and knees through the thick jungle growth.

Campisciano talked rather freely as the train carried them all back to New Orleans. Walter had been killed on the Wednesday following the kidnaping. During most of the days before he had been kept locked up in the shack. Campisciano continued to deny killing the child himself. This, he insisted, was done by Incaratera, of whose whereabouts he had no idea.

Mrs. Campisciano sat with her own child in her arms, in silence. The men grouped about her on the train and tried to make her speak. She would not open her mouth. Even her husband seemed to urge her to speak. Once he turned his eyes on her and said, "Don't you remember last Wednesday night you asked me why I could not sleep—why I got up and went back to bed so often—and I told you the child had been killed by Angelo and that was the cause, because the boy's face was always before me?"

She did not answer him.

Someone asked her, in Italian, for neither of the Campiscianos understood much English, "How could you, a mother, with a child of your own, take part in murdering a small child?"

She still would not answer.

Peter Lamana had to go to the morgue to identify his son. He entered the room where the remains were exposed on a slab with James Laughlin, the coroner's chief clerk. There was little more than the tiny limbs and the featureless face, yet the father knew beyond a doubt that no mistake had been made. The big man sobbed like a child. "My God, how could they do it?" was all he could say. He had to go home then and tell the mother.

What followed was one of the most ghastly performances by some residents of the city that had ever occurred in its history. A mob gathered outside the morgue early Sunday morning, demanding in loud voices to see the remains. The *Daily Picayune* said the next day:

> When the yard gates were opened to let the Lamana undertaking wagon, bearing the corpse, pass out, the crowd surged in, and the driver had to check his horses several times to prevent the trampling of some of the people. Some of this crowd followed the wagon in a wild, aimless race down Franklin Street, while most of the mob thronged through the yard and pressed and jammed through the narrow door of the deadhouse. There, the insane desire to possess some gruesome souvenir of the most horrible crime that has shocked New Orleans since the Hennessy assassination by the Mafia took hold of the people, and they fought and fell over each other in an effort to tear off pieces of the clothes in which the body had been found, and which still lay, reeking with maggots and shreds of rotting flesh, on the slab.
>
> Mr. Laughlin was equal to the occasion and, with the assistance of several policemen, he pushed the ghouls from the morgue and locked the door. Those of the crowd, who had managed in the brief space of time to tear off a strip of the befouled cloth, were excited over their trophies, and passed them around for their less fortunate fellows to gaze upon with widely distended eyes.

Other crowds were gathering in the Vieux Carré. The Sicilians in the Lamana neighborhood kept indoors, for once more there was fear for their safety. Men stood on corners in groups and talked of lynchings and of "Dagos." There were those who believed it would be a good idea to "kill all Dagos," and those who said "all Dagos are Black Hand." Reports came of mass meetings to be held that night. The mob had tasted blood.

No mass meetings were held, and the fever slowly subsided, although there were the informal corner groups to be seen for days.

That Sunday afternoon, June 23, the funeral for little Walter Lamana was held. More than five hundred persons followed the cortege to the cemetery, and the whole city grieved. It is said that Orleanians walked the streets with tears streaming down their cheeks. Parents would not let their children out of their sight. Churches tolled their bells.

Although some of the gang were still at large, many of the important ones were now behind the bars of Parish Prison, and the public in general felt that Tony Costa, Frank Gendusa, Ignazio and Maria Campisciano, and Nicolina and Leonardo Gebbia were as important and as guilty in the committing of both the kidnaping and the murder as the four men who had escaped—Luchesi, Monfre, Tony Gendusa, and Incaratera.

Sunday morning, as soon as possible after Campisciano had described Incaratera's murder of the child, two of Angelo's brothers were arrested and taken to Parish Prison. It was hoped that they might reveal the hiding place of the murderer. There was a rumor that Stefano Monfre had been seen in a city in Kansas, but police did not place much credence upon it, and were inclined to believe that all the missing members of the gang were hiding in the New Orleans vicinity.

Scares of riots and lynchings still persisted, not only in New Orleans, but in the parishes of St. Charles and Jefferson as well, where some of the kidnapers were being held. Precautions were taken everywhere. Special deputies were appointed in the outlying parishes, and the New Orleans police strengthened the guard at the Parish Prison in the city.

Governor Blanchard promised the authorities that the militia would be in readiness for any emergency. The governor spoke on the telephone with Sheriff Long of St. Charles Parish. Long informed him that seventy deputies were on constant duty at the St. Charles Parish Jail, many being stationed outside, others inside. All were armed and prepared for any emergency. In New Orleans special police were spread out in a circle surrounding Parish Prison.

All visitors except newspapermen were barred from the prison. Soon talk of lynching the "Dagos" subsided.

At his request Peter Lamana was permitted to see Campisciano and his wife. He stood outside the bars of the man's cell, staring as if he could not believe anyone capable of this monstrous crime upon his son. When he reached the woman's cell he looked at her and at the child in her arms.

"You have a child of your own," he said. "How could you take part in the murder of another man's child?"

There was no answer.

Maria Campisciano had two children. Besides the nine-month-old baby girl she had brought to the prison with her, there was Vincent, aged four years, who remained behind with neighbors in St. Rose. A few days after her arrest Vincent was brought to his mother, and allowed to remain with her in the women's ward for the time being.

Campisciano denied any part in the killing, and insisted he had been forced to keep the child on his property against his will. He had seen Incaratera kill the little fellow, yes, but he had not even been in the room. He had been standing out in the field near the window of the shack, and a man he knew only as "Joe" had held a pistol to his head so that he could not interfere with the deed Incaratera was committing. Through the window, Campisciano said, he saw Incaratera strangle Walter then attack him with a length of pipe.

This, the police insisted, was impossible. The window Campisciano mentioned was too high to permit a view of the interior of the shack. And who was "Joe"? He might, it was thought, be Luchesi. However, they were not inclined to believe Campisciano's story at all.

Nicolina Gebbia's part in the crime now became a matter of speculation. Nicolina now said that she was to have married Tony Gendusa in the following month. Yet her love life seems to have been somewhat complicated. Francesco Luchesi, she said, who boarded with her mother at 613 St. Philip Street, was also in love with her. Nicolina had just received a divorce from Joseph Congenni. One day she was angry and depressed, and she remarked in Luchesi's presence that she would marry anyone who asked her. "I'll marry you," said Luchesi. "All right," Nicolina had replied impulsively. "I will marry you." Afterward she had regretted this. She said she did not like Luchesi, but she feared him.

"Frank would not work," she explained. "He was no account, and when I told my family I was going to marry him, they became so mad that they put Frank out of the house. He owed my mother for five weeks' board anyway.

"I didn't see him for about two weeks, then I met him on the Saturday afternoon of the kidnaping on Decatur Street near St. Philip. He took hold of my arm and said, 'Your mother kicked me out; your brothers won't speak to me. I have no money so I'm going to give myself to the break.' "

Nicolina explained that the expression "give myself to the break" meant he was going to the bad—that he would do something dishonest.

"He kept saying that and staring at me like he was going crazy. 'Why are you going to give yourself to the break?' I asked him. He said, 'I can't find no work and I ain't got no money. I will steal children and make thousands.' I called him a dirty dog, and he said, 'If you dare to say anything I've told you I'll kill you.'

"I met him again Sunday, the next day, when I was going to the fish market. It was about eleven o'clock—I know the hour because I heard the bells of the Cathedral ringing for high mass. He stopped me, and said, 'Didn't I tell you I was going to give myself to the break? Well, I done it, and don't you say anything. I'm going away, but soon I'll have lots of money, and then I'll write to tell you where to come and marry me. If you don't come, I'll come for you and kill you.'

"I told him again he was a dirty dog, and asked him if he had kidnaped a child where he had taken it. He said to the home of Ignazio Campisciano."

At this point in her story Nicolina began to weep. "They say they'll hang me," she said. "That would be murder. Maybe I should have told the police what Frank said to me, but I was so afraid. I swear to God I had nothing to do with the kidnaping or the murder of that poor child. Neither did my mother or my brothers. We were all afraid of Frank Luchesi."

Nicolina was later taken to the Denechaud Hotel for questioning by members of the Italian Vigilance Committee, who had established headquarters there. She repeated this story, but it was believed that she was protecting both Luchesi and Tony Gendusa. "I am a mother," she kept protesting. "Would I take part in the murder of a child?"

The next day Nicolina's two children, George and Nolan Congenni, and her small brother, Vincent, aged seven, were found wandering the streets of the Vieux Carré. The entire Gebbia family was in jail. The children had had nothing to eat for days. Charitable organizations took them in charge.

Leonardo Gebbia denied knowing any of the accused except Luchesi and the Gendusas. He and Costa were brought face to face in the Parish Prison, and Costa was asked if he knew the other man. "Of course," he replied. "That is Leon Gebbia."

Gebbia rushed to Costa in a rage and shoved his face to within a few inches of Costa's. He beat his breast, and shouted, in Italian, "You don't know me! Do you mean to say you recognize me?"

A newspaper reporter thought he tried to wink at Costa.

"What's the matter with you?" Costa asked. "Of course I know you. You are Gebbia."

Now the police revealed a story that had hitherto been kept secret. Some days after the disappearance of Walter Lamana a well-known and highly respected merchant of New Orleans, Frank Clesi, had come to them with the suggestion that he call on Frank Gendusa, who he believed might know something. Gendusa had offered to turn the child over to him for $2,000. Clesi replied that Mr. Lamana did not have that much money and suggested that $500 be accepted. It was this story that cast the heaviest pall of guilt upon Frank Gendusa.

On Wednesday, June 26, Mayor Martin Behrman called on Frank, and heard his version of the story.

"The Monday after the kidnaping," he said, "Mr. Lamana and

Judge Patorno came to see me and tell me they think my brother Antonino steal little Walter. Me, I curse and swear, call Antonino a son of a bitch. I tell the gentlemen that I try to find Antonino and make him give the boy up.

"Then Mr. Clesi come and I tell him I do what I can. Wednesday I'm out near the track in Algiers and who I see but Antonino, standing just like a loafer, his hands in his pockets, and I go up to him and say, 'Antonino, you son of a bitch, what you do with that boy?'

"Antonino, he look at me and smile. Then he say, 'The baby, he well. He sleep well. He eat well. Nobody gonna hurt him.' I tell him then he better give the baby back. He smile and say he give him back for $6,000. I say, 'Antonino, Mr. Lamana is not as rich a man as that.' And he say, 'Well, we give him back for $2,000 then. Tell him to sell his carriages and horses. He raise that much if he wants his boy.' Then he laugh and walk away. I never see him again. After Mr. Clesi comes back I try to find him, but I can't. Then they put me in jail. Mister, you take my hand, I swear to God, I kill Antonino myself you bring him here."

Mayor Behrman and other men interviewed Campisciano again. His story remained the same, but he added details and told of watching Incaratera and "Joe" carry the body of the child into the swamp. "I could not stand it," he said. "I could not sleep."

A careful search of Campisciano's property had now been made. A trunk was found which contained new, cheap lace curtains, some bolts of material, a number of watches, and several boxes of shotgun shells. In the bottom of the trunk were found letters that did not belong to Campisciano nor to anyone else in the neighborhood. The trunk and its contents were of the sort carried by peddlers who frequently traveled through southern Louisiana. Indeed, one such peddler had recently disappeared. He had last been seen near the Campisciano farm.

What else might that swamp conceal?

The belief that Campisciano had played a larger role in the actual murder of the child grew steadily.

The coroner's report of the examination of the body indicated that the little boy had not died of strangulation, but of a blow from some instrument resembling a hatchet. The skull was split in front, and it was easy to deduce that the blow had probably been struck as Walter stood facing his assailant.

Both those neighbors of Campisciano who were being held in jail at Hahnville—and there were many of them, several new arrests seeming to have taken place nearby every day—and those who were still at liberty believed that Campisciano had killed the child himself. Soon the New Orleans police were inclined to consider his story of Incaratera strangling the boy a fabrication.

Another strange circumstance arose. Acquaintances of Campisciano told of how he had concealed the identity of the assassin of his brother. The name of that killer they said was Gendusa. Tony Gendusa?

Then the hatchet was found. It was concealed under old clothes in a bureau in the Campisciano home. An attempt had been made to wash away dark stains, but this had not been altogether successful.

Peter Lamana went to the shack himself, to see the place where his small son had been killed. It was a damp, ill-lighted place, containing no furnishings. In one corner was a heap of corn shucks. It was here the boy had probably slept—if he slept at all. Two of the boards in the flooring were stained with blood. Mr. Lamana asked for instruments, and himself removed the sections of the boards on which were marked this evidence of what had been done to Walter. He wrapped them in newspaper to take back to City Chemist Metz for analysis.

Lamana talked to many people who lived near Campisciano. He visited the Hahnville jail and spoke to others there, among them Rose Pauella and a relative of Rose's, whose name was "Joe." A beaten path stretched from the Campisciano farm to Rose's house, and the Pauellas had refused to talk freely after Campisciano's arrest. Both were very suspicious, and it was wondered for a time if Joe might not be the Joe mentioned as helping Incaratera carry Walter's body to his place of hiding. It was believed, too, that the Pauellas did not maintain their attitude because of fear, as it was known many of those who had been arrested did, but, rather, that they were friends of the Campiscianos, and sought to aid them.

In regard to the four participants in the kidnaping who had not been apprehended, every rumor was traced, every trail followed to the end.

Angelo Incaratero was thought for a time to be in St. Bernard Parish, for instance, but this proved to be without foundation. Various strangers were arrested and held in many places near New Orleans, each of whom was suspected as being one or the other of the missing men, but each time the man held was innocent.

At last there came definite information that Stefano Monfre was in Pittsburgh, Kansas. James Di Vincenza, Monfre's brother-in-law, and himself a man of fine reputation, brought this information to the police, and offered to accompany officials from New Orleans so as to make a positive identification.

But Di Vincenza and the others arrived in Pittsburgh too late. Monfre had arrived there a few days after the kidnaping and had lived with a brother, Rafael, even had worked for a week in the mines. Then, Rafael told them, he had read of the Lamana case in the newspapers and had seen Stefano's name mentioned as being one of the men implicated. He had ordered his brother from his home, and Stefano had fled.

Stefano Monfre's record was a very bad one. He had been suspected of having murdered his wife's first husband and of other crimes. All the others of the Monfre family were said to be good, hard-working citizens, to whom Stefano was a source of acute embarrassment.

The hunt continued. Governor Blanchard offered a reward of a thousand dollars for the apprehension of any of the fugitives, and canceled an engagement to speak at a Fourth of July celebration at Tammany Hall in New York City so that he might be in Louisiana when the men were found.

Proof that Incaratero had been seen in Meridian, Mississippi was now given by two men, Bolivar Hyde, a grocer, and Tony Caruso, a fruit merchant, who had seen him and talked to him. Incaratero told them he was going to Cincinnati and then to Chicago. Police in both those cities promised to co-operate with New Orleans authorities in every way.

The next alarm came from Pointe a la Hache, not far from New Orleans. A suspect arrested there was identified by a Mrs. Lala and a Mrs. Foto as Tony Gendusa. Photographs were sent to New Orleans. The resemblance must have been strong: Frank Gendusa, when shown the pictures, said he wasn't sure, "it looks like Antonino, huh?" Nicolina said it was not Tony at all. Costa thought it might be. The man was finally identified as someone else and was released by Sheriff Mevers of Plaquemines Parish.

Most of the authorities thought that Tony Gendusa and Luchesi were hiding in the swamps near the city—perhaps in those very ones where Walter's body had been found. It was fairly certain that neither of the men had any money. Monfre and Incaratero, it was conceded, had probably managed to make temporary escapes to other parts of the country.

Ignazio and Maria Campisciano, Tony Costa, Frank Gendusa, Nicolina Gebbia, and Leonardo Gebbia were arraigned before the St. Charles Parish Grand Jury at Hahnville on July 1. True bills of murder were returned against these persons and against Francisco Luchesi, Tony Gendusa, Stefano Monfre, and Angelo Incaratero, the four men still to be apprehended.

The reactions of those in custody varied. Campisciano seemed to accept his fate most readily. He told his guards at the Parish Prison that he expected to be lynched as soon as he reached Hahnville. He wrote his will and said that he was not afraid to die.

Gebbia made the somewhat absurd mistake of sending for Chandler C. Luzenberg and asking Mr. Luzenberg to act as his defense attorney, to which the latter replied he intended to prosecute him and to see that he was hanged. Mr. Luzenberg was the district attorney in New Orleans.

Nicolina could not understand why she was being indicted, and continued to insist that she was innocent. What guilty knowledge she had kept secret had been done so because she was afraid for her life. Would not anyone do that?

Maria Campisciano was silent until representatives of a charitable organization came to take her son Vincent away from her. Then this hitherto quiet and somewhat enigmatic woman fought like a tigress. Backing against a wall in her cell, she screamed at and fought with those who tried to take away the child she held clutched in her arms. Vincent howled. "Oh, Christ!" cried his mother. "Holy Son of the Blessed Mother, if they hang me, others must hang. Now you take my son from me. Must all mothers suffer so? Do you think I, a mother, killed that little Lamana boy? Oh, Christ, tear out my eyes, strike my baby dead, if I killed anyone!"

Vincent was finally taken away. Maria crouched beside the cot on which the baby daughter she had been allowed to keep lay sleeping, and covered the infant's face with kisses. "Santa Maria," she insisted, "I know nothing of this. I swear to you I did not even see the boy Walter Lamana—I did not even see him."

It was against Mrs. Campisciano that the hate of the crowd who awaited the train seemed to turn with the most venom. Women hooted and jeered at her.

"Hang her!" they cried.

"How could she be so cruel?"

"They ought to burn her at the stake!"

Maria seemed to ignore her husband, as they were all taken from their coach and led to the courthouse. Once she turned on him a look of complete contempt, as if she despised him for having talked so freely and blamed him for her own predicament. In court she said not a word, but kept her eyes closed most of the time, her baby nursing at her breast.

Both Costa and Leonardo Gebbia protested their innocence to Judge Edrington. Nicolina again inquired why she was being indicted. Campisciano still seemed to have accepted his doom.

L. Robert Rivarde was appointed to defend the four who were to be tried first—the Campiscianos, Costa, and Frank Gendusa. Mr. Rivarde was optimistic about the outcome. He issued a statement in which he said that Maria had been only a tool of the others and had been guiltless of any real participation in the crime of murdering Walter Lamana, so she would probably go free. The three men he thought might escape with light sentences.

The six prisoners were returned to New Orleans on Wednesday, July 5, it being thought they were safer from any outbreak of mob violence in the larger city than they would be in the Hahnville jail.

Statements from Judge Patorno and Captain Capo promised the angry public that everything would be done to hang all the accused, including the women, Maria Campisciano and Nicolina Gebbia.

There was still no success in capturing the four men at large. News came now from Italy that Tony Gendusa had served eight years in prison there for blackmail, coming to the United States after his release.

The trial in Hahnville's little courthouse began on Monday, July 15, 1907. No time had been wasted. The Lamana boy had been dead only a few days more than a month. This was the trial of the four mentioned above. The Gebbias were scheduled to be tried on July 22.

New Orleans newspapers noted carefully the reactions of those now going on trial for their lives. Campisciano had reached a state of melancholia, and it was feared that he might try to end his life. All metal instruments were kept out of his reach; he was not even allowed to shave for days before the trial. Costa, always emotional and given to explosive expression and wild gesticulation, had become a cringing coward who huddled in a corner of his cell alternately muttering to himself and screaming his innocence to everyone within earshot. On the evening before the quartet were to be transported to Hahnville Costa knotted his pocket handkerchief about his throat, fastened the other end to the grill covering the door of his cell and threw himself forward. His groans attracted deputy sheriffs. He was half strangled, but alive. After that all the men were stripped naked and kept in that condition until an hour before departure.

They came to take Maria Campisciano's baby. This time she was better controlled. She wept bitterly, holding little Anina pressed to her breasts until the last moment, gazing into the face of the infant as if she were never to see it again. When the baby was gone, she sank to the edge of her cot, her arms still folded as if they held Anina, tears streaming from beneath the lashes of her closed eyes. All the women in the ward crowded about her, most of them weeping with her. The baby had become the pet of the women's ward. Little Anina's gurgles could be heard far down the corridors as she was carried away.

Gendusa and the Gebbias were quiet. Although the Gebbias were not to be tried on the fifteenth, they were going along to be called as witnesses. Leonardo had promised to aid the State.

Old Mrs. Gebbia was interviewed by Judge Patorno the day before the trial. Mrs. Gebbia could not understand why she and her family were imprisoned. They were innocent—innocent.

The morning they were to leave the men were given their clothes, the women were permitted to change. It is doubtful that Parish Prison was ever noisier than that morning. As Maria and Nicolina were led away by deputies, Mrs. Gebbia began to shriek, and Nicolina soon joined in. Costa began to yell loudly in Italian, flinging his arms about so that he had to be physically restrained. Mrs. Monteleone screamed too.

Outside the streets were crowded as the prisoners entered the police van. The jolting of the wagon and excitement made Costa's nose bleed. Leonardo Gebbia and Campisciano began to quarrel violently. Maria wept. Nicolina howled. At the train Campisciano turned from his abuse of Gebbia to a reporter for the *Daily Picayune.*

"You are the murderers," he said in Italian. "The child would be alive if it were not for you. I won't forget you. You made a great man of me. The courts ought to be trying you instead of me."

The reporter showed him a picture of Anina in the morning paper. The baby was sitting on the lap of Mrs. Agnew, the matron of the New Orleans Waifs' Home. The baby was smiling and looked happy.

Campisciano liked it, and when the reporter told him he could keep it, he folded it roughly and shoved it in his pocket. "You killed the child, not me," he said. "Maybe you will kill my baby, too."

Leonardo Gebbia, the most American of the crowd, tried to act tough. "You see, pal," he told the reporters, in that Brooklyn-like accent that for some reason is common in New Orleans, "I just can't talk. I know youse reporters want to treat me square. I'll tell youse this. I never did associate with them Dagos. My sister mixes up with trash, but not me. They always said I was stuck up because I never did speak to none of them." Given a cigar, young Gebbia— he was just past twenty—bit off the end, spat it to the pavement, and boarded the train with a jaunty, self-confident air.

Peter Lamana was aboard that train. Sheriff Madere asked him if he were armed. Mr. Lamana handed over a revolver, but contended that he had not intended to use it. "I am satisfied that the law should take its course," he said.

In its entire history the little village of Hahnville had never had such a crowd. People came from all over Louisiana, special trains having been run out from New Orleans. Vendors had set up tents in the streets near the courthouse, in which they sold sandwiches, coffee, and cold drinks. Street vendors offered ice cream and candy, and there was, generally, a carnival atmosphere.

The trial opened at eleven o'clock, with District Attorney L. H. Marrero, Jr. of St. Rose Parish and Chandler C. Luzenberg representing the State, L. Robert Rivarde acting for the defense, and Judge Prentiss E. Edrington presiding.

The jury was selected the first day. The four who were on trial sat silently watching. Costa kept twitching and jerking. The others seemed composed and resigned to the outcome.

The next day, Tuesday, July 16, Coroner O'Hara of New Orleans was the first witness to be summoned by the State. He told of the condition of the body, of the evidence that death had been caused by some instrument such as a hatchet.

Then came the report of Dr. A. L. Metz. The hatchet that had been turned over to him did not hold any blood stains. The dark blemishes upon it had been caused by something else. It could easily have been washed, contended the State.

Mrs. Peter Lamana took the stand. At the sight of Walter's bloodstained clothing, which was spread out upon a table within sight, she burst into tears. When her sobs subsided she described the Saturday afternoon and evening of the day Walter had disappeared. At five-thirty in the afternoon Mrs. Gebbia had come over and given Walter a nickel for candy. Sunday the elderly woman had called again. She had told Mrs. Lamana that her boy was not drowned as the mother had feared, but had been taken by some "bad men," and that it would be well to pay them money. Mrs. Gebbia had seemed very certain of this, and this had astonished Mrs. Lamana, though she had not at the time thought the woman was implicated. On Tuesday the entire Gebbia family visited her. This was surprising since the Lamanas were friendly only with Leonardo.

Peter Lamana was called next. His testimony was brief, as he told of his efforts to find his son before it was too late. He was well controlled while on the stand, although afterward he said, "I wanted to jump at the throat of Campisciano every time I looked at him. I had a hard time to keep still."

After lunch Leonardo Gebbia was called. A witness for the State, he described seeing Costa walk off with the child. Luchesi had lifted Walter into the wagon. The little boy had cried and tried to get away, but they held him fast. He added one new and rather startling bit of evidence. When all the men involved were occupying a row of cells, Leonardo said a man with a bushy red beard, whose name was Georgio Guzzardo, had visited Campisciano. Trembling and in tears, Guzzardo took Campisciano's hand and covered it with kisses. "Oh, Christ!" Guzzardo had said. "Promise me you won't give me away. Promise me that." Campisciano had answered, saying, "You must promise me in turn that if they hang me you will take my children and raise them as your own. They may hang my wife, too. You must support my children until they are grown." Guzzardo had given his word to do this in payment for Campisciano's silence, Gebbia said.

Jennie Gariffo, the pretty fifteen-year-old neighbor of the Campiscianos, told of seeing the curtained wagon arrive at daylight on June 9. Campisciano and another man had taken a small boy from the wagon. Later that Sunday afternoon Jennie had heard the child crying. She and several members of the family had gone over to investigate, but Mrs. Campisciano had met them at the edge of the property and told them what they heard was a neighborhood boy out hunting cows.

Other neighbors of the Campiscianos were called. Sheriff F. O. Weaver told of the first arrest of Campisciano, and Sheriff Marrero of Jefferson Parish described how the man had led them through the swamp to the body.

Mr. Rivarde cross-examined all the witnesses, but accomplished very little.

During the first day there was only one outbreak from any of the prisoners. When a Mrs. Fontana testified that she had seen two men and a boy crossing the Campisçiano fields, Maria sprang to her feet and screamed in Italian, "Tell the truth!" and had to be silenced by Judge Edrington.

Some of the witnesses who had come from New Orleans were angry because they were barred from the courtroom, in particular Judge Patorno, who was very indignant. Interviewed after the court closed for the day, Patorno expressed some criticism of the way things were going, although he was confident all the accused would be hanged. He added that the Italian Vigilance Committee would ask for the indictment of the older Gebbias and the Monteleones later. "These people are just as guilty as the others," he said, "and should be hanged with them."

It was reported that all the prisoners slept well that night. Costa, however, had entered upon a hunger strike, and stated that he was going to starve himself to death.

Campisciano announced that evening that when the Gebbias went to trial he would testify as State's witness against them. Leonardo, he said, was only trying to save his own life. It had been Leonardo who had suggested that Incaratero murder the child, Campisciano now swore. Each day Luchesi and Incaratero had taken Walter out of the shack, where he was locked at night, and kept him with them when they spent the day in hiding behind the sugarhouse, watching for anyone who might approach. On the Wednesday after the kidnaping Walter made so much noise that Leonardo, who had come out to the farm, told Incaratero to take him into the shack and "finish him."

The State concluded its case Wednesday morning. The defense now summoned Frank Clesi, who related the details of his visit with Frank Gendusa. Mr. Rivarde then tried to prove that Frank Gendusa had endeavored to persuade his brother Tony to return the boy, and therefore had not been guilty of the crime with which he was charged.

Leonardo's younger brother, Frank Gebbia, was Mr. Rivarde's next witness. His testimony, however, was not to the advantage of the defense. He told how every day Costa, Incaratero, Luchesi, Monfre, Tony Gendusa, and Nicolina and Leonardo Gebbia met in his home and held long and secretive conferences. Tony Gendusa, Luchesi, and Monfre, Frank said, had been spending days at his home long before the kidnaping. Frank said, too, that he was badly treated at home. His parents and brother and sister would not allow him to attend school, but made him work and bring home all his money.

Leonardo Gebbia took the stand for a few minutes, while Mr. Rivarde tried to show that his story of the conversation between Campisciano and Guzzardo was fantastic and a figment of the young man's imagination. However, Leonardo could not be persuaded to alter his testimony.

Sheriff Weaver and Sheriff John Fitzgerald followed a procession of minor witnesses, mostly consisting of Campisciano's neighbors. The sheriffs described the arrest of Campisciano. Ignacio Caravello was summoned for a few questions. He had seen the wagon, but he had never seen a child. He told again of watching Campisciano ride down the road leading to New Orleans. Caravello, a young man of excellent reputation, had been held in jail at Hahnville until now for his own protection. That evening he was released.

Captain Capo was now questioned by Mr. Rivarde as to the

circumstances of Campisciano's confession. The defense attorney made good use of the fact that stringent methods had been employed to obtain the confession, and accused Captain Capo and Judge Patorno of torturing Campisciano. They had not tortured the man, the police captain testified, but merely frightened him. The captain then related an account of the finding of Walter's body, and with what certainty Campisciano had led them to its hiding place. Mr. Rivarde returned to the forcing of the confession. Here Mr. Luzenberg objected, saying to review that would take much time and all necessary facts were already known to everyone.

When Costa took the stand he testified that he had known Peter Lamana, but not the children. Over and over again he babbled that he had not murdered Walter—that he had harmed no one. He said he had visited the Gebbias, but he did not know Monfre, Luchesi, Incaratero, or Campisciano. He had nothing to do with the crime at all. By *Santa Maria*, he was innocent as a babe.

The defense called Campisciano.

"Who killed Walter Lamana?"

"Angelo Incaratero."

Campisciano then described in detail the events leading to the murder. Tony Gendusa had told him to expect Luchesi and Monfre, who were bringing the boy, and had warned him that he would be killed if he did not co-operate with them or if he talked. On Wednesday Leonardo Gebbia had come out to the farm and advised them to kill the child.

After Incaratero had committed the murder he and Luchesi had emerged from the shack with a bundle. Campisciano was plowing his field. Incaratero and Luchesi had made him accompany them into the swamp to hide the bundle.

"Who is responsible for this crime?"

"Incaratero, Luchesi, Monfre, Tony Gendusa, and the Gebbias."

Campisciano named no one who was then on trial.

Mr. Rivarde now closed the case for the defense.

The arguments of the counsel and the address of Judge Edrington were brief. The jury was out from 5:12 to 6:03. Just before the jury was readmitted to the courtroom Judge Edrington addressed those present.

"The court will ask everybody in the court to keep quiet when the jury comes in,'" he said, "and to make no demonstrations. Do not give expression to your thoughts or feelings by making any remarks or indulging in any demonstration whatever. Make no sign of your feelings whatever. Mr. Sheriff, bring in the jury."

The *Daily Picayune* of July 19, 1907, described what followed.

"They took their seats, and the Judge asked the clerk to inquire if they had agreed on a verdict. They all answered in the affirmative. Mr. Crespo handed the document, on which the indictment had been written, to the Judge, who pondered over it quite a while, holding his fan in front of him, so that none of those around could see what it was. An ominous silence continued. The Judge ordered the clerk to hand it over to the District Attorney, who also studied it quite a while.

"Mr. Triche was then handed the document and instructed to read it aloud. The verdict was, 'Guilty without capital punishment.' "

The silence in the courtroom was unbroken.

But that silence was only for the moment. Within an hour the town of Hahnville was seething with indignation. When the jurymen emerged from the courthouse they had to be protected by deputies. All held their fans over their faces (the day was hot and all the men and women present seemed to have carried palmetto fans) to avoid being photographed. That very afternoon many of the jurymen left town. Within their cells in the town jail the prisoners shivered with terror of the angry hum of voices that penetrated the walls of the prison.

By nightfall Governor Blanchard had ordered three companies of the State Militia to Hahnville to prevent the threatened lynchings. Soldiers with drawn bayonets circled the jail and were quartered within the high wood fence surrounding it. Others were stationed along the streets of the town.

In neighboring towns—Gretna, Kenner, and Harvey—meetings

were held and it was reported that mobs were being organized to march on Hahnville and to take the prisoners away from the militia if necessary.

A crowd from New Orleans then seized a Texas and Pacific freight train and rode it the twenty miles to Hahnville. There they were met by officers of the militia, who after long and hot arguments, and threats with drawn guns, persuaded the angry Orleanians to return to the city. The night of the nineteenth Mayor Behrman of New Orleans ordered all saloons, hotel bars, and clubs closed. Special police had to be assigned again to the Vieux Carré. All night long jeering mobs gathered before the city hall and the offices of the several newspapers in the city.

The papers all expressed opinions that the verdict was an outrage. The Italian Vigilance Committee offered the statement that there had never been such a miscarriage of justice in the history of the nation. Judge Patorno said, "It is time for the good people of the Italian colony to rise to the occasion and let Judge Lynch have an inning. We have worked day and night on the case, and I was sure that each of the Italians who were placed on trial would have soared higher than Jasper's kite. I have always been an advocate of law and order. I have opposed violence when I was sure that the law would vindicate an outrage perpetrated on a community, but in this case I am sure that the law did not receive the least bit of consideration."

Peter Lamana was even more furious.

"It is an outrage," he said. "I cannot believe that twelve men would dare to face this community after rendering such a verdict. The law appeared clear. I am sure that Campisciano killed my boy. I am positive that he was aided by his wife. Gendusa and Costa were the men who stole the child. I am disgusted. If I had them here I would shoot them all down like dogs."

On the twentieth the four who had been sentenced were smuggled out of Hahnville and transferred to the state penitentiary at Angola, Louisiana, far from the Hahnville-New Orleans vicinity. The Gebbias were taken back to the Parish Prison in New Orleans, to await their trial. After that Hahnville gradually quieted to its former tranquility, but some members of the jury remained away for weeks.

On the twenty-second, the day the Gebbia trial was to begin, their attorney, John Q. Flynn, asked for a continuance on the grounds that public opinion was too inflamed for there to be any possibility of a fair hearing at that time. The date was then postponed until November 12.

In the meantime, Frank Gendusa and the Campiscianos began their life terms at hard labor. Tony Costa had to be hospitalized upon his arrival at Angola. In September he died in the prison hospital.

All was quiet by November, but the public had by no means forgotten its disappointment in the verdict that was the result of the first trial, and perhaps Nicolina and Leonardo Gebbia knew that they could not expect but to suffer from the consequences. When they were brought into the Hahnville courtroom Nicolina looked frail and worn from the long months in prison, and Leonardo, although he did his best to swagger, also was haggard and thin.

During the summer months following the other trial all the prisoners but the young Gebbias had been released, including their parents—a fact violently opposed by the Lamanas, who felt the elder Gebbias to be as responsible, at least in a moral sense, as the brother and sister now on trial. The Monteleones had gone to Chicago, from where they sent Nicolina and Leonardo money and presents.

It was the afternoon of the second day of the trial, November 13, before the jury was selected. Then the first witness, Coroner O'Hara, again told his story of the condition of the child's body. His testimony was followed by that of John Davis, a night clerk in the morgue at New Orleans, who identified the ghastly shreds of clothing that had been found upon the small corpse. Oscar Antoine told of seeing the boy as he returned from the funeral the day of the kidnaping. There followed a series of less important witnesses.

During the testimony the Gebbias sat together, facing the witness box. Nicolina, small and rather pretty, wearing a cheap black dress with a high collar and no hat on her pile of fair hair, twisted her handkerchief continually, and now and then turned to whisper to her brother, who unshaven and untidy, viewed the proceedings with sullen, sleepy eyes. When Mrs. Lamana was called Nicolina began to cry.

Mrs. Lamana told of the several visits of the Gebbias and other details of the days following the kidnaping. Not only Nicolina but also members of the jury wept as she spoke. Then Mr. Lamana followed his wife, to tell the same stories as he had offered in the trial in July.

There were only two events during the whole of the Gebbia trial that created excitement. One was the appearance of Ignazio Campisciano, who was brought from Angola by armed guards, and who endeavored to testify for the State, swearing under oath that it had been Leonardo Gebbia who had ordered that Walter be killed.

The other testimony that caused a stir was that of Frank Gebbia, the young brother, who retracted all the statements he had made in the other trial and vowed that Judge Patorno had come to his cell in Parish Prison, placed a gun to his head and forced him to promise to give such evidence.

It is doubtful that anyone following the case could fail to guess what the outcome would be. The defense attorney, Mr. Flynn, offered an excellent argument at the conclusion, pointing out that there was no proof that either of the Gebbias had murdered the child, and that they were on trial for murder, not for conspiracy in the kidnaping. The only thing the State had proven, said Mr. Flynn, was that some of the Gebbias had visited Mrs. Lamana. There was no evidence at all against Nicolina. She had feared Luchesi, and for that reason had kept silent. Leonardo Gebbia was a young ruffian, who mixed with bad company perhaps, but this did not make him a murderer.

District Attorney Marrero spoke of the horrible nature of the crime and reminded the jury that Campisciano, on whose property the child had been murdered, had testified that it was at the insistence of Gebbia that the slaying had been committed.

The jury was out less than thirty minutes. The decision came quickly and was unanimous: "Guilty as charged."

"Does this apply to both the accused?" asked the judge.

The foreman replied, "Yes, sir."

The citizens of Hahnville were jubilant. This time justice had been done. The Gebbias would hang. Crowds gathered outside the courthouse once more, but the attitude was quite different now. The jury, as they emerged, were congratulated for their decision.

And the Italians in New Orleans were equally pleased. Now they were free of the Black Hand and need no longer live in fear of extortion and death should they not obey the orders of secret societies. The Italian Vigilance Committee announced the formation of a National Italian Protective League. To this organization could come all good Italians who received threats of any kind. Ships bringing immigrants from Europe would be boarded by members, and no more Sicilian criminals would be allowed to enter the United States.

The reactions of the newspapers were somewhat curious. The verdict against the Gebbias was called "the strangest ever heard." If they were guilty of a capital offense and were to be executed, were not the others equally as guilty? Had not excitement and public sentiment after the result of the last trial played a larger part in the decision of this one than the evidence?

Mr. Flynn announced that he would ask for a new trial. "The verdict is a sham on justice," he said. "The evidence against Nicolina was especially feeble."

But Nicolina seemed not too worried. She believed firmly that her sex would save her.

"They may hang my brother," she said, "but never me. I may die in prison, but not this way." Here Nicolina drew a finger across her throat. "All I ever did was to keep my mouth shut."

Leonardo said simply, "I've been the fall guy in the whole case. They've punished me for what somebody else did."

Mr. Lamana felt that at least in part his son was to be avenged.

"Thank God that some of the scoundrels will get their just deserts," he said. "I believe the Gebbias were the prime movers in the whole affair, and I would rather have them hung than any of the others."

On November 18 the Gebbias were returned to New Orleans. Nicolina was reported to be ill.

There is little point in describing the brief second trial of the Gebbias. There was almost no new evidence. The resulting verdict was the same.

However, the Gebbias were determined to fight until the last. They now employed Mr. Rivarde, who had defended the first four of the kidnapers tried. The Supreme Court refused Mr. Rivarde a hearing of the case, but in the spring of 1908 he appeared before the Board of Pardons. Here he won a commutation of sentence for Nicolina to life imprisonment.

"Sure I'm glad for her," said Leonardo, when he was told of this. "She didn't have nothing to do with killing the kid. But I didn't either. I told you I was going to be the fall guy."

On Friday, July 16, 1909, at one o'clock in the afternoon, Leonardo Gebbia climbed the scaffold in the prison yard at Hahnville. He retained his swagger until the end, and until the end protested his innocence.

"Why ain't they caught the others?" he demanded the morning of the execution. "How about Tony Gendusa, Incaratero, Monfre, and Frank Luchesi? It's more than two years and they ain't caught 'em. They never will now, but they're satisfied just so long as they're hanging me."

At the foot of the gallows he turned to the sheriff, and said, "Do a good job, big boy." He then handed the sheriff his half-smoked cigar.

Hahnville was filled with nearly as many visitors for the execution of Gebbia as had come for the trial. Again there was the town fair atmosphere, with tents along the streets serving food and soft drinks, and it was a field day for the newspapers. Everyone of importance was interviewed, columns alone being devoted to Mr. Johnston, the executioner, who boasted of his proficiency in his profession. He promised to take special care in the hanging of Leonardo Gebbia.

Mr. Lamana, accompanied by Philip Geraci and a party of friends, arrived, bringing, said the newspapers, a lunch of roast beef, bread, condiments, and wine.

At precisely one o'clock Leonardo Gebbia stood upon the trap door. While Mr. Johnston adjusted the noose about his neck Leonardo chatted calmly. He was still trying to talk when the trap was sprung. His neck was broken instantly. Mr. Johnston had done his job well.

Philip Geraci secured the noose from the hangman and gave it to Peter Lamana.

Not until the Lindbergh kidnaping was there to be a crime in that category that contained so many shocking details. Because of the prominence of the Lindbergh family the case attracted more national attention, but even that brutal crime did not contain elements as sinister and as frightful as the murder of Walter Lamana.

Here suspicion was cast upon a whole neighborhood, and many mysteries remain unsolved. Many people must have seen Costa walk off with the boy, yet fear kept them quiet. Many other than those who came to trial were involved, yet they went free. A life was paid for a life and then police and public seemed satisfied.

However, Walter Lamana did not die in vain. With the conclusion of the case fear of the Black Hand and the Mafia vanished from New Orleans, and recipients of threatening letters took them to the police from then on.

LET THE POOR GIRL SLEEP!

Murder interests us most when it occurs in the least expected place. News of sudden death within the criminal world may shock us by its quality of violence, but we are scarcely surprised. However, when one member of that portion of society we call respectable kills one or more persons among his intimates, or even should he be suspected of having killed them, our interest reaches a higher pitch. In part at least, it is the absence of the unusual, the very commonplaceness of the backgrounds of the Lizzie Bordens and the Ruth Snyders that makes these cases fascinating. It could happen to our friends, or to ourselves.

In September, 1911, it would have been difficult indeed to have selected any family less likely to be destined for the ordeal they were to undergo than the Crawfords, who lived on Peters Avenue in New Orleans. The family then consisted of Mr. and Mrs. Robert Crawford and their three young nieces, Annie, Elsie, and Gertrude. Mr. Crawford had been for many years a motorman on a streetcar, "well-known for his patience and his kind attention to his public duty," as the newspapers were later to phrase it, "who quite recently opened a small café near the Audubon Park." Elise was a stenographer for the New Orleans, Fort Jackson, and Grand Isle Railroad Company, "a competent employee, really brilliant in her work, and a favorite among her associates." Annie was out of work, after having been employed for more than six years at the New Orleans Sanitarium. Gertrude, only nineteen, had recently arrived from Port Arthur, Texas, where she had lived for a time with a married sister.

The three girls had, not long before, been subjected to a series of sad experiences. In June, 1910, the eldest girl of the family, Mary

Agnes, who was always called "Mamie," died suddenly. In the following month, July, both their parents, first the father, Walter Crawford, then the mother, were taken from them within thirteen days of each other, both deaths coming quickly and almost without warning. A few months after that Annie and Elise went to board with their aunt and uncle, to be joined later by Gertrude.

The neighbors on Peter Avenue considered the girls brave and somewhat pathetic. All three were still in deep mourning. They wore nothing but black with an occasional touch of white. They were said to go nowhere except to church and to the cemetery where the rest of their family was buried. This seemed particularly dismal for Miss Elise and Miss Gertrude, who were pretty girls with cheerful dispositions. Even as it was, both had young men callers.

In the case of Miss Annie, she was often heard to say that she would never wear anything other than the identical costume in which she always appeared, and it was difficult to remember her, or to imagine her, in anything else. She always wore a black cloth skirt that not only reached to the ground but trailed a little behind her, a shirtwaist of dull black silk, and, in the street, a large mourning hat from which fell a thick black veil that almost entirely concealed her features. At her belt there was always pinned a crisp white handkerchief.

The eldest of the trio, she was twenty-eight. Her features were heavy and she was plain. The eyes behind the spectacles that she never removed in public were prominent and a cold blue. She wore her pale yellow hair done up in a severe knot with bangs upon her forehead. Miss Annie had no beaux and it was generally considered that she was already an old maid.

However, Miss Annie was highly respected by the Crawfords' acquaintances, for it was said that it had been she who had taken on the responsibility of looking after the other girls, and of replacing their mother insofar as it was possible. It was Miss Annie who saw that they attended Mass and paid periodic visits to the family grave in St. Patrick's Cemetery No. 3. It was Miss Annie who decided whether the young men who came to call upon Miss

Elise and Miss Gertrude were proper associates for them. It was Miss Annie who always nursed the sick in the household.

The Crawfords' house, which they rented, was half of what is called in New Orleans a "double camelback," that is, two apartments divided by a single wall with duplicate front yards, front galleries, backyards, and wash sheds, with four downstairs rooms on each side and an upstairs, consisting of two bedrooms and a bath, over the rear half of the house giving the camel's hump effect. The cottage was neat and clean, painted white with bright green shutters, and further adorned with an iron picket fence, a modest amount of gingerbread, and a small flower garden in the front yard. Annie had the front bedroom upstairs and Elise and Gertrude shared the back one—at least until Elise became ill. Then, at Annie's suggestion, she and Gertrude swapped places, so that Annie might be with Elise at night.

It was on Monday afternoon, September 18, that Elise came home from work in a taxicab, a somewhat unusual occurrence for persons in the moderate financial circumstances of the Crawfords at that period. With her was a Mr. Muller, who worked in her office, and, after turning her over to Mrs. Crawford, he departed.

Annie was in the backyard washing clothes, but she came into the house at once, took Elise in charge and put her to bed. Elise had a violent attack of vomiting, very similar to several she had suffered recently, so Annie went next door and telephoned Dr. Marion H. McGuire, who had been treating Elise for nervousness during the past few months. When Annie returned she told her Aunt Mary that Dr. McGuire had prescribed capsules of calomel and soda for Elise, then, dressing herself for the street, Annie went to Walsdorf's Drug Store, a few blocks away, to get them.

Mrs. Crawford had retired downstairs when Annie called her that night. When the aunt reached the room upstairs Elise appeared to be in a coma. Annie again ran next door and telephoned the doctor. He arrived a short time later, pricked Elise's arm with a needle, made some other tests, and then, with the aid of the aunt and Annie, got the girl to her feet and forced her to walk about the room until she was partially aroused.

All day Tuesday Elise remained in a semiconscious state. However, she was so recovered on Wednesday that Annie took her downtown for electric treatments. One symptom of Elise's nervous trouble had been either real or imaginary difficulty with her left leg. Dr. McGuire had prescribed the application of an electric battery.

Elise remained in bed Thursday, but on Friday she came downstairs, took some broth prepared by her aunt, then fell asleep on a sofa in the dining room. When she awakened Annie helped her to her room, gave her another capsule, and put her to bed. At five o'clock Dr. McGuire made a brief visit, and at about six, Elise's young man, Edward Zahn, called and talked with the sick girl for about a half hour. While he was there Annie went down to the kitchen and prepared some grits, toast, and a cup of tea for her patient.

It was while she was gone that Elise made what was later to be considered a significant request.

"Aunt Mary," she asked, "will you sleep with me tonight?" And when Aunt Mary asked why, Elise added, "You think Annie stays with me at night, but she doesn't. Often I wake up and she isn't here."

When Mr. Zahn left, Annie brought in Elise's supper. A few minutes later Gertrude came into the room. Elise tasted the tea and complained that it was bitter. She then requested that Gertrude make her a fresh cup.

Gertrude returned with the tea, and this time Elise drank it. Annie had gone into the other bedroom, and the two younger sisters were alone. Elise took two rings from her fingers and unfastened her chain and locket from her throat. She handed them to Gertrude, saying, "Gertie, I want you to have these." Gertrude objected, but Elise was so insistent that at last the younger girl put the rings on her own fingers and the chain and locket about her own throat. "I won't need them any more," said Elise. Annie then came into the room, but if she noticed that Elise had given away her jewelry she said nothing about it.

At about eleven o'clock that night Aunt Mary, after explaining to her husband that she was going to spend the night with Elise, entered the girl's room to find her sitting in a rocking chair near the window. She was asleep and her breathing made a harsh, rasping sound. Aunt Mary called to Annie, who, together with Gertrude, had already retired in the other upstairs room, and Annie came in wearing a nightgown and a kimono.

"Does Elise always snore that way?" asked Aunt Mary.

"Sometimes she does," was Annie's reply. "Don't worry about it."

Then, according to Aunt Mary's own story, told later: "I went over and felt Elise's head, and I found it cold and clammy. I raised her arm and it dropped limply to her side. I called out, 'Oh, Elise has another spell. Go for the doctor!'"

Once more Annie went next door to telephone. The room in which the neighbor's telephone was placed had windows opposite those of Elise's room. After Annie had talked to Dr. McGuire, she went to the window and called to her aunt. Her exact words were to be the subject of much discussion later. Aunt Mary and Gertrude both insisted that what Annie said was, "Is Elise still breathing?" Annie's own version was that she had asked, "Is Elise still breathing loud?"

When she returned to the room, Annie found her aunt shaking Elise and trying to arouse her in other ways.

"Why don't you let her alone?" Annie said. "Let the poor girl sleep."

Both Annie and her aunt knelt and said some prayers. A few seconds later Annie looked up and said to her aunt, "She's better off than I am."

Aunt Mary, again according to her own account, then "sprang forward like a wild woman," and cried, "Annie, did you do this?"

Robert Crawford appeared in the door. Annie said to him, "Aunt Mary's going crazy!"

Annie went into the bathroom and returned with some liquid in a cup, which she proffered to her aunt. In Aunt Mary's own words, "I dashed it to the floor!"

Dr. McGuire summoned an ambulance almost immediately upon

his arrival. The interns first used a stomach pump, then rushed Elise to the Charity Hospital, Annie and Dr. McGuire following in his carriage.

At nine-thirty the following morning Elise died. Annie was at her side.

The next day, Sunday, the *Daily Picayune* carried a brief account to the effect that an inquiry was being made "into the death of Miss Elise Crawford, a pretty young woman who resided at 1011 Peters Avenue, who passed away in the hospital yesterday morning," adding, "Members of the family interviewed at the wake Saturday night could not offer a suggestion. They knew of no unhappiness in the young lady's life, for she was a pretty young woman, brilliant in her work and beloved by all."

Assistant Coroner C. William Groetsch had been summoned to the hospital by Dr. McGuire even before Elise died. To him the doctor gave over two cups containing the fluids extracted from the girl's stomach and bladder. These, in turn, were given to City Chemist Metz. Dr. Metz, even before he had made his analysis of the fluids, told newspaper reporters that the death of Elise might be due to opium poison.

Elise was buried on Sunday afternoon in the family grave with her parents and Mamie. Annie had recently purchased extra ground so that the grave might be enlarged and, at the same time, had a fine granite coping placed about the plot. Annie was always assiduous in her attention to such matters.

On Tuesday afternoon City Chemist Metz notified District Attorney St. Clair Adams that there were three grains of morphine in the two cups of fluid taken from Elise. After a conference with Police Inspector James C. Reynolds and Assistant Chief of Detectives Dan Mouney, the three officials, along with several policemen, set out in a taxicab for the Crawford residence.

What the gentlemen found upon their arrival must have startled them. When they were admitted by Mrs. Crawford they saw at once that the entire house was in a state of disarray. Pictures were down, carpets were rolled up, and boxes and crates filled with household effects were about. There was every indication that the Crawford family was about to depart the premises.

Yet Mrs. Crawford's explanation was simple enough, although it indicated that the relationship within the family group was not precisely as had been thought. They were, Mrs. Crawford said, "breaking up." She and her husband had rented a smaller place in Octavia Street, and were moving there. Annie was returning to Port Arthur, Texas, with her married sister, Mrs. Edward Leo, who had arrived on Sunday for the funeral. Gertrude had not yet decided what she would do.

The entire family was at once escorted to police headquarters, and in a manner that now seems curious. A policeman was sent out to stop one of the streetcars that then operated on a line running along Peters Avenue. All the passengers were requested to leave the car and aboard it were placed the Crawfords. The next day the New Orleans *Item* published a photograph of the family boarding the trolley for the bumpy ride downtown.

Robert Crawford was the first of the group to be questioned. Evidently a man who paid small attention to his womenfolk, he had little information to offer the district attorney, and, after a few minutes, he was permitted to take a chair in an anteroom to await the time when he might escort the ladies home.

Miss Gertrude was more helpful. After describing Elise's last illness, she told of quarrels between her Aunt Mary and Annie. Gertrude had gone to live in Texas with Mrs. Leo after their parents had died, and when she wanted to return Annie had opposed the idea. In the end Aunt Mary won the argument and Gertrude was allowed to come back to New Orleans. Then on Friday, when Elise was so ill, Aunt Mary insisted on sending for Mrs. Leo. Again Annie became angry. She did not want, said Gertrude, "to be burdened with any more of the family."

Despite the fact that she displayed obvious fear of Annie, Gertrude answered questions with a frankness that amazed her interrogators. It had been Annie who had nursed each member of the family before death. Each time, too, when the suggestion was made that Mrs. Leo be summoned from Texas, Annie tried to prevent it. It was soon clear that Annie Crawford had dominated the household, and, in particular, Miss Elise, Miss Gertrude, and, before her death, Miss Mamie.

Gertrude was questioned about life insurance. Annie, said Gertrude, had only that morning gone to the offices of the Metropolitan Life Insurance Company with Mrs. Leo to attempt to collect from a policy on Elise's life. She had been refused.

Mrs. Crawford was questioned next. She said that "when Annie spoke the whole family trembled." Then she told in great detail of that Friday night, emphasizing her own suspicions of Annie. Wednesday night, she said, while attending to Elise, she had to leave the room hurriedly because she had been attacked by a sudden and unexplainable sleepiness. "It was not as if I had not been sleeping well," she said. "It was unnatural."

At nine o'clock that evening all the Crawfords except Annie were allowed to go home. Mrs. Leo, probably because she had not been in the house when Elise died, was not questioned at this time. The district attorney must have by now been certain that the mystery it was his duty to unravel would not prove too difficult. The newspapers were already saying that the case was without a doubt one of murder by poison, "not only in the case of Miss Elise," as the *Daily Picayune* put it on September 28, "but perhaps of Mr. and Mrs. Walter Crawford, the unfortunate stenographer's parents, and of the sister, Miss Mamie, who also passed away about a year ago." Even the motive seemed simple and commonplace, in view of Miss Annie's hurried trip to the offices of the life insurance company.

It is interesting to wonder what St. Clair Adams and Annie Crawford really thought of each other during the first ordeal of tedious questioning that took place that night. Mr. Adams was young, handsome, and brilliant, and there were moments when Annie played the coquette with him. He must have realized almost at once that this tiny, plain girl, dressed in her funereal black and carrying a large black lacquer fan, was far from simple and that his job had just begun.

Annie was ushered into the office by a deputy and took her seat in a chair facing Messrs. Adams, Reynolds, and Mouney. She was so short that her feet did not touch the floor, but, crossed at the ankles, swung back and forth. She fanned herself as if she was warm, but there was no indication of nervousness and the blue eyes behind the spectacles were cold and hard.

She took advantage of every opportunity to command the situation. When a newspaper photographer attempted to take her picture she immediately raised her fan to conceal her face, and refused to answer any questions until he was ejected from the room. Then she smiled graciously upon Mr. Adams and thanked him in a calm voice. When other men entered the room (they were Assistant District Attorneys Warren Doyle and A. D. Henriques) she insisted on knowing who they were before continuing.

The questions came fast and she answered them without hesitancy and in a clear strong voice. Once three men did ask questions in almost the same instant. Then, quite suddenly, a lens from her spectacles dropped on the floor. Despite her lack of beauty Annie must have had a way with her, for the inquisitors all joined in the search, while Annie sat fanning and smiling at St. Clair Adams, who alone had retained his seat. When the lens was found she took time to fit it into the frame, and, when this was done, she had her answers ready.

She denied ever giving Elise morphine. Once, she said, she believed Elise had asked for a dangerous drug, the name of which she did not recall, but she had of course refused it.

"But you were in charge of the narcotics at the New Orleans Sanitarium," said Mr. Adams. "Surely you cannot deny you are familiar with such drugs as morphine."

Annie admitted she was familiar with morphine, in so far as having handled it in her work.

Mr. Adams then asked her if she were an addict herself.

"I will stay here for a hundred days," Annie said, according to the record, "and I can show you that I do not use the drug. Get any physician you want and let him draw blood from my veins, and see if I use drugs of any kind."

One of the men present told her it was known to the police that she had once purchased a poison from Walsdorf's Drug Store.

"It was oxalic acid," Annie said quietly. "We use it for bleaching. Elise, you say, died from morphine?"

The question of the capsules of calomel and soda was brought into the inquisition. A statement from Dr. McGuire asserting that he had not prescribed them for Elise was read to Annie.

She took it calmly. "The doctor has forgotten," she said. "He advised me to give them to Elise when I spoke to him on the telephone."

After five hours, at two o'clock in the morning, Annie, after being advised that she was to be held under suspicion of murder, was turned over to Mrs. O. C. Kennelly, woman probation officer of the Juvenile Court. Annie went with Mrs. Kennelly not to a cell, but to one of the district attorney's offices, where she lay down upon a sofa and went to sleep.

The questioning was continued the next morning, but Mr. Adams did not have any further success. Annie dismissed the idea of life insurance as a motive as being absurd. Her parents, she said, had only $1,300 of insurance between them, Mamie but $300, and Elise only $132. She, Annie, had not been the sole beneficiary in any case. In all but that of Elise the money had been divided with other sisters. In the instance of Elise, her funeral had, indeed, cost more than the amount of insurance she carried. In nearly all cases Annie had added to the insurance on each of the deceased from her own savings in order that the funeral expenses might be paid.

Annie returned to the care of Mrs. Kennelly. During the day she ate nothing, but drank many cups of black coffee. It was late that afternoon when Annie quite abruptly turned to Mrs. Kennelly and admitted her use of drugs.

"I was ashamed to tell Mr. Adams," said Annie. "I've been taking morphine for three or four years."

Having abandoned hope of ever gaining her confidence, Mrs. Kennelly waited now with renewed hope.

"I might," said Annie at last, "have given morphine tablets to

Elise by mistake. I might have mixed them with the ones of calomel and soda."

It was as unexpected and as simple a statement as that.

That night Annie made a formal statement to St. Clair Adams, still insisting, however, that it had been a mistake that had caused her to give Elise the morphine. But before she said a word Annie made a characteristic demand. Pointing to Assistant Chief of Detectives Dan Mouney, who was present in Mr. Adams' office when Annie was brought in, she said, "I don't want that man in here." Chief Mouney departed.

The record of this confession takes the form of answers to questions put to Annie by the district attorney.

"I've treated you kindly, haven't I?" asked Mr. Adams.

"Oh, yes. I have no complaint about your treatment."

"Miss Annie, you admit that you take morphine tablets?"

"Yes."

"You take morphine by mouth and not hypodermically?"

"Yes."

"How long have you been addicted to the habit?"

"For some time. Three or four years, I think. I stopped for a while. Then we got into trouble again, and I simply had to go back."

"Where did you get the drug?"

"At the New Orleans Sanitarium."

"Did they know you were getting them?"

"Not that I know of."

"On Friday morning did you give your sister, Elise, any of them?"

"Yes, I gave her three of them."

"Three morphine tablets?"

"Yes."

"Half-grain tablets in capsules?"

"Yes, Mr. Adams."

"How did you happen to do that?"

"Because I wanted to give her calomel, and I got them mixed up."

"Did you see the effect it had upon her?"

"I did."

"Why didn't you call a doctor and tell him what you had done?"

"I thought she would get over it, and my aunt would not do anything to me. I was afraid of her."

"You are afraid of your aunt?"

"Yes, sir."

"Where did you get the tablets you gave Elise?"

Annie now told of visiting the sanitarium on the Wednesday before Elise died. She explained that she often went there, and had been doing so during the sixteen months since she had left the hospital's employ. However, on Wednesday she had not been able to obtain any morphine. The tablets she gave Elise were some she already had in the house. There had been a dozen or more in the bottle.

"And what did you do with the others?"

"I threw them into the toilet, Mr. Adams."

"After you discovered your mistake?"

"Yes, sir."

"When did you last have morphine?"

"On Saturday morning."

"Have you wanted it since?"

"No."

"Miss Annie," said Mr. Adams now, "I want you to tell me the truth. Tell me the whole thing—everything that happened."

"After my mother died," Annie said, "and we broke up house, and my eldest sister took the youngest one to live with her, Elise and I went boarding. She was not satisfied then, and Gertie was out there, and we were down here. Finally, some young man wrote to Gertie. He simply addressed her a postal card. Gertie showed it to my eldest sister, and she did not approve of it. She wrote to Elise, and Elise wrote to this young man to ask what he wanted and who he was. Then she wrote Gertie and told her it was all right to keep company with this young man. But Gertie was not satisfied with that. She had to get on a train and come down here. Then we went to board with Aunt Mary. I was not able to take care of Gertie. She was just a child. Elise thought I was unjust to her because I said I did not want her. It wasn't that I have a hard heart, but she was in better hands where she was. Gertie always wanted to be around, and I could not stand a child of that age."

"Is that why you gave Elise the morphine?"

"No. That is why these people do not like me, simply on that account—because I tried to keep the youngest one out there."

"Elise was always interfering with you?"

"Yes, Mr. Adams. I would tell Gertie this and that, and she would tell me to mind my own business."

"In what other ways would she interfere with you?"

"She would tell Gertie to go ahead and see a young man if she wanted to. I had no objection if he were a nice young man. Another thing, I thought it was not right to go to Spanish Fort and West End* just after our mother died. You know it was not right to go places and have a good time. They had a grudge against me because I would not allow it, and because I would not go myself."

"Did Elise interfere with you in any other way?"

"The only other trouble was that she wrote to Aunt Mary when we were boarding on St. Andrew Street. She wrote that if Aunt Mary would take Gertie and let her come from Texas she would be willing to pay one half the board, which she never did. Aunt Mary got tired. That's why we were all moving. Last Sunday I asked Elise how much she paid Aunt Mary, and she said she had paid nothing, and that I was unjust to treat her that way when she was sick. I told her I had not said anything to hurt her feelings, and she said that when she got out of that house she wanted me never to claim her as a sister."

"Elise told you that?"

"Elise told me that. She has never treated me right, Mr. Adams, but that is not why I gave her the morphine. That was a mistake. I could be in the house from Monday until Sunday and she would never talk to me, and that is no way to treat a sister. When she was sick I waited on her, and no matter what she wanted I gave it to her."

* Amusement parks near New Orleans.

"You waited on her almost entirely?"

"Almost entirely."

"You brought her medicine, food, and drink?"

"Yes."

"You gave her only three tablets of morphine?"

"Yes, Mr. Adams."

"Did she ever complain about the food you brought her?"

"No, Mr. Adams. But once when Aunt Mary brought her some broth she complained to me that it was bitter. But that was because some of the oil we had put around in the kitchen safe had gotten on the spoon. I tasted it myself."

"You gave her the morphine by mistake?"

"Yes."

"Intending to give her calomel and soda?"

"Yes."

"You did not call the doctor in and tell him of the mistake because you were afraid of your aunt?"

"Yes."

That was all. District Attorney Adams then told Annie she must go to prison to be held for trial. She displayed no emotion. She said quietly, "Mr. Adams, I must have some lawyers, but I can't afford to pay for them. Can you arrange that for me?"

He told her that the court would appoint counsel for her.

"I must have the best in the city," she said. "None but the very best will suit me."

Adams replied that she could be assured of worthy representation in court.

As she departed for the Parish Prison with the deputies Annie gave every indication of enjoying the situation. She held herself very erect, her black skirt trailing slightly behind her, as it always did. Outside, photographers tried to take her picture, but she used her fan to elude them, and those that appeared in the papers the next day show not a trace of her features, only the black-garbed figure, diminutive under the immense mourning hat, from which streamed the heavy black veil, and before the veil the inevitable black lacquer fan.

The stories that appeared in the newspapers the next day were not kind to Annie. The *Daily Picayune* did comment, "She proved a marvelous character to the men who were seeking to question her, and aside from that she showed a great deal of smartness in evading photographers who camped about to get a snapshot of her."

Photographs appeared in all the papers during the following few days, grotesque ones of Annie shielding her face with veil and fan, others that showed her caught unawares in open-mouthed expressions. In headlines she was sometimes called a "fiend," a very popular word in 1911, and occasionally a "monster." On September 30 the New Orleans *Item* called her "the woman with the cold blue eyes," and the same day the *Daily States* said her eyes "flashed sparks of yellow fire." Headlines such as "Is Annie Crawford a Lucrezia Borgia of the Twentieth Century?" were very popular. She was compared to De Brinvilliers and LaVoison.

Officials of the Presbyterian Hospital (its name had been changed from New Orleans Sanitarium) gave out statements. Annie, they said, had been discharged for incompetency. A nurse employed there believed that Annie's inability to do her work with efficiency had been due to addiction to drugs, although no one had suspected that she was stealing them. Annie had been employed in the narcotics department for years, but for about the last six months she had worked at the hospital she had been in the office. The president of the hospital was interviewed by a *States* reporter. He was quoted in that paper on the twenty-seventh as saying that although Annie had been discharged she had for a long time before that been "a good clerk, who rose from a $12 a month position through sheer industry and attention to her duties to a $50 a month position." He revealed, too, that Mamie Crawford had also been employed in the hospital for some time before her death. This story ended by calling Annie "a sinister genius."

In the same edition of the same newspaper was another piece headed "A *Cause Célèbre*," which stated, "The case promises to develop into one of the sensations of the century throughout the country, and representatives of out-of-town newspapers are in the city, busy flashing headline stories about the case over the wires to all parts of the United States." Added was the comment, "By-standers laugh at the cameramen as Miss Crawford lifts the big black fan she carries before her face each time an attempt is made to take her picture. District Attorney Adams has given orders that no photographers be permitted to take her picture in the future without her consent."

All the newspapers revealed the fact that in each case of a fatal illness within the Crawford family a different doctor had been called in, and it was always Annie who summoned them. Dr. Edward F. Bacon attended the father; Dr. P. W. Falls, the mother; and Dr. H. B. Gessner had treated Mamie. All the doctors were questioned. All admitted that in each case there were symptoms of uremic poisoning, although Mamie's death had been diagnosed as spinal meningitis, that of Walter Crawford as "brain trouble," and that of the mother of the family as tubercular peritonitis.

According to the *Daily Picayune* of September 28, St. Clair Adams made the statement that "perhaps Annie Crawford is one of the great criminals of history."

Annie showed no unwillingness to give interviews during the first few days of her imprisonment. The first night she talked with a representative of the *Daily Picayune*. The next day there was the headline "'That Aunt of Mine Never Liked Me,' Declared Miss Annie Crawford." In this story Annie was reported as saying that her aunt had always disliked her because she was independent. After leaving her position (she insisted she had resigned) Annie said she had enough money in the Hibernia Bank to maintain herself. This fact angered her Aunt Mary.

"Yes, I know I am charged with murder," said Annie, "the murder of my sister who just died, but that is a charge which cannot be proven, for it is foolish to think that I, a sister, would murder one of my own, and the idea of them thinking I am also responsible for the deaths of my mother and father and my other sister is preposterous. What would be my gain? Perhaps if one of the policies had been for $10,000, I could reason out that some might harbor such a thought."

Annie was asked why she had never married.

"I have simply never found a man I liked well enough," she said. "Not that I would not like to marry, but I value my independence. I have some money in the bank, not very much, but a woman like me can live on it a long time. I am a woman who is not interested in rich dressing, I like plain and clean clothes and that style suits me best."

The body of Elise Crawford was exhumed on September 29. No autopsy had been performed before interment, a fact that, under the circumstances, appears somewhat strange. Now experts admitted to Assistant District Attorney Doyle that the embalming fluids might have by this time made the finding of morphine in any of the organs difficult. Nevertheless the liver, the stomach, and part of the lower intestines were removed, and Dr. Groetsch delivered these organs, sealed separately in jars, into the hands of Dr. Metz.

That same day Annie was arraigned before Judge John B. Fisher of the First City Criminal Court.

When she was asked for her plea Annie did not answer at all, but stood before the judge, her face concealed as usual by the thick veil, the fan clutched in one black-gloved hand. The judge repeated his formal question, "Are you guilty or not guilty?"

Annie looked up at him through her veil and said, "I'd like to have a word with you alone, Judge."

Judge Fisher replied that such a request could not be granted and that if she did not answer he would enter the plea as "not guilty."

Annie said nothing, so the plea was entered and she was remanded to be held without bail.

The next morning the Daily Picayune carried a statement from St. Clair Adams to the effect that Annie Crawford would be tried only on the one charge of poisoning Elise, as medical authorities agreed that it would be useless to exhume the bodies of her parents and Mamie. They had been dead more than a year. Vegetable poison would have long ago reached a state of decomposition. Now only a confession by Annie Crawford could prove she killed her parents and other sister, said Mr. Adams, and such a confession was extremely unlikely.

Annie Crawford was now the center of interest throughout the city. The morning she left Judge Fisher's court, leaning on the arm of Police Inspector Reynolds and holding her fan up before her face, excited cries went up from the curious, as she approached the crowd that lined the street outside.

"Here she comes!"

"Annie, put down your fan!"

But no one saw her face.

Horror piled upon horror when Dr. Metz announced his findings. Eight grains of morphine were extraced from Elise's organs, enough, said the chemist, to kill five men. What then did Annie's confession of having given her sister three half-grain capsules mean?

The reporters continued to interview Annie. One account in the *Daily Picayune* on the twenty-ninth said that Annie now "looked tired and careworn, but her eyes still flash out with a peculiar yellow gleam from behind her spectacles, which she wears constantly. Her mouth takes on resolute curves at times which show the will with which report says she dominated her family. Her hands are very small and white—frail, soft hands that seem made for soothing the brow of a dying sister—not the hands to deal out death draughts to the youth and innocence that should have been sheltered."

This reporter asked Annie if there was anything she cared to say that might place her in a better light. Annie replied that she had told the district attorney everything there was to know. The reporter insisted that there might be something that would alter public opinion. "Again the black fan was raised, and Miss Crawford leaned back and closed her eyes, holding the fan meanwhile before her lips. She seemed asleep. Once the interviewer turned toward her, however, and found the eyes open, regarding the interrogator with a fixed steadiness, as though to decide whether the proffer of help came from a friend or foe."

Annie then said, "Everything will be all right. I place my faith in God."

The interview was ended by the entrance of Mrs. Mary O'Connor, "the warm-hearted prison matron," bearing two glasses of lemonade. Mrs. O'Connor said Annie Crawford was a model prisoner.

Meanwhile, the Crawfords had moved from Peters Avenue to Octavia Street, and the house they had vacated was still empty. The owner had leased it, but the new tenant refused to move his family into it because. of the unpleasant notoriety. The Crawfords had led a miserable existence since Annie's arrest. They were stared at upon the streets and followed by reporters. They gave out no statements after the first few days, but the neighbors supplied some curious stories. One of these said that Annie's behavior had been peculiar for the past several months.

"She would arise in the morning and barely bidding her sisters and her aunt and uncle good morning, she would seat herself in a chair and, bending her head down, remain silent and motionless for hours. If she did rouse herself from this position, and go out into the street, when she came back she would resume her former attitude and remain thus until bedtime. This, however, was not attributed to any but natural causes." This from an acquaintance, according to a story in the *Daily Picayune*. It was added that, "Miss Annie kept her vice a secret from her family."

On the Saturday after she entered that Parish Prison cell Annie was visited by Mrs. Leo, who brought her a suitcase of clothes, conversed for some time with Mrs. O'Connor, and then wept bitterly at the sight of Annie. Annie does not seem to have displayed any emotion whatsoever.

But on Sunday, when Mrs. Leo returned, bringing with her Edward Leo, her husband, who had just arrived from Port Arthur, Annie underwent a complete change. The prison authorities allowed the little family group to meet in the prison chapel. With her brother-in-law Annie seemed a different person. For the first time since her arrest she smiled frequently, and once or twice burst into laughter. When they departed Annie embraced both the Leos, and then began to cry. These were her first tears.

After that Annie was much more cheerful. Three young women came to interview her. She chatted with them as if they were intimate friends. Evidently to them she was quite other than a fiend, for as they departed her cell all three kissed her cheek.

She seemed more normal in every respect now. Each morning she dressed herself with care, spending a long time in arranging her pale yellow hair. She did not associate with the other prisoners, but read during a good portion of the day, and devoted much time to her rosary. Whenever her dead relatives were mentioned she wept. She expressed complete confidence in the district attorney, upon whom she seemed to look as a friend, rather than the man who was going to prosecute her in court for murder. Most astonishing of all to everyone was the fact that never did she express the slightest desire for the drug to which she professed to be addicted.

One day of the week following she quite suddenly expressed a desire to be photographed. Ever since her arrest she had protested that the newspaper pictures showed her at her worst. She said it was because of this that she had hitherto used her veil and fan to elude the cameramen. Now she wanted her picture published, provided she had time to prepare for the sitting.

The morning the photographers came she spent two hours trying to curl her bangs. They could not be managed, so she insisted upon being photographed wearing her mourning hat. She moved when the first picture was taken, and when the photographers told her she had spoiled it, she burst into a gale of laughter. The second attempt was successful.

The picture, when published, showed a vastly different Annie. The veil was pushed back, her spectacles were absent, and she was revealed as a rather pleasant-looking young woman with a thin face, high cheekbones and large eyes.

On October 20 it was announced that Lionel Adams and Joseph Generelly, two of the city's most distinguished criminal attorneys, would defend Annie Crawford when she went to trial. She had asked for the best representation and she got it, the lawyers accepting the case without fee because of their interest in its complexities.

Now it seemed to the general public in New Orleans that Annie's chances of going free were good.

Her trial opened on March 12, 1912. Annie had been in prison six months and she showed evidence of this when she entered the courtroom over which presided Judge Frank D. Chretien.

She came into the room resting heavily upon the arm of a deputy sheriff, who towered over her small figure. She still wore a black cloth skirt, a shirtwaist of black silk, and the mourning hat. The neat white handkerchief was pinned as usual at her belt. Her veil was down, and when every pair of eyes in the room turned in her direction, she lowered her head and raised the black lacquer fan to her lips. She did not look up until she took her seat beside her attorneys at the long table before the dais where Judge Chretien waited. As Court Crier Conrad's pronouncement: "The State vs. Annie Crawford!" faded, she slumped in her chair. She seemed to have no interest in her surroundings. Even when her lawyers leaned toward her and whispered something she seemed not to hear them. The veil remained down, and her features could scarcely be seen.

"This figure at the bar in its sable habit and marks of mourning was gloomy and dismal enough to awaken even hard hearts to a little pity and there were those in court who hoped that the evidence soon to be heard would establish the woman's innocence," wrote a *Daily Picayune* reporter on March 13. "If her crimes are proven she might well rank with the fiendish Marquise De Brinvilliers who expiated her guilt in the torture chamber of the Chalet and with the hangman's sword in the *Place de Greve* in Paris."

For Annie that courtroom must have been a torture chamber indeed. Her attitude during the three days it took to select the jury was one of complete isolation and resignation. Hour after hour, day after day, she sat there, scarcely moving, almost as it was said she had sat during those days before Elise died. Bent and silent, everything about her impressed those who watched that she considered herself an object of a terrible persecution. Not once did she so much as glance at the men who were being interviewed for jury duty. She seemed unconscious of their existence or whether they were accepted or rejected.

On the morning of the second day, with only three jurors selected,

Mr. Generelly asked the court that all spectators be barred except attorneys, doctors, and newspapermen.

The jury was completed on the afternoon of the third day. Then Judge Chretien asked Annie to raise her veil so that the gentlemen might see her face, and for the first time she lifted it. She was pale and there were deep circles under the huge blue eyes, but her mouth was firm, her jaw set.

The State called its first witness on Friday, March 15. Mrs. Robert Crawford took the stand. St. Clair Adams had laid his plans well. He brought first his strongest witness.

Even Annie seemed shocked into attentiveness. She raised her head and stared after her aunt's back as the woman passed her. When her Aunt Mary turned Annie looked down for a moment, then gazed at her aunt, not with malice, but with frank speculation as to what course the testimony of this witness would take.

Mrs. Crawford was dressed in black and wore a veil. With a tired and unhappy face she first described the illness of Elise, once breaking into sobs. She told the court how, some months before the girl's death, the three nieces had come to live with her and her husband. Elise had worked and Annie was living on her savings and between them they paid Gertrude's board as well as their own. She then described Elise as a "lively girl" who was never melancholy.

Elise had started to complain of nervousness late in August. She had gone to Dr. McGuire for treatment, and a week after that returned to work. One thing of which she had complained was that her left leg was shorter than her right. It was for this that Dr. McGuire had prescribed the application of an electric battery.

Mrs. Crawford was questioned in detail about the days immediately preceding the death of Elise, and particularly about the last night of her life. Then she told of the arrival of the ambulance. She did not see Elise again until her body was brought home by the undertaker.

Mr. Generelly cross-examined her. She admitted Elise had been ill the March before. "We thought it was only a spell of indigestion," she said.

The Crawford family bought all their drugs at Walsdorf's Drug

Store. Annie had said she had purchased the calomel and soda there. Mrs. Crawford insisted Elise was and had always been a healthy girl until the last illness, except that she sometimes had headaches "just like any other woman."

She left the stand a few minutes before noon, and court adjourned for lunch.

At two o'clock Gertrude was called. The district attorney made her review the events of Friday night, and her story almost duplicated that of her aunt's. Mr. Adams asked about the tea Elise had refused to drink.

"Annie brought up tea and toast after Mr. Zahn had left," she said. "Elise complained the tea was bitter and I made her a fresh cup."

"Did you use her same pot and cup?"

"Yes, sir."

The district attorney asked her to continue.

"At about ten o'clock I was undressing for bed. I saw Annie give Elise something then—something she mixed in a glass with a spoon. Some time later my aunt found Elise in the chair, unconscious. Annie went next door and called Dr. McGuire. Then she leaned out of the window and asked my aunt if Elise was still breathing."

"Tell me her exact words, Miss Gertrude."

"Annie called to my aunt, 'Aunt Mary, is Elise still breathing?'"

"Go on, Miss Gertrude."

"When Annie returned my aunt was crying. Annie knelt down beside her to say a prayer. My aunt took hold of her arm and said, 'Annie, did you do this?' Annie then said to my uncle, who was just coming into the room, 'Aunt Mary's losing her mind. She's going crazy!' Annie went out of the room and came back with some liquid in a cup for my aunt to drink. Aunt Mary dashed it out of her hand."

Mr. Generelly took the cross-examination. He questioned Gertrude in detail about the tea. She did not remember whether or not Annie had put sugar in it. Was she sure that she could recall the words Annie had used when she called out from the house next door? Was it not a fact that Annie had asked if Elise was still breathing loudly?

Gertrude was insistent. "She merely asked, 'Is Elise still breathing?' "

"You are sure she did not ask, 'Is Elise still breathing heavily or hard?' "

Gertrude was positive.

After receiving an admission from the girl that she may have been excited at the time, Mr. Generelly dismissed the witness.

Dr. Marion H. McGuire was the State's third witness. He had known Elise since April 1911. She was frail and only weighed 115 pounds, but she was suffering from no organic disorder. She was in a nervous state and complained of some difficulty with her left leg. He had recommended electric massage.

The doctor then made a rather startling statement.

"When Elise came to me in June," he said, "she was suffering from the effects of a drug of the belladonna type."

"Do you mean that the deceased was a drug addict?" asked the district attorney.

Dr. McGuire would not be committed to a direct answer to this question. However, he admitted to Mr. Adams that when he was called during the final illness of the girl he had concluded that her comatose condition was due to drugs. There was evidence of opium poison. He had told the family at about midnight that her condition was grave. He had remained by the sickbed in the hospital until six o'clock in the morning. The pupils of the patient's eyes were contracted and her breathing was irregular.

Lionel Adams cross-examined the witness. No relation to St. Clair Adams, this Mr. Adams had been one of the city's best-known criminal lawyers for decades. It was he who defended Troisville Sykes.

"Dr. McGuire," he asked, "do you know whether or not Elise Crawford took drugs?"

"I do not."

Mr. Adams then questioned the doctor as to the nervous spells of the deceased. The doctor had thought these probably due to the three deaths that had occurred in the family in such rapid succession.

There now followed a long series of questions involving many medical terms. One of the jurors requested that the terms be explained and defined, which Judge Chretien agreed was a reasonable request. Mr. Adams explained to the court that these terms were entirely foreign to him, but that he had been instructed in their usage by Drs. Gustave Mann and Howard H. King of Tulane University, who were present to serve as medical advisors for the defense, and that he was doing his best. At this point Dr. McGuire asked Judge Chretien if he might be excused from answering such professional questions, as he had not been called as a medical expert, but merely to give testimony related to the death of Elise Crawford.

Lionel Adams then asked the doctor if Elise's difficulty with her left leg, which the doctor admitted she "threw out in a peculiar sweep," could not have been due to aneurysm, an enlargement of the blood vessels of the brain. The doctor replied this was possible, also that such a condition might be due to an addiction to drugs. He said that he had never heard of belladonna as a habit-forming drug. He refused to be forced into an admission that he had at any time thought Elise an addict of morphine.

St. Clair Adams called a Dr. Stafford of the Charity Hospital, who testified that he had noted, "The woman's pupils were contracted, and I treated her for some kind of opium poison. We used strychnine and atrophine and put the patient under the faratic current in the battery room." He would not testify as an expert nor answer Mr. Generelly's question, during the cross-examination, "Is it dangerous to put a person who has paralysis of the heart under the faratic current?"

Dr. William C. Groetsch told of his part in the removal of Elise's organs after the exhumation of her body. Mr. Generelly demanded to know why an autopsy had not been performed immediately after death. Dr. Groetsch asked, "May I tell the usual procedure?"

"The coroner's duty is required by law, and the coroner knows his duty!" cried Generelly.

St. Clair Adams rose. "There is no law in this State requiring a coroner to hold an autopsy," he said.

Dr. Groetsch then explained that no autopsy had been held at death because there were at that time no suspicious circumstances involved, or at least they were not sufficient to warrant such an examination. The body had been buried without a death certificate as a tentative burial, awaiting the analysis of the fluids that had been extracted prior to death.

Mr. Generelly placed great stress on the importance of an autopsy in the matter of proving a corpus delicti, and several times made Dr. Groetsch admit that Elise Crawford had been buried for days before the removal of her organs. Then the defense lawyer asked if it were not likely that the lungs would have been congested in a case of morphine poisoning, and asked why they had not been removed along with the other organs. Dr. Groetsch replied that he had taken only those organs from the body for which he had been requested. He admitted that the body had been embalmed, and this was the cue for Mr. Generelly to ask if the organs might not have been impaired by the chemicals used in the embalming process. The coroner answered in the affirmative.

Dr. Groetsch admitted that he had received an impression that Dr. McGuire had thought Elise Crawford a suicide. "I asked Dr. McGuire who she was," he said. "He told me she was Annie's sister. 'Who is Annie?' I asked. He said, 'Oh, you know. Sanitarium Annie.'"

Dr. McGuire had then added that Miss Elise had been despondent lately and in a very nervous condition.

Henry Tharpe, the undertaker who had handled the funeral of Elise, Miss V. C. Auburtin, described in the records as "the well-known lady embalmer," and several other minor witnesses were called that day. Court was adjourned at five-twenty. The jury asked if night sessions might be held so that their length of service could be shortened. This request was refused.

When Dr. A. L. Metz, the city chemist, was called the next morning, Saturday, he was positive that the death of Elise Crawford had been due to morphine poisoning. He was questioned by the State for several hours. At noon the defense asked that court be adjourned until Monday, so that the cross-examination might be prepared.

Lionel Adams questioned Dr. Metz for two hours on Monday morning. Coached by Drs. Mann and King, the attorney explored every medical possibility that the death of the girl might have occurred as the result of long usage of morphine rather than by large doses administered without her knowledge. Unable to force an answer from the chemist, Adams then implied the possibility that the records of the morphine contents of Elise's organs might not be reliable.

The district attorney demanded loudly, "Does the attorney for the defense mean to say that the records might be false?"

"Yes, sir, I do!" was the reply.

"Your Honor," said the district attorney, "the counsel for the defense has persistently insulted this witness and I do not think it should be tolerated."

Judge Chretien commented that he did not believe the defense intended to insult the witness.

Lionel Adams then requested that his medical advisors be allowed to examine the organs of the deceased, whereupon court was adjourned until Wednesday.

On Tuesday the jury was taken fishing at Little Woods, a resort a few miles from New Orleans, by an appointed body of deputy sheriffs. "A fine lunch was served and there was the usual quota of beverages," we are told by the *Daily Picayune* the next day.

Dr. Groetsch was recalled to the stand Wednesday morning. He made the astounding revelation that the body of Elise Crawford had again been exhumed on the Sunday just past. This had been done upon an order from the district attorney. Dr. Groetsch had gone to the cemetery early on Sunday morning along with Dr. O'Hara, the coroner, Dr. McGuire, Dr. Charles Duval of Tulane University, and Miss Auburtin. The coffin had been taken to a shed in the rear of the graveyard and there Dr. Duval had opened the body. He admitted this had been done without a court order and that Dr. Duval had no connection with the police.

Dr. Duval was called to the stand at once. He said he had, during his career, performed some three thousand autopsies. He then described how he had gone about this last one. Mr. St. Clair Adams asked that he give the jury full details.

"I first had the body washed," he said, "and then proceeded to hold the autopsy. The sides of the coffin were quite rotten. We tore these away and rested the body on the bottom of the coffin, which was laid upon two barrels in the shed. The head was still in a good state of preservation, but the legs were decomposed.

"I removed the brain and the middle ear, cutting the cord holding the brain to the rest of the body with a knife. Then I started on the body. There was an incision below the breast extending down, which was held together by a cord. I extended this up to the Adam's apple. I laid back the flaps of the skin and exposed the organs. I removed the lungs and heart, which were in a perfect state. Next I removed the diaphragm and all the intestines. I took out the spleen and found it impaired by lesions.

"All these organs I had removed to my laboratory, where I subjected them to a microscopic test. I found a piece of liver about an inch long in the abdominal cavity. Now, sir, I have brought these organs into court with me and I should like to show them."

At this point men came forward from the rear of the courtroom carrying a number of boxes and packages, which were placed upon the State's table. The spectators in the room had to be quieted before Dr. Duval could proceed. Annie Crawford pulled down her veil, but she leaned forward toward the horrible exhibits for a moment, as if she could not help staring at them. Then she bent her head and put a hand over her eyes.

Dr. Duval descended from the witness stand and, going to the table, unwrapped the brown paper covering the exhibits. He lifted jar after jar toward the jury, each vessel containing a human organ floating in aclohol.

"Note the heart carefully," he said, holding one jar high. "It is one of the finest I have ever seen in my life."

He was standing so close to Annie she could have touched him. Her whole body slumped in the chair. Her shoulders rose and fell in shudders.

Dr. Duval continued to comment upon each specimen. At one point he was asked a question by the district attorney the answer to which was destined for the next day's newspaper headlines.

"What," asked the district attorney, "was the womanly state of Elise Crawford?"

"She was not a virgin, if that is what you mean," replied Dr. Duval.

Again the courtroom had to be silenced.

The doctor continued, "There were changes in the spleen and kidneys due to opium poisoning. The holes in some of the organs were caused of course by the embalmer's needle. There is no evidence of arteriosclerosis, no diabetes, not even malaria. The diagnosis is death by opium poison."

"Doctor, can you state as a fact that this girl did not die of a brain disorder?" asked the district attorney.

"She did not die of any brain trouble," replied Dr. Duval.

Mr. Generelly objected to the methods of the State.

"They went in secret to take the body from its grave!"

He was supported by Lionel Adams, who rose and ordered Dr. Duval, "Step down, sir, and sit over here!"

St. Clair Adams pointed a finger that trembled with rage at Lionel Adams.

"Stay where you are, doctor!" he cried. "That man has no right to instruct my witness. He's not running this case."

"No, nor are you running this court!" shouted Lionel Adams with equal vigor.

Mr. Generelly joined the argument.

"These people go out to the graveyard at daybreak," he charged, "dig up the corpse, and reach their own conclusions. It is the most disgraceful procedure that I have ever heard of in my life!"

Judge Chretien then demanded that both the State and the

defense "cease their bickering" and return to the examination of the witness.

At two o'clock that afternoon another quarrel ensued between the Messrs. Adams. The defense lawyer charged that the district attorney was interfering with his cross-examination of Dr. Duval.

"The witness is being plagued," he said.

St. Clair Adams retorted, "See here, Mr. Adams, don't you dare to holler at me in court, or to lecture me. I won't stand for it, sir!"

"Well, I'll do so out of court then," Mr. Lionel Adams replied.

"You can do that, sir, any time you desire, and well you know what to expect," said the district attorney.

"Gentlemen! Gentlemen!" interrupted Judge Chretien. "You must stop this quarreling."

Court adjourned near six o'clock that evening. The two men met near the table where lay the organs of the deceased. St. Clair Adams asked Lionel Adams, "Do you want to see me downstairs?"

The attorney for the defense glared over his gold-rimmed spectacles at the district attorney. "If you're looking for trouble, Mr. Adams," he said, "I'll send my friends to you."

"You know very well," replied St. Clair Adams, "that I would never fight a duel with a man of your character."

It was then, according to all reports, that the defense attorney slapped the representative of the State upon the cheek with his open palm. The next day the *Daily Picayune* said, "Mr. St. Clair Adams sprang forward like a raging bull and swung right and left at Mr. Lionel Adams, who for the moment gave way. Doctors, lawyers and deputies tried to get between the two men. District Attorney Adams had to be overpowered by several men, while Lionel Adams was also held. In the middle of the fracas Dr. Gustave Mann, who had been sitting in conversation with Annie Crawford, joined the fracas, striking District Attorney Adams with his fist. Then the district attorney's brother, Sturgis Adams, also an attorney, charged like a roaring lion at Dr. Mann, calling him a 'miserable coward.' Dr. Oscar Solomon came running up, waving his walking stick in the face of Lionel Adams and shouting, "Take off your glasses! Take off your glasses!'"

Some of the men stumbled against the table holding the jars and microscopic slides of Elise Crawford's organs. Jars went crashing to the floor and the glass slides were smashed and ground to bits beneath the feet of the struggling men. The contents of the jars spilled upon the floor. Annie Crawford shrieked. She was taken from the room by deputies and turned over to a police matron.

Judge Chretien ordered District Attorney Adams, Lionel Adams, Sturgis Adams, and Dr. Gustave Mann placed under arrest. They were escorted downstairs to the First Precinct Police Station, where, after giving their promises that they would not renew the fight, they were paroled.

Meanwhile the coroner and his assistants carefully gathered together Elise's organs and bore them away to safety.

The next day the Messrs. Adams observed a studied politeness toward each other. Commented the *Daily Picayune*, "Each seemed to avoid the occasion of speaking to the other, but when the occasion did arise both were cultured, formal gentlemen, holding to the most exacting laws of etiquette and the usages of polite society."

The State now summoned a number of attachés of the Presbyterian Hospital. Miss Helena Parker, a nurse, testified that while Annie Crawford had been employed there, during the days the institution was known as the New Orleans Sanitarium, she had always had access to morphine. Miss Emma Durans, another nurse, had seen Annie at the hospital on the Wednesday preceding the death of Elise. She added that Annie was a regular visitor. Miss Winnie Landry had, on Wednesday, noticed Annie standing about two feet from the cabinets containing narcotics, and said that she had also noted that Annie was left alone near those cabinets for at least fifteen minutes.

St. Clair Adams took the stand next. He told of Annie's arrest and confession. Mrs. Mary O'Connor then testified that Annie had "always said the district attorney was more than kind to her, and that her confession was of her own free will."

When the afternoon session opened Assistant District Attorney

Warren Doyle read Annie Crawford's confession to the group of men who had questioned her.

C. F. Laws, a bookkeeper for the Hibernia Bank and Trust Company, was the next witness. He said that the accused had a checking account in the bank, but that during the month of September, 1911, it contained only $1.27. In March, 1910, it had amounted to slightly more than five hundred dollars.

Gertrude Crawford was recalled. She told the State that she, too, had an account at the Hibernia Bank.

The district attorney exhibited a check dated June 23, 1911, in the amount of twenty dollars.

"Did you sign it?" he asked.

"No, sir."

"Who did, then?"

"My sister Annie," said Gertrude. "She kept my checkbook."

"Did she write it with your authority?"

"No, sir."

Gertrude, in reply to questions, accused Annie of drawing more than one hundred dollars from her account without her knowledge. She said she had known nothing of this until after Annie was arrested. On other occasions she had signed checks over to Annie, after Annie had filled them in for her.

Mr. Generelly took the witness.

"Isn't it true," he asked, "that fifty dollars of the money you accuse your sister of taking from your account went as your share toward payment for the coping placed around the grave of your parents?"

"Yes, sir," said Gertrude.

Generelly was angry.

"Why didn't you say that before?" he asked. "Don't you realize your sister is being tried for her life?"

"I didn't think of it," said Gertrude.

"Now, Miss Gertrude, your sister Elise had two rings and a necklace that she would never remove, but wore even when she went to bed. Is that not so?"

"Yes, sir." This was the first time the jewelry was mentioned in court.

"On the night she died did she not take them off and give them to you?"

"Yes, sir."

"Elise thought a great deal of those rings?"

"Yes, sir."

"She never took them off?"

"Only when she washed."

"But that night she gave them to you?"

"Yes, sir."

The defense dismissed the witness.

All during the examination of Gertrude, Annie Crawford had kept her veil down. It remained over her face when the district attorney exhibited checks drawn against an account that Elise had kept in the Hibernia Bank, and while S. I. Jay, of that institution, testified that the handwriting on the checks was probably not that of Elise Crawford, and while St. Clair Adams charged that Annie had forged checks against the accounts of both Gertrude and Elise.

In the checking account Elise had maintained there remained only $5.98. Annie, said the newspapers, was now suspected of theft as well as murder.

However, it was Saturday morning, March 23, that the newspapers carried their most scandalous headlines, at least from the point of view of many Orleanians, now wondering what new and even more exciting development would come from the trial of Annie Crawford. That morning the *Daily Picayune* announced in large print:

ELISE CRAWFORD'S PAST LAID BARE; SIN OF EARLY DAYS REVEALED

Poor Elise! She was to be spared nothing.

Late Friday afternoon Joseph Generelly had asked that Mrs. Robert Crawford be recalled. When the lady took the stand the first question "startled the court."

"Mrs. Crawford," he asked, "isn't it true that when Elise had her child you told Annie that if you had your way you would destroy it?"

Judge Chretien had to use his gavel before Mrs. Crawford's answer could be heard. The fact that Elise Crawford had once borne a child had not entered the testimony before.

The aunt leaned forward now, as if to be certain that her answer would be heard. "No, sir," she said in a loud voice.

The State objected to the question.

"It's six years since the deceased had that child," said St. Clair Adams, "and it has nothing to do with this case."

"Your Honor," said Mr. Generelly, "I propose to show that it does have something to do with this case."

"Why, sir, you are slandering the dead!" cried the district attorney.   •

"I most strenuously object to such language as that, Mr. Adams," said Generelly. "We are not slandering the dead. It was you who dragged her from the grave, and it was your expert who first mentioned that Elise Crawford was not a virgin."

Judge Chretien ruled in favor of the defense. The district attorney resumed his seat.

"Now, madam," said Generelly, "when Elise came home sick and vomiting a few days before her death, did you not go to Annie and say to her that you would like to know whether Elise might be pregnant again?"

"Yes, sir," said Mrs. Crawford. "I asked Elise that and she denied it. Annie said she was going to ask her, too."

"Did you say if it were true you were going to do away with the child?"

"No, sir. I did not."

"And did not Annie say, 'For God's sake, Aunt Mary, don't do that. If it is there, let it stay'?"

"No, sir. That is not true. What Annie said was that Elise should have died when the first child was born."

The attorney for the defense said, "That is all I have to ask this witness."

St. Clair Adams had only one question. "Mrs. Crawford, did

Annie say that Elise should have died when her child was born?"

"Yes, sir. She did."

"You may step down, madam," said Mr. Adams.

He turned to the bench and announced that the State had no more witnesses.

Mrs. James Dunn was called by the defense on Saturday. Mrs. Dunn said she had been a neighbor of the Crawford girls when they lived with their parents on Constance Street near Napoleon Avenue. She had remained friendly with them after they moved away. Elise came to see her frequently.

The last time she had seen Elise was a few months after the girls had gone to live with their Aunt Mary. She thought Elise looked tired.

"Mrs. Dunn," Elise said, "if I remain in that house much longer I'll be dead just like poor Mamie."

Then she told Mrs. Dunn she was expecting to be married soon.

According to Mrs. Dunn, Elise added, "Then I won't have to wear black any more. I hate black, but Annie makes me wear it."

"And what did you tell her?" asked Lionel Adams.

"I told her," said Mrs. Dunn, "to remember that there was many a slip twixt the cup and the lip."

"And she replied?"

"She said, 'Oh, Mrs. Dunn, if he goes back on me it's very easy for me to be wrapped in the arms of Mother Earth. I prefer death a thousand times to being separated from the one I love.' "

St. Clair Adams cross-examined Mrs. Dunn. He told her that that last speech she attributed to Elise Crawford sounded like something from a bad play. Mrs. Dunn was very angry when she stepped down from the witness stand.

The defense called Dr. E. P. Lowe. He testified that he had treated Elise in March, 1911, for belladonna poison. He admitted it was possible she had been an addict to morphine.

"Would you have said Elise Crawford was a nice girl?" asked Lionel Adams. In those days the phrase had a definite meaning.

"No, sir," replied Dr. Lowe. "I would not."

"Please explain, doctor."

"She was careless in her language," said Dr. Lowe. "I do not mean that it was ever vulgar. It was not what she said, but how she said it. Any man would know."

Max Samson, a New Orleans druggist, was summoned. He recalled that in July, 1911, the deceased had come into his store, and had appeared to be in a peculiar state. He offered her a chair, and she sat down and wept hysterically.

Edward H. Walsdorf testified that the Crawford family bought their medicines from his drugstore. Henry Tharp, the undertaker, stated that Miss Annie was the person who had the responsibility of paying Elise's funeral expenses.

Mrs. Leo was then questioned briefly. She admitted having gone with Annie to the offices of the Metropolitan Life Insurance Company. Annie had wanted to collect the amount of the policy on Elise's life at once, so that all bills could be paid and they might leave for Port Arthur as soon as possible. The policy was only for $132, and it would be necessary to add twelve dollars in order to pay the undertaker, whose bill was $144. The insurance company had refused to pay the policy upon that visit.

At four o'clock that afternoon Lionel Adams finally asked Annie Crawford to take the stand.

Annie seated herself, crossing her ankles, her short legs swinging a little as usual, as her feet failed to reach the floor, the small train of her black skirt dripping behind her restless feet. All day her veil had been down, but now she raised it and arranged it neatly behind her huge hat. Black-gloved hands gripped the fan, as if they needed something to cling to, and sometimes she raised the fan and bit it. Her face was pale, even her lips, and her eyes were heavily circled, but, except for the grip on her fan, she seemed as self-assured as ever.

Lionel Adams began the questioning.

"Now, Miss Crawford, tell us your age and the ages of your two younger sisters."

"I am twenty-nine, and Gertrude is nineteen," said Annie. Her voice was low, but perfectly steady. "My sister Elise, who is dead, was twenty-five."

"When did your mother die?"

"In July, 1910. My father had died a few days before that, and Mamie in June. We lived at that time at 4423 Constance Street. When mother died we broke up housekeeping. I think it was a month or so later. I went to board on St. Andrew Street with Elise. Gertrude went to Texas with my married sister. Then, in January, 1911, Aunt Mary took the house on Peters Avenue and we moved there."

"Miss Crawford, please tell the court this. Was Elise addicted to the use of morphine?"

"Yes, sir. She was."

"When did you first learn of this?"

"In August, 1910. I found her with a bottle containing the drug in capsule form in her hand. There were seven or eight capsules in the bottle."

"Did you say anything to your sister?"

"Yes, sir. I asked her if she used the drug, and she admitted it. I advised her against its use, because I knew what it was like, and she told me to let her alone, that she would use the drug as long as she liked."

"Did you ever see her in any of her spells?"

"On several occasions."

Annie then told of begging Elise to stop taking morphine. On one other occasion before the final illness Elise had come home in a taxicab. Elise's last illness had really begun the last day of August. Annie had nursed her then, and again during the spell that began on the Monday preceding death, although it was Aunt Mary who was with her just before she had been taken to the hospital. Annie had followed her to the hospital that night with Dr. McGuire. Aunt Mary and Gertrude had remained at home. Annie had been by her side when death came.

"What are your relations with your aunt?"

"What do you mean?"

"Were you friendly with her?"

"Now and then we would have little spats about Gertrude, but nothing of a serious nature. Gertrude wanted to go places where I did not think she had any business to go."

"Is it so that your Aunt Mary, Mrs. Robert Crawford, heard you say that it would have been better if Elise had died when she had her child?"

"Yes, I think she might have heard me say that, because at the time I thought so."

"Did your Aunt Mary at any time make accusations against you, or even hint that she thought you had killed Elise?"

"No, sir. She did not."

"Did she ask you, 'Annie, did you do this?' "

"No, sir, she said nothing of the sort."

"Where was your Aunt Mary?"

"When I went to bed about eleven o'clock I left her in Elise's room. She called me at about a quarter to twelve, telling me that Elise was snoring. I ran into the room and I found Elise looking just as if she was lifeless. Aunt Mary was shaking her and calling to her, and I told Aunt Mary not to disturb her and to let her alone until the doctor came. I then ran out to telephone Dr. McGuire from the neighbors'. When I got back Aunt Mary was jumping up and down as if she had gone wild. She cried out that she was going to throw herself down the stairs. I called her husband and he quieted her."

"What time was it when you called the doctor?"

"It was nearly twelve o'clock. I went next door to use the telephone. The people were in bed, but they let me in."

"Was there any talking from the house next door?"

"Yes, there was. I stood at the window and called over. I asked, 'Is Elise still breathing loud?' "

"Are you positive of the exact words you used?"

"Yes, sir. I asked, 'Is Elise still breathing loud?' "

"Miss Crawford, who had charge of your mother's funeral?"

"I did, Mr. Adams."

"You arranged everything? You attended to the embalming and to the burial?"

"Yes, sir."

"Your sister, Mrs. Leo, was in Port Arthur, Texas?"

"Yes, sir. She came down here, but I had arranged everything before she arrived."

"Did you give your sister anything in a glass on the night preceding her death?"

"Yes, sir. I gave her some cracked ice in a glass."

"Positively nothing else?"

"On the morning she died Elise asked for some calomel and soda. It is possible that at that time I mixed the capsules of calomel with some I had containing morphine."

"What else did you give her during that illness?"

Annie then went into details. Friday morning Elise had seemed better. She came downstairs and her Aunt Mary had given her some broth. In the afternoon Annie gave her a glass of citrate of magnesia. At six that evening Annie fixed her some grits, buttered toast, and tea. At six-thirty Elise was sitting up in bed, and at nine o'clock she asked Annie to help her change her nightgown. At that time Annie had noticed that Elise was not wearing her rings or her necklace. This was most unusual.

"I went across the hall to the room I shared with Gertrude," Annie said, "and I asked her about Elise's jewelry. Gertrude said Elise had given it to her. I thought this was very strange, since Elise was so fond of her rings and necklace. However, I said nothing. I undressed and read for about fifteen minutes. Then I went to bed, but I couldn't sleep because I was so worried about Elise. I was still awake when Aunt Mary called me and asked me to telephone Dr. McGuire."

"Now, Miss Annie, can you say that you did give your sister a capsule containing calomel, or a capsule containing morphine?"

"I can't say, Mr. Adams. I had the capsules on the dresser, both kinds, and I don't know which kind I gave her."

"Did you ever give Elise morphine in any previous illness?"

"No, sir. I never did."

"Take the witness," said Lionel Adams.

St. Clair Adams rose and faced Annie Crawford. She raised a

hand and tucked a lock of yellow hair in place. She continued to swing her feet.

"Miss Crawford, how long did you work at the New Orleans Sanitarium?" asked the district attorney.

"About six and a half years, I think it was, Mr. Adams." She tapped her chin with the fan.

"What were your duties there?"

"When I first went there I was on the telephones. Then I was in the drug room. I stayed in the drug room for several years."

"Did you see the nurses every day?"

"Oh, yes, sir."

"Did you seek to learn the nurses' duties?"

"I object!" interrupted Lionel Adams.

St. Clair Adams changed his question. "Well, Miss Annie, do you know the effects of morphine on the human system?"

Lionel Adams objected again, but was overruled by the Bench.

The district attorney repeated, "Do you know the effects of morphine upon the human system?"

"I don't think so."

"Didn't you admit as much in your signed statement? Let me read that statement to you."

Mr. Adams then read her confession, slowly and in a clear voice.

"Now, what have you to say, Miss Annie?" he asked.

"I might have said it. You asked me so many questions that night, Mr. Adams."

"Well, you were just as cool and collected that night as you are now, were you not?"

"I don't think so, Mr. Adams. I might have been more nervous."

"Miss Crawford, what was in the capsules you gave Elise?"

"I don't know, sir. It might have been calomel or it might have been morphine."

"I'll now reread one part of your confession," he said. He read again the section in which Annie had replied in the affirmative to his question, "You gave her the morphine by mistake?" When he was through, he asked. "Miss Annie, you told me that without qualification of any sort, did you not?"

"Perhaps I did."

He flung out an arm and waved the papers toward the jury. "We know you did. It is there."

"I might have been confused, Mr. Adams."

"Wasn't it the truth?"

"The truth is I don't know whether I mixed them or not."

"Didn't you tell me before you made this statement that you gave Elise calomel?"

"Yes, sir."

"Didn't you tell me in the statement that you gave her morphine?"

"I said I might have mixed them."

"You said you had mixed them, didn't you?"

"Maybe I did."

"Didn't you tell your Aunt Mary and Gertrude that Dr. McGuire had instructed you to give Elise calomel and soda?"

"No, sir. I did not say that. Dr. McGuire told me to give them to her on the telephone when I talked to him, but when he called at the house he told me not to give her any after that."

"When was that?"

"When he came at five o'clock Friday afternoon."

"Did you give her any after that?"

"No, sir. I did not give her any after that."

"Miss Crawford, did you not tell me that you discovered you had given Elise the wrong capsules?"

"Perhaps I told you that."

"You discovered your mistake by the results, did you not?"

"I thought of that after Elise went to sleep. But as she was so used to the drug I thought she would get over it."

"Did Dr. McGuire tell you or the other members of the family that Elise was dying of opium poison?"

"If he said that it must have been when I was not in the room."

"When you went to the hospital with Dr. McGuire did you not know that Elise was dying of morphine poison?"

"No, sir."

"Were you in the room when they were giving Elise artificial respiration, and when Dr. McGuire stuck a needle through her tongue?"

"No, sir."

"Well, then, when were you in the room?"

"I was in the room when Dr. McGuire came that night. I went downstairs and fixed him some hot water which he said he needed. Then I went to my room to dress."

"You were not dressed when he came, Miss Crawford?"

"No, sir. I had on a nightgown and a kimono. I ran over to the neighbors' house to telephone in my kimono."

Mr. Adams then made Annie describe more details of that night. Annie said she had fetched the jar and cups for the interns when they arrived, these to be used for the fluids extracted from the stomach of the dying girl. Annie had heard no one mention morphine poison at any time. She had not known until the next day that morphine had killed her sister.

"How did you hear then?" asked the district attorney.

"A friend came to call on us," said Annie, "and told us she had read it in the newspapers."

"You were at the hosiptal where you were formerly employed on Wednesday of the week your sister died, Miss Annie. Did you take the morphine at that time?"

"No, sir. The last time I got the drug was on September the sixth, or the seventh."

"You were in the habit of taking the morphine when you visited at the hospital?"

"Sometimes I did, and sometimes I did not."

"Why did you not tell Dr. McGuire that you thought you had given Elise morphine?"

"I did not want him to know that I took the drug, and I thought Elise would get over it."

"Did your aunt know you took it?"

"No, sir."

"Had you ever told your sister, Mrs. Leo, about it?"

"No, sir."

"How long have you been taking morphine, Miss Crawford?"

"About four years. I stopped once, then went back to it."

"Miss Crawford, did you love Elise?"

"Certainly."

"Very dearly?"

"Yes, very dearly."

"You were a sort of little mother to her?"

"Yes, I certainly was."

"Well, then, why did you not seek to save her from using morphine, knowing the drug to be a vice?"

"I tried to get her to stop, but she would not. She was old enough to think and act for herself, and I did not think it was my duty to tell Dr. McGuire."

"You stated you had more morphine tablets—about a dozen in a bottle. What did you do with them?"

"I threw them in the toilet."

"When was that?"

"On the evening of September 22."

"Did you have any more morphine?"

"That was all I knew was in the house."

"Did you take morphine yourself Saturday morning?"

"I don't remember."

"You told me that you did."

"Well, I don't know whether I did or not."

"Why did you throw the bottle away?"

"I thought I had better leave the thing alone."

"How did you procure your morphine?"

"I told you once before."

"Tell me again."

"I took it from the hospital."

"Did you not resent Elise's interference with your control of Gertrude?"

"No, sir."

"Were you not always quarreling?"

"No, we were not."

"Did you not resent Elise advising Gertrude to keep company

with young men to whom you might have some kind of objections?"

"Yes, that is true."

"Did you not quarrel with Elise about her going to West End and Spanish Fort?"

"No."

"Did you have a serious quarrel with Elise about paying Gertrude's board?"

"Not a serious quarrel. I spoke to her once about paying half of Gertrude's board, which she had promised to do. It was really not a quarrel."

"How did you take morphine?"

"I always took it by capsule and never used a hypodermic. I have never used a hypodermic."

"How did Elise take it?"

"By capsule, I think."

"Do you know that one of the most efficient ways to counteract the effects of opium poison is to irritate the patient so as to keep him from going deeper into a coma?"

"I know absolutely nothing about it."

"Why did you tell your aunt not to disturb Elise?"

"Because I wanted the doctor to see her that way."

"Did you know that opium poison causes a coma?"

"I did not."

"Did not Elise give Gertrude her rings because her fingers had become so thin that the rings slipped off?"

"No, sir."

"Did not Elise give Gertrude those rings fully ten days before she died?"

"No, she gave them to her in the evening of the day she passed away."

"When was the last time you took morphine, Miss Annie?"

"I think it was September 22, in the morning."

"You did not take it the next day—Saturday?"

"Perhaps I did. I am not sure."

"Have you had none since?"

"None since, sir."

"How much morphine were you in the habit of taking each day?"

"Three or four half-grain capsules."

"Did you not suffer any inconvenience when you stopped?"

"For a while I did, but not any more."

"I am through," announced the district attorney.

The defense was invited to ask further questions of the accused. Mr. Lionel Adams replied that he thought she had "had enough."

Sunday the jury were taken for another outing. This time it was for an automobile ride through the parks and to the shores of Lake Pontchartrain. At the lake front they were served food and drinks, and played baseball and other games. That night Coroner O'Hara had to be called in to give one man treatment for an attack of indigestion. Ten others received strychnine to relieve their fatigue. By now all the newspapers were expressing the wish that the trial would come to an early end for the sake of the jury, reported exhausted.

Edward Zahn was the first witness to be called on Monday morning, having been summoned at the request of the State.

When Mr. Zahn had taken his seat, St. Clair Adams told him apologetically that he must ask him a personal question, then proceeded to ask, "Mr. Zahn, what were your relations with Elise Crawford?"

Lionel Adams objected and was sustained by Judge Chretien. Mr. Zahn stepped down.

The defense now recalled Mrs. Leo.

No one connected with the case had suffered more, and more innocently, than had this member of the Crawford family. "Of all the family," said the *Daily States* on March 20, 1912, "it is she who has stuck by her sister Annie during the ordeal. Scarcely older than Annie, what she has endured has aged her beyond her years. Her sensitive face is pale and careworn. Four times death struck her family in rapid succession, and four times did she journey from her home in Port Arthur, Texas, to do what she could for the surviving members. Now she must see her younger sister on trial for her life, charged with the heinous crime of murdering one sister and suspected of slaying the other one and their parents. Yet she seems to have given this sister Annie her faith, and has done all in her power to ease the lot of the accused!"

Lionel Adams questioned Mrs. Leo about a letter she had received from Elise just before her death. What had Elise meant when she had said, "Ed's eyes are opened"?

Mrs. Leo replied that she did not know, except that it was possible that Elise had meant that Mr. Zahn knew of her past.

"Might not she have meant that Mr. Zahn was not going to marry her because he had found out about her past?"

"I do not know, sir."

District Attorney Adams rephrased the same question when he cross-examined her.

"Isn't it true, Mrs. Leo, that Elise meant that she had told Edward Zahn about her past and that he had forgiven her?"

Again Mrs. Leo's reply was that she did not know what Elise had meant.

Mr. Muller was next. He stated that Elise Crawford was "a girl of fine character, a modest girl, and an extremely faithful stenographer." He had not found her despondent at any time.

Shortly after lunch that afternoon both the State and the defense announced that all evidence in the case had now been presented.

The arguments began at about three o'clock that same afternoon, Assistant District Attorney Warren Doyle opening for the prosecution.

After reviewing all details, Mr. Doyle pointed out that it had been established beyond doubt that the deceased had come to her death from morphine poisoning. He concentrated for some time upon the fact that Annie Crawford was a confessed addict to the drug, and that all medical authorities agreed that morphine fiends were unworthy of belief and entirely incapable of differentiating between truth and falsehood. The accused admitted to theft of the drug from the hospital where she had worked in the past. She was a woman, apparently, who would stoop to any crime.

There was one most important thing. Why had the accused urged her aunt not to awaken Elise Crawford from her comatose state? "Let the poor girl sleep," Annie had said. Indeed, let her sleep forever!

"The demon of murder always betrays his votaries," then asserted Mr. Doyle. Why had Annie, if her deed had been an accident, concealed the means? Throwing the morphine capsules into the toilet had given her crime the element of concealment.

The defense had changed their plans suddenly, and had endeavored to prove Elise Crawford a drug addict, who had ended her misery by suicide. They had badgered Dr. Duval repeatedly. They had brought in such witnesses as Mrs. Dunn, who had used phrases heard only on the stage and never in life. If it were true that Elise had reason for suicide, why was the man she loved by her side the night of the fatal illness? As to a motive for murder, it was not essential that one be proven, but, nevertheless, the State had its motive. As small as was the amount, Annie Crawford had killed her sister for the life insurance.

Joseph Generelly began the discussions for the defense. He reminded the jury that their decision meant life or death to the accused girl. Either this was murder in the first degree or she was innocent. He then referred to the exhumation of the body of Elise Crawford and described the "so-called autopsy" as nothing more or less than "an awful mutilation of a dead body, for it was not until the body was a second time exhumed and cut up, that the State's attorneys really knew the cause of death . . . not until Dr. Duval took the stand." He added, "They went without orders from the court. They went like grave robbers, performing their ghastly deeds in a back shed in the cemetery." He then asked why "a stranger like Dr. Duval" had performed the final autopsy, instead of the coroner.

Mr. Generelly reminded the jury that he and Mr. Adams had taken this case without a fee because they believed implicitly, he said, in the innocence of Annie Crawford. Dr. Mann and Dr. King had offered their services for the same reason.

"Now, that aunt," said Mr. Generelly. "Let us speak of her. You have been told how noble she was to have sheltered three motherless girls, but don't forget she sheltered them at so much a head, and when the money was not forthcoming she was breaking up the home to get rid of them."

He referred to the question Mrs. Crawford said she had asked, "Annie, did you do this?" How could she have known the true condition of Elise—unless she was familiar with the effects of morphine? Why should she, otherwise, have made such a statement?

"It was first brought out by the State," he continued, "that the unfortunate dead girl was not a virgin. They dragged the dark secret from its grave. They made much of Annie's statement that it would have been better had poor Elise died when her child was born. Did Annie deny this? She did not deny it. She only expressed a sentiment that any man in this court who has a daughter might express. Who of us would not rather see his daughter dead than the victim of such shame?"

He commented briefly upon the State's claim that the insurance had been the motive for the crime and dismissed it as absurd, reminding the jury that Annie spent more than the amount of the insurance policy upon the funeral. He criticized Gertrude Crawford for testifying that Annie had drawn money from her account without her consent. "She knew in her heart," he said, "that the money was her contribution to the cost of the coping Annie Crawford was having placed about their parents' grave."

The defense, Generelly argued, had established well the fact that Elise had committed suicide.

"It was not brought out in the trial," he said, "who years ago wronged this unfortunate girl. The name of the scoundrel was not revealed, but whoever he is, wherever he is, the hand of God will reach out to strike him down, for to him may be traced the origin of the trouble which had its tragic climax in the death by poison of this poor Elise.

"Who followed Elise to the hospital? It was Annie. Where were the aunt and Gertrude? What was the first thought of this aunt, who claimed to love Elise so much, when she saw the girl was sick, and vomiting? Was she pregnant again? Not whether she might be seriously ill."

After a few concluding remarks Mr. Generelly closed his argument.

Lionel Adams began his argument a little after four-thirty that afternoon. He asked the jury to visualize the intense suffering Annie Crawford had already endured. He did not claim she had ever been the subject of coercion on the part of the State, but even before that first statement she had made she had undergone such an ordeal as few strong men could have withstood.

"A poor, frail, delicate creature such as this," said Mr. Adams, with a sweeping gesture toward Annie. "A morphine fiend, an opium eater, denied the use of the drug she craved and sitting under the grilling of the district attorney until two o'clock in the morning. Was it any wonder she confessed?"

He then sketched briefly "the wretched life of the young woman —all that trouble and grief, the death of her parents and sister. Is it any wonder she sought solace in drugs?" He said he could not be convinced her confession had been entirely voluntary. He described her "throbbing nerves and seething brain, crying out for the lethal touch of the drug which had enslaved her."

He spoke of "the body dragged from the grave a second time, taken from the crumbling coffin—the body with the limbs rotting from the torso and its organs filled with formalin, the embalmer's fluid, preserved, laid out, and again mutilated, without order from the court, or any notice to the prisoner whose life is at stake.

"Why I've been in these courts as man and boy for fifty years," said Mr. Adams, "and in all that half century of experience I have never heard of such a procedure."

At five-ten he asked Judge Chretien to call a recess as he was tired.

Lionel Adams resumed his argument at seven-thirty.

"If morphine caused the death of Elise Crawford," he said, "and it is not admitted who administered it, it was murder, suicide, or an accident. Unless you can find a motive it is suicide or an accident. There is no murder without a motive." He reviewed the past life of Annie and Elise, and dwelt at some length upon Elise's courtship, "which the poor girl hoped would end at God's altar with the holy sacrament of marriage." He reminded the jury of "the gloomy touches of the mind disturbed, the mind which saw but darkly through the sunlight of present hopes, and which inclined toward the melancholy goal of suicide."

Why had Elise given away her most prized possessions? She had valued her rings and her necklace above all she had in the world.

Mr. Adams had spoken for forty minutes before recess. Now he talked for more than two hours. At times he had to stop to catch his breath. Once he was forced to lean heavily upon the stenographer's table and rest, apologizing for this to the jury.

In his concluding remarks Mr. Adams referred especially to Mrs. Dunn's report of her last conversation with Elise. He asked, "Is it not natural to suppose that Elise was only carrying out her threat to end her days should her lover ever leave her? The giving away of the rings and the necklace, would it not indicate this?"

St. Clair Adams arose a little after ten o'clock that night. He first said that he was not going to deal in personalities, nor was he going to "call people such names as grave robbers."

He described obtaining the original statement from the accused. It had been spontaneous and freely given. Only routine questioning had been used in the interrogation. "I ask you gentlemen," he said. "if I can be accused of unjust treatment to an innocent girl? Do you think I would stoop to put the noose around the neck of a woman I knew to be guiltless of the crime with which she is charged?

"I have been accused of desecrating a grave in the gray of early morning, without the knowledge or consent of the court. I have been charged further with disturbing the body of the deceased, not in the interests of justice, but simply to gratify a desire to

ghoulishly tear open graves and mutilate and insult the grim relics
of mortality.

"Do you gentlemen believe that I, your district attorney, would
be capable of such a despicable crime? Do you believe that an
honest, reputable physician like Dr. Duval would lend himself to
such a deed?"

The district attorney added that he, too, had a charge to make,
and that was that all the attacks of the defense "had been cruel
and vicious." And they were made obviously unnecessary by
the fact that the first findings of Dr. Metz had been in themselves
conclusive.

Elise Crawford, he said, had held no thoughts of suicide. She
had looked, not backward to misfortunes that nearly all had now
forgotten, but ahead to life and marriage and happiness with a fine
young man, Edward Zahn. Her fiancé had known of her past and
had forgiven her. She had made a mistake that any girl might make.

"It is not suicide," said Mr. Adams. "No. Black murder has been
done!"

He described Annie Crawford as "a heartless, callous little
woman, who hovered like a black angel of death in the drug room
of the hospital, taking poison with which to effect her dark deeds."
After seven years she well knew how to use the drug and how "to
accomplish the hellish deed, the foul and cruel murder of her
sister, Elise."

The motive was clear. Annie Crawford was desperately in need
of money. The amount did not matter. The most heinous crimes
in history had been committed for small sums or for some unim-
portant or inadequate reason. Crime was never logical, averred Mr.
Adams. All crimes were blunders.

"We have undertaken to establish this case as secret murders
can alone be establised—by circumstantial evidence," he said.

In conclusion the district attorney stated that the guilt of Annie
Crawford had been proven beyond all doubt, and that he asked
for a verdict of murder in the first degree.

When Judge Chretien completed his charge to the jury it was
nearly eleven-thirty. The weary men filed out of the room slowly.

Annie required the support of a deputy as she was conducted back to her cell to await the final decision.

Perhaps it can be guessed what Annie was thinking that night, though, by all reports, she slept well, despite the fact that she drank several cups of strong black coffee before retiring.

What was in the minds of the citizens of New Orleans and the persons in other parts of the country who had followed the trial closely seems to have varied a great deal. It can be safely said that the majority of Orleanians thought her guilty. But not all. Numerous attorneys, criminologists, and churchmen, as well as ordinary citizens, expressed themselves freely, in print and in private, and seem to have held the most divergent opinions. For instance, the Rev. J. L. Sutton, a former chaplain of the Louisiana State Penitentiary and at the time of the Crawford trial superintendent of the Home for Destitute Boys in New Orleans, described Annie as "a gentlewoman with a tender heart, and one who finds balm in praying to her Maker." The Rev. Sutton had visited her frequently in her cell, and had known her for years before the deaths in her family. He now accused the newspapers of having made a monster of a girl who "was really polished, polite, gentle, and sweet."

Those who in their own judgment had already convicted Annie almost invariably believed her guilty not only of the murder of Elise, but of her mother and father and of Mamie, despite the fact that she was not on trial for these other mysterious deaths.

It has been said many times and in many places that it is not the duty of any American court to ascertain or to decide who has committed a crime, and Annie's jury, like any other, now was charged with but one purpose—to decide only whether the accused had killed the deceased with malice aforethought, according to the legal definition of murder. Yet nothing can prevent any private citizen from holding his own little individual trial within his own mind, and such was the case here. Four persons in the same family, treated by four different physicians, had died of four maladies, that though diagnosed as different illnesses, bore curious resemblances, and all this within a short time, the first three within five weeks of each other. To some this was all coincidence. For others belief in such coincidence was impossible.

Many things were debated. Annie said Elise had been a morphine addict. If that were so, why had she waited until the trial to offer this evidence, instead of doing so in her initial statement to the district attorney? Yet both Dr. Lowe and Dr. McGuire had implied that Elise might have been. Then, if Elise were an addict, and death had come because of an accidental dose of morphine administered by Annie, why had not her system, not unused to the drug, been able to overcome the relatively small amount Annie had, or thought she might have, given her?

Was Elise Crawford a suicide? If so, why should she have been? Admittedly, she had had trouble in the past, but that was six years before. Perhaps she was not happy in the circumstances under which she was living, but the Crawford household was dissolving, and there was at least a reasonable chance that a happy married life lay ahead of her. Her fiancé had come to see her in her illness, and they were, despite whatever meaning may be placed upon the passage in the letter Elise had written Mrs. Leo, on the best of terms.

If Elise were not a suicide why had she given her rings and her necklace, things she treasured, to Gertrude? Was she suspicious that Annie was murdering her? Had she a premonition of death?

Was Annie Crawford a morphine addict? If she were, why had she shown not the least discomfort when imprisoned and deprived of the drug? If she were not an addict, why did she claim to be, unless it was to account for having the drug in her possession so that she might be able to pretend to have made a mistake in the matter of mixing the capsules? If she were not an addict, had she been stealing the drug from the hospital all these months to use in a series of murders?

Would Annie, having planned the murder of Elise so carefully, have blundered to the extent of calling from next door, "Is Elise still breathing?" Would she have blundered again in trying to prevent her aunt from arousing the girl from her coma? Annie Crawford was anything but a stupid woman. And if she had not done these things why had her aunt and Gertrude been so insistent that she had?

Lastly, there is the lack of motive for murder. The one regarding the insurance policies does not hold up, or at least is so weak as to be extremely doubtful. Annie had spent more for the funerals than she had gained.

If Annie was guilty, then one must decide that she killed out of pure hatred of her family, a hatred that amounted almost to insanity, and that was born out of a warped, egocentric determination to triumph over them all, to dominate them to the extent of ending their lives. But there is no indication in the records that Annie Crawford was insane. Everything points to the fact that she had the strongest mind in the family.

The court reconvened at ten-thirty the next morning, Tuesday, March 26, 1912. Annie, we are told, entered the room looking refreshed and rested. She took her seat "and threw back her veil with a quick, impulsive sweep of her arm."

Judge Chretien requested that Mr. Jewell, the foreman of the jury, rise and speak.

Mr. Jewell arose and informed the court that the jury had been unable to reach a verdict. Three of the men stood for conviction, nine for acquittal.

Judge Chretien asked if there were any hope that further voting and discussion might reconcile these varying opinions.

Mr. Jewell said there was no such hope.

It was a mistrial.

Later it was revealed that the jury had faced a deadlock from the beginning. Seven of the jurymen had announced their decisions, immediately after the closing of the case, that Annie was innocent. A little later two more had joined them. The other three had remained unshaken in their conviction that she was guilty.

Annie took the verdict as a triumph. She sprang from her chair and wrung the hands of her attorneys, laughing and weeping hysterically. She regained her poise a few minutes later, however, and, when cameras began to click about her, she pulled down her heavy black veil and raised her fan before her face.

By the time she reached her cell she was trembling and Mrs. O'Connor removed her hat and shoes and made her lie down. The matron now revealed that Annie had not eaten for days. Hot soup was brought in and newspaper reporters were shut out. Mrs. Leo came to visit her and the two sisters cried together.

The newspapermen found it almost impossible now to interview anyone who had been connected with the case. The Crawford family, having suffered so much, refused to see them. St. Clair Adams could not be found and the next day it was announced that he had gone fishing. Judge Chretien and Messrs. Lionel Adams and Joseph Generelly refused to make statements of any kind.

Annie Crawford was released at once. Mrs. Leo was waiting for her. That afternoon they boarded a train for Port Arthur.

THE AXMAN WORE WINGS

Probably there are few human beings who have not considered the murderer who might come for them in the night. All of us would like to cherish the illusion that when we retire, and all the lights are out and all the doors fastened, that we are safe until the next day. Yet who has not awakened in the night to lie listening to strange unexplainable noises, to his own pounding heart? Who has not, at least on occasion, risen and gone about the house in search of a sound, usually, and with relief, to find nothing?

But it is not always nothing that people find, and not all persons have a chance to search, or even to leave their beds. What of he who awakens to see a dark shadow hovering above him? There can be few worse terrors in human experience. The mere fact that the intruder is unknown and nearly invisible, is silent, is for at least an eternal second motionless, is enough to make the moment one of sheer horror. The worst must be the waiting, while the heart bursts with fear, while the panic of the nightmare that is no dream strangles the scream in the throat. Then there is a second waiting, for the blow—perhaps of an ax.

Thousands of Orleanians knew what it meant to fear such an experience all through 1918 and 1919 when the Axman terrorized the city, and some did awaken—if they had been able to sleep at all—to glimpse the killer and to know that the ax was falling, that their skull was going to feel its sharp edge. Not many cities have known such a time of terror.

In 1918 New Orleans like all other American cities was busy thinking and reading about and devoting itself to the news and the duties of World War I. In the spring of that year no one knew it

193

would end in November, although there was hope that it would not go on too much longer and a great deal of optimism that the Allies would win. Headlines in a New Orleans newspaper on May 3 read, "Lull in Flanders; Allies Lines Holding," yet by May 23 the same newspaper warned, "Massed Germans Awaiting Orders Now To Open Drive," and Orleanians were instructed to "Kill The Germ In Germany—Liberty Bonds Will Help!" On May 24 another headline announced, "Senate Rejects Dry Amendment by 20 to 20 Vote." At New Orleans moving picture theaters Charlie Chaplin was starring in *A Dog's Life* and Theda Bara in *The Soul of Buddha*. Also on that day a woman was arrested in New Orleans for wearing trousers on the street. But on the same day there was another headline in all the papers in the city. A couple named Maggio, who operated a small grocery at the corner of Upperline and Magnolia streets, had been attacked during the night before by an unknown assailant who was armed with an ax. It had begun, although most Orleanians must have thought of it as a shocking but isolated case, and they could hardly have dreamed of what lay ahead.

On that morning of May 24, 1918, the *Times-Picayune* devoted a good portion of its front page to the story, and in the center of the page was a photograph of the room where the Maggios had been sleeping, a room in their living quarters behind their store, with inset pictures of the couple as they had looked at their wedding fifteen years before. According to the account, police thought it was just before dawn when someone had chiseled out a panel in a rear door of the apartment and entered. He had struck each of the sleepers once with an ax, then slit their throats with a razor. Mrs. Maggio lay on the floor, her head nearly severed from her body, Joseph Maggio was sprawled half out of bed. The razor lay on the floor in a pool of blood. The ax, as bloodstained as the razor, was found on the steps going out into the back yard. The ax had been Maggio's own property. There was a small safe in the room which was open and empty, yet a hundred dollars or more in cash was found beneath Maggio's blood-soaked pillow and on the dresser in a little pile was Mrs. Maggio's jewelry, including several diamond rings. The police were reported to have already stated that they did not believe robbery was a motive, but that the murderer had opened the safe to make it appear that it was.

In rooms on the other side of the house lived Joseph's brothers, Andrew and Jake. They had discovered the bodies. Jake told police that he awakened at about five o'clock and heard groaning and strange noises on the other side of the wall separating his bedroom from that of Joseph and his wife. He aroused Andrew and together they went into the room. Joseph was on the bed then, and still alive. He even tried to rise and fell half out of the bed. Andrew and Jake called the police at once. The police put them both under arrest, after a neighbor who rushed into the house along with them said he had seen Andrew come home some time between two and three in the morning. Later in the morning there was another curious discovery. Chalked on the sidewalk a block away were these words: "Mrs. Maggio is going to sit up tonight just like Mrs. Toney."

The police went to work. In 1911 there had been three ax murders, similar to the Maggio case, all of Italian grocers and their wives. There had been a grocer named Cruti, then one named Rosetti, whose wife was murdered with him, finally a Tony Schiambra and his wife. Was the last the "Mrs. Toney" referred to in the sidewalk writing? People began talking of Mafia and of Black Hand. The Italian population was particularly worried and some of them demanded police protection.

In the meantime Andrew and Jake Maggio were in jail swearing their innocence. Andrew said it was true he had been out late the night before. He had been celebrating for he had just received his draft call. He had come home drunk and he would not have been able to notice anything strange if there had been anything to notice. Jake verified this and said he had had a hard time arousing Andrew. They were respectable, hard-working young men—Andrew was a barber, Jake a cobbler.

Jake was released the following day and Andrew on May 26. Andrew told a *Times-Picayune* reporter with "tear-filled eyes" that he would never get over this. "It's a terrible thing to be charged with the murder of your own brother when your heart is already broken by his death," he said. "When I'm about to go to war, too. I had been drinking heavily. I was too drunk even to have heard any noise next door." But he and Jake were free and were cleared of any suspicion.

The papers of May 26 announced that Detective Theodore Obitz had charge of the case and had "many theories." On the evening of May 26 Detective Obitz was shot through the heart by a Negro he was arresting for burglary. It had no connection with the Maggio murders.

Weeks passed and nothing more happened. The newspapers informed Orleanians that the Allies had been forced to retire on the Aisne and that the Russian Czar had been murdered. Many citizens probably almost forgot the Maggio case. They were rushing to the Strand Theater to see James W. Gerard's *My Four Years in Germany* at road show prices and talking about putting New Orleans "over the top" in the new Red Cross Drive.

Then on June 28 a baker, John Zanca, made his morning call to deliver bread and cakes to the grocery of Louis Besumer. It was after seven o'clock when he arrived, and as Besumer's store was still closed, Zanca went around to the living quarters in the rear to leave his bread there rather than risk having it stolen from the front of the store. When he reached the back door he stopped and stared in horror. A lower panel of the door was neatly chiseled out. Perhaps half-consciously Zanca knocked on the door. He said later, "There seemed nothing else to do."

And Louis Besumer opened the door. Blood streamed from a wound in his head. He said, "My God! My God!"

Zanca rushed past him and found the woman he had always thought Mrs. Besumer on the bed covered with a bloodstained sheet, unconscious and with a terrible head wound. He called the Charity Hospital and the police.

The newspapers announced the next day that "Mrs. Besumer" was in a serious condition, but still alive, and that Besumer had been released. Detectives believed the woman had been attacked on the gallery leading across one side of the living quarters, for there was much blood there, then had dragged herself or been carried back to the bed, possibly by Besumer. An ax, Besumer's property, was discovered in the bathroom, still bright, bright red with blood. Besumer, it was said, was Polish, and had lived in New Orleans only three months. He had come to the city from Jacksonville, Florida, and before that had operated a farm in South America.

On June 29 there were further developments. That morning the *Times-Picayune* carried a headline reading, "Spy Nest Suspected!" It was stated that letters to Besumer written in German, Russian and Yiddish had been found in a trunk in his apartment. The New Orleans *States* the same day asked the question, "Is Besumer a German Agent" and "Was the Besumer Grocery a Front for a Spy Ring?" On June 30, a Sunday, a great deal of space was devoted to this, and it was hinted darkly that federal authorities were interested in the case. One reporter did note, however, that Besumer was not Italian and asked, "What of the Mafia theory in the ax killings?" It was also noted that Lewis Oubicon, a Negro employee of Besumer, was being held for questioning.

Besumer's own statements were made public on July 1. The first thing he is reported to have said was "That woman is not my wife." He said the woman who had been attacked was named Mrs. Harriet Lowe and that she had come to New Orleans from Jacksonville with him, and that they had lived together ever since. His own wife was ill, he said, and with relatives in Cincinnati. He swore he did not know what had happened. Someone had struck him while he slept. When he regained consciousness he found Mrs. Lowe on the gallery and he had carried her to the bed. He had been about to summon an ambulance when Zanca knocked at the back door. He was not a German, but a Pole, and he had no use for the Germans. He spoke and received mail in a half dozen languages. He was certainly no spy, he vowed. He offered the police his full co-operation.

But federal authorities did come into the case. Carrying a bathrobe for her, Besumer went to see Harriet Lowe at the hospital. He was refused admittance and the bathrobe was taken away from him and ripped open at the seams by government agents. The next day his grocery and living quarters were ransacked. Nothing was found.

Mrs. Lowe made her first statement on July 5, having by then regained consciousness. She said, "I've long suspected that Mr. Besumer was a German spy." Besumer was arrested at once.

On July 6 Mrs. Lowe was interviewed again. She said, "I am married to Mr. Besumer. If I am not I don't know what I'll do." Then she added, "I did not say Mr. Besumer is a German spy. That is perfectly ridiculous." A few days later Besumer was freed from government custody.

Mrs. Lowe at last talked of the attacks. She said that Besumer was working on his accounts about midnight, sitting at a table with a lot of money before him. She always worried about how careless he was with money, she said, and she warned him and asked him to put it in the safe. Then she smelled some prunes she was cooking in the kitchen and she went into the kitchen to look at them. There her memory left her. She supposed it was the blow on the head. She could not even remember going to bed. Her next memory was of awakening. "I don't even know what made me wake up," she told police, "but I opened my eyes and in the light from outside I saw a man standing over me, making some sort of motions with his hands. I saw the ax. I recall screaming, 'Go away! Don't push me that way!' He was a rather tall man, and heavy-set. He was a white man and he wore no hat or cap. I remember his hair was dark brown and almost stood on end. He wore a white shirt, opened at the neck. He just stood there, making motions with the ax, but not hitting me. The next thing I remember is lying out on the gallery with my face in a pool of blood."

The story changed on July 15. In another police interview that day Mrs. Lowe said she was not in bed when she was struck. She was on the gallery. Police thought this made more sense and again looked toward Besumer with suspicion. They questioned neighbors. Yes, the Besumers had had violent quarrels, they were told. Besumer was fifty-nine and Mrs. Lowe twenty-nine. He was jealous and they quarreled over money, too. Police began asking one question. Could Besumer's own wound have been self-inflicted? A check with authorities in Jacksonville and in Cincinnati proved that Besumer and Mrs. Lowe had never been married and that Besumer had a living wife. That did not help matters, and they were far from convinced that Besumer was not a German agent. Neighbors gossiped about the foreigner who had odd ways and spoke German fluently, as well as other languages, who looked like a simple peasant and had the manners and airs of a cultured gentleman. People began saying that perhaps Besumer had attacked Mrs. Lowe, then wounded himself, all in imitation of the Axman, perhaps because Mrs. Lowe knew too much of his activities as a spy.

Then on August 3 the doctors at Charity Hospital performed surgery upon Mrs. Lowe. Two days later she died, and, dying, mumbled that Besumer had struck her with the ax. He was arrested at once and charged with murder.

The Axman chose that night, August 5, to strike again.

Edward Schneider, a young married man, was working late that night, and it was after midnight when he turned the key in the front door of his home in Elmira Street. When he reached his bedroom and turned on the light he was almost paralyzed with horror. His wife lay unconscious, her face and head covered with blood.

Mrs. Schneider, who was expecting a baby within a few days, was rushed to Charity Hospital. She regained consciousness and remembered awakening to see a dark form bending over her, an ax swung high. She recalled shrieking as the ax fell.

She recovered and a week later was delivered of a healthy baby girl. She was never able to tell more about what had occurred, however, and although the police searched diligently for clues none was found. To add to the general confusion were deviations from the Axman's habits. No ax was about. The intruder seemed to have entered by a window, for no door panel was chiseled out. As usual, however, nothing was stolen.

The day after the attack upon Mrs. Schneider a newspaper for the first time put into a headline what Orleanians had been asking each other for months. The *Times-Picayune* asked, in large and dramatic type: IS AN AXMAN AT LARGE IN NEW ORLEANS?

Pauline Bruno, aged 18, and Mary, her sister, aged 13, awoke shortly after three in the morning of August 10 when they heard strange noises coming from the next room, where their uncle, Joseph Romano, was sleeping. Pauline crawled out of bed, turned on her light, and opened the door between the rooms. A man, whom she later described as " dark, tall, heavy-set, wearing a dark suit and a black slouch hat," was standing by her uncle's bed. Pauline screamed and then the man seemed to vanish. As if it were all a fantastic nightmare, her uncle rose from the bed, staggered through a door at the other side of the room, and crashed to the floor there, which was the parlor. Pauline ran after him.

Later she told the following story to an *Item* reporter: "I've been nervous about the Axman for weeks," she said, "and I haven't been sleeping much. I was dozing when I heard blows and scuffling in Uncle Joe's room. I sat up in bed and my sister woke up too. When I looked into my uncle's room this big heavy-set man was standing at the foot of his bed. I think he was a white man, but I couldn't swear to it. I screamed. My little sister screamed too. We were horribly scared. Then he vanished. It was almost as if he had wings!

"We rushed into the parlor, where my uncle had staggered. He had two big cuts on his head. We got him up and propped him in a chair. 'I've been hit,' he groaned. 'I don't know who did it. Call the Charity Hospital.' Then he fainted. Later he was able to walk to the ambulance with some help. I don't know that he had any enemies."

Romano died two days later in the hospital, without being able to make further statements. Police reported that this time there were all the Axman's signatures. An ax was found in Romano's back yard, bloodstained and fearful. The panel of a rear door had been cut out. Nothing in the house was stolen, although Romano's room seemed to have been ransacked. The only thing that made it unlike some of the other cases was that Romano was a barber, not a grocer.

Now there was a new wave of hysteria among the Italians in New Orleans. Some of the families set up regular watches, taking turns standing guard over their sleeping relatives. A few were said to be leaving the city.

Police began to be flooded with reports about the Axman after the Romano incident. Al Durand, a grocer, reported finding an ax and a chisel outside his back door on the morning of August 11. Joseph LeBeouf, a grocer at Gravier and Miro streets, only a block from the Romano home, came forward with the story that someone had chiseled out a panel of his back door on July 28, a day when he was not home. Still another grocer, Arthur Recknagel, told of finding a panel in one of his doors removed back in June, and of finding an ax in the grass of his rear yard. Recknagel lived only a half dozen blocks from the Romano home. On August 15 several persons called police to tell them the Axman was wandering around in the neighborhood of Tulane Avenue and Broad Street disguised as a woman!

On August 21 a man was seen leaping a back fence at Gravier and South White streets. A woman reported she clearly saw an ax in this man's hand. Immediately the neighbors formed a kind of posse, as other people ran from their houses screaming that the Axman had just jumped their fence! A young man named Joseph Garry vowed he had fired at the Axman with his shotgun. Police arrived on the scene, but no one was apprehended, and the excitement quieted down about midnight, although it is doubtful if many people in the vicinity slept well that night or for several nights thereafter. The New Orleans *States* reported the next day:

Armed men are keeping watch over their sleeping families while the police are seeking to solve the mysteries of the ax attacks. Five victims have fallen under the dreadful blows of this weapon within the last few months. Extra police are being put to work daily.

At least four persons saw the Axman this morning in the

neighborhood of Iberville and Rendon. He was first seen in front
of an Italian grocery. Twice he fled when citizens armed themselves and gave chase. There was something, agreed all, in the
prowler's hand. Was it an ax? . . .

On August 30 a man named Nick Asunto called the police to
tell them he had awakened and heard strange noises downstairs. He
lived in a two-storied house. He went to the head of his stairs and
saw a dark, heavy-set man standing below, an ax in his hand. When
Asunto yelled at him the Axman ran out the front door. On August
31 Paul Lobella, a notions store proprietor at 7420 Zimple Street,
found an ax in his alley. There were a dozen similar reports.

Now police made statements to the effect that they did not
believe the Besumer case was of the now ordinary variety. They
made public Mrs. Lowe's confession. Her memory cleared after the
operation, they said, and she had told them that Besumer struck
her with an ax after she had asked him for money. He chased her
down the gallery, screaming, "I am going to make fire for you in
the bottom of the ocean!" She had reiterated, too, that Besumer
was a German spy. Therefore they were sure this was not the Axman
at work, although they believed all the other attacks, including that
upon Mrs. Schneider, were the crimes of a single person, perhaps a
homicidal maniac.

Joseph Dantonio, a retired detective, long an authority on Mafia
activities, was questioned by a *States* reporter, and was quoted in
that newspaper as saying, "The Axman is a modern 'Dr. Jekyll and
Mr. Hyde.' A criminal of this type may be a respectable, law-abiding
citizen when his normal self. Compelled by an impulse to kill, he
must obey this urge. Some years ago there were a number of similar
cases, all bearing such strong resemblance to this outbreak that the
same fiend may be responsible. Like Jack-the-Ripper, this sadist may
go on with his periodic outbreaks until his death. For months, even
for years, he may be normal, then go on another rampage. It is a
mistake to blame the Mafia. Several of the victims have been other
than Italians, and the Mafia never attacks women, as this murderer
has done."

Then, as if he were exactly as Detective Dantonio had theorized, the Axman did disappear. After the Romano killing and the other unauthenticated attacks and scares, nothing happened at all for a long time. Weeks and months passed, the fighting of World War I ended, Christmas came and then the New Year and no more attacks occurred. Orleanians, even the Italians, breathed freely again, and the police, still mystified, found nothing more to work with in solving the crimes. From time to time suspects were arrested, but all had to be released. Only Besumer remained in jail awaiting trial, the only real suspect they had in connection with any of the crimes.

Then, on March 10, 1919, Iorlando Jordano, a grocer in Gretna, just across the river from New Orleans, heard screams coming from the living quarters of another grocer across the street, a man named Charles Cortimiglia. He rushed over and into the Cortimiglia apartment. Mrs. Cortimiglia sat on the floor, still shrieking, blood gushing from her head and the body of her two-year-old daughter Mary clasped in her arms. Also bleeding frightfully, Charles Cortimiglia lay on the floor nearby.

Jordano tried to take Mary from her mother's arms, but she wouldn't let him, so he got wet towels from the bathroom and tried to bathe her face and that of her husband. Cortimiglia groaned, but did not regain full consciousness. Then Frank Jordano, young son of Iorlando, rushed in and began assisting his father. The father sent him to call an ambulance. Both the Cortimiglia parents had to be taken to the Charity Hospital with fractured skulls. Little Mary was dead.

When the police searched the property they found the familiar Axman pattern—the back door panel chiseled, the bloody ax, Charles Cortimiglia's own, on the back steps, nothing stolen. Reading the newspapers the next morning Orleanians and the citizens of Gretna all knew the worst. The Axman was back!

As soon as she could talk coherently Rosie Cortimiglia told of awakening to see her husband struggling with a large white man wearing dark clothes, who was armed with an ax. The man tore himself loose from Cortimiglia, sprang backward and struck once with the ax. When her husband fell to the floor and the Axman swung around Mrs. Cortimiglia seized Mary, who was asleep in her crib beside the parents' bed, clasped her to her and screamed, "Not my baby! Not my baby!" The Axman struck twice more, then fled. Mary was killed instantly.

Both the Cortimiglias were badly injured, but Charles recovered first and left the hospital. A few days later Rosie made another statement, an accusation that amazed the police. "It was the Jordanos!" she said. "It was Frank Jordano and the old man helped him. It was those Jordanos!"

Charles Cortimiglia was questioned. He looked as astounded as the police. "It was not the Jordanos," he said. "I saw the man well and he was a stranger. No, it was not Frank Jordano."

Nevertheless, both Jordanos were arrested, charged with the murder of Mary Cortimiglia and placed in the Gretna jail.

Both denied their innocence fervently. Frank, who was only eighteen and about to be married, said at first he had been home all night, then admitted he had been to a dance with his girl and that he had lied because he did not want her name brought into the affair. The elder Jordano, sixty-nine and in poor health, told his story of finding the Cortimiglias over and over again.

Yet Rosie Cortimiglia told her story over and over, too. Frank and Iorlando had both been in the room. It was Frank who had struck them all, had murdered her baby. She said the Jordanos had hated her husband and herself a long time because both families were in the grocery business in the same block. It was jealousy, she said. She gave the police everything they needed—eyewitness identification and motive. Charles Cortimiglia continued to deny it all. "My wife must be out of her mind," he said. "It was a stranger." Rosie retaliated, "He is afraid for his own neck, that husband of mine. It was the Jordanos."

One thing seems to have bothered detectives working on the case more than anything else. For all his youth Frank Jordano was more than six feet tall and weighed over two hundred pounds. Making a test with a man of similar size, they admitted a man that size could not squeeze through the panel of a door. A giddy reporter on the *Times-Picayune* wanted to know if it were possible the Axman was really a midget.

When Rosie was released from the hospital she was taken to the Gretna jail. There she identified the Jordanos again. Pointing a finger at them she screamed, "You murdered my baby!" and fainted. It was announced that the Jordanos would go to trial for the murder in May.

But before that Louis Besumer went on trial. The trial opened on April 30. It was brief and few witnesses were called. District Attorney Chandler Luzenberg summoned Coroner Joseph O'Hara for the State, who described Mrs. Lowe's wounds and the cause of her death. Zanca, the baker, said that Besumer did not seem to know what he was doing that morning when he had opened the door or even to realize Mrs. Lowe was hurt. Federal officers admitted they had no evidence that Besumer had ever been a German agent. Besumer's attorney, George Rhodes, said it was a reflection on the United States Secret Service to say that Besumer had been a spy, and that Besumer was not being tried on that charge in any case and, besides, the war was over. The police to whom Mrs. Lowe had made her accusation of Besumer admitted that even then she had not been very coherent. Dr. H. W. Kostmayer said that only a very powerful man could have inflicted himself with the wound Besumer had received and he did not consider the accused strong enough to have accomplished it.

The next morning the jury debated but ten minutes and Besumer was found not guilty. Released, Besumer told reporters that he believed the same Axman had attacked Mrs. Lowe and himself as had attacked the others and that his imprisonment had been due almost entirely to "war feeling," because he had been thought to be a German, although he was really a Pole and had never been a German sympathizer.

In the meantime the Cortimiglia case had brought on a new series of Axman reports. Immediately after the attack upon the Gretna family New Orleans police received numerous reports of chiseled panels, axes being found, dark, heavy-set men lurking in neighborhoods, particularly around grocery stores, and many

Orleanians, particularly Italian grocers, appealed once more for police protection. The newspapers reviewed all the cases of 1918 and editorialized upon the mystery. It was announced that Police Superintendent Frank Mooney had again assigned special men to the task of uncovering the perpetrators of the crimes, despite the fact that the Jordanos were in the Gretna jail and that Superintendent Mooney had expressed the opinion that he ". . . was sure that all the crimes were committed by the same man, probably a bloodthirsty maniac, filled with a passion for human slaughter."

A *States* editor wrote, on March 11:

> Who is the Axman; what are his motives?
>
> Is the fiend who butchered the Cortimiglias in Gretna Sunday the same man who committed the Maggio, Besumer and Romano crimes? Is he the same who has made all the attempts on other families?
>
> If so, is he madman, robber, vendetta agent, sadist or some supernatural spirit of evil?
>
> If a madman, why so cunning and careful in the execution of his crimes? If a robber, why the wanton shedding of blood and the fact that money and valuables have often been left in full view? If a vendetta agent of the Mafia, why include among victims persons of nationalities other than Italian?
>
> The possibilities in searching for the motives in this extraordinary series of axe butcheries are unlimited. The records show no details of importance which vary. There is always the door panel as a means of entrance, always the axe, always the frightful effusion of blood. In these three essentials the work of the Axeman is practically identical.

But the reaction of Orleanians to the 1919 outbreak of the Axman was by no means all fearful and grim. Probably because the war was over and people were in a gayer mood than they had been the year before, there were some who joked about him and even found a kind of humor in the situation. There were reports of "Axman parties" and a New Orleans composer wrote a song entitled "The Mysterious Axman's Jazz" or "Don't Scare Me, Papa!" which

Orleanians played on their pianos. Then, on March 14, a letter purporting to be from the Axman appeared in a newspaper, which read as follows:

Hell, March 13, 1919

Editor of the *Times-Picayune*
New Orleans, Louisiana

Esteemed Mortal:
They have never caught me and they never will. They have never seen me, for I am invisible, even as the ether that surrounds your earth. I am not a human being, but a spirit and a fell demon from the hottest hell. I am what you Orleanians and your foolish police call the Axeman.

When I see fit, I shall come again and claim other victims. I alone know who they shall be. I shall leave no clue except my bloody axe, besmeared with the blood and brains of him whom I have sent below to keep me company.

If you wish you may tell the police not to rile me. Of course I am a reasonable spirit. I take no offense at the way they have conducted their investigations in the past. In fact, they have been so utterly stupid as to amuse not only me, but His Satanic Majesty, Francis Josef, etc. But tell them to beware. Let them not try to discover what I am, for it were better that they were never born than to incur the wrath of the Axeman. I don't think there is any need of such a warning, for I feel sure the police will always dodge me, as they have in the past. They are wise and know how to keep away from all harm.

Undoubtedly, you Orleanians think of me as a most horrible murderer, which I am, but I could be much worse if I wanted to. If I wished, I could pay a visit to your city every night. At will I could slay thousands of your best citizens, for I am in close relationship to the Angel of Death.

Now, to be exact, at 12:15 (earthly time) on next Tuesday night, I am going to visit New Orleans again. In my infinite mercy, I am going to make a proposition to you people. Here it is:

I am very fond of jazz music, and I swear by all the devils in the nether regions that every person shall be spared in whose home a jazz band is in full swing at the time I have mentioned. If everyone has a jazz band going, well, then, so much the better for you people. One thing is certain and that is that some of those people who do not jazz it on Tuesday night (if there be any) will get the axe.

Well, as I am cold and crave the warmth of my native Tartarus, and as it is about time that I leave your earthly home, I will cease my discourse. Hoping that thou wilt publish this, that it may go well with thee, I have been, am and will be the worst spirit that ever existed either in fact or realm of fancy.

THE AXEMAN

The Tuesday on which this "Axeman" promised to visit the city was March 19, St. Joseph's Night, a night when many Orleanians, and even more in 1919 than now, give parties and dances to celebrate a break in Lent.

That St. Joseph's Night in New Orelans seems to have been the loudest and most hilarious of any on record. All over the city Orleanians obeyed the instructions in the letter. Cabarets and clubs were jammed and friends and neighbors gathered in homes to "jazz it," according to the letter's edict. Bands and phonographs and inner-player pianos all over the city created bedlam, and every owner of a piano seemed to have on hand sheet music of "The Mysterious Axman's Jazz" or "Don't Scare Me, Papa!"

Young men living in a fraternity house at 552 Lowerline Street even inserted an advertisement in the *Times-Picayune* inviting the Axman to call. Appearing in the morning of Tuesday, March 19, the advertisement was signed by "Oscar Williams, William Schulze, A. M. La Fleur and William Simpson," and it informed the Axman that a bathroom window would be left open for him, so that it would not be necessary for him to mar any doors; and that all doors would be left unlocked if he would stoop to making such a conventional entrance. He was told there would be, however, no jazz music, but only a rendering of "Nearer, My God, To Thee," which his hosts considered more suitable for the occasion. They concluded the advertisement by stating. "There is a sincere cordiality about this invitation that not even an Axman can fail to recognize."

But the Axman failed everybody that night and made no appearances. Apparently he was satisfied with the amount of jazz music being played all over the city.

Frank and Iorlando Jordano went to trial on May 21 for the murder of Mary Cortimiglia. The Gretna courtroom of Judge John H. Fleury was packed with friends and neighbors of both the victims and the accused.

The first witness was Coroner J. R. Fernandez, who went through the routine of describing the cause of Mary's death. In the front row sat Rosie Cortimiglia, dressed in black, tense and obviously near hysteria from the moment the proceedings began. Not far away sat her husband, but they did not look at each other or speak, for they had separated immediately after their disagreement over the identification of the Jordanos. Besumer was in the room, having been called because he was a survivor of a visitiation of the Axman. He was summoned to the stand early in the trial. He said he could not identify either Frank or Iorlando Jordano as the man who had attacked him and Mrs. Lowe. He could have identified no one, he concluded, because he had not seen the Axman.

Rosie burst into tears when she took the stand, but she reiterated her identification, pointing to the men again. Some of the people in the courtroom hooted her and Judge Fleury had to ask for order and threaten to clear the room. Still whispering and angry noises could be heard from friends of the Jordanos.

Charles Cortimiglia once again flatly denied the man with whom he had struggled was either of the Jordanos. He could not understand his wife's insistence on placing the blame on them, he said. He had seen the man. He had not been Frank; he had not been Iorlando Jordano. No! It was all wrong!

Defense Attorney William F. Byrnes summoned a stream of character witnesses for almost all of two days. All testified both the accused were respectable men of fine reputation in the town. Mrs. Iorlando Jordano took the stand. She was nervous and tense and

she was kept only a moment. She said, "My old man was home all ·
night and my boy was out with his girl."

During the second day Andrew Ojeda, a *States* reporter, was
called by the defense. He testified that he had interviewed Mrs.
Rosie Cortimiglia soon after she regained consciousness. At that
time she had said, "I don't know who killed Mary. I believe my
husband did it!"

This caused another commotion in the courtroom. A woman
screamed in the rear. People who must have been friends of the
Jordanos applauded; friends of the Cortimiglias hooted and hissed.
Again the judge had to threaten to clear the room. Charles Cortimiglia sprang to his feet, then sat down again.

The defense summoned Dr. Jerome E. Landry, who had treated
Mrs. Cortimiglia. Did Dr. Landry consider Rosie Cortimiglia's
mental condition such that she would make a reliable witness? He
stated that in his opinion it was. District Attorney Robert Rivarde
summoned Dr. C. V. Unsworth. Did he consider Rosie Cortimiglia
sane? He did. The defense then brought Dr. Joseph H. O'Hara to
the stand and asked the same question. Dr. O'Hara stated that in
his opinion she was suffering from paranoia.

As the trial went on more and more people fought their way
inside, bringing small children, babies, and box lunches. Several
times a day Judge Fleury had to issue threats because of the bedlam
in the room.

On the fourth day the defense issued new character witnesses for
the Jordanos, one another Gretna grocer, Santo Vicari, who testified that someone had tried to chisel through a panel in one of his
doors only two nights before the attack upon the Cortimiglias and
at a time when he knew the whereabouts of the Jordanos. When
Iorlando Jordano took the stand he said that he thought Rosie
Cortimiglia was not in her right mind. He had loved little Mary.
She had called him "Grampa." Only a lunatic could imagine he
would have harmed her. He had been as shocked and grieved by the
cruel attack as if he had been the child's grandfather. He had run
to the Cortimiglias' home in answer to Rosie's screams, then his

son had come, later his wife. All they had tried to do was help. Now they were accused of the attack. His boy was a good boy.

Frank Jordano was on the stand two hours. He answered Mr. Byrnes's questions in a strong clear voice and he did not waver under the district attorney's cross-examination. He had been at a dance with his girl that night. He had lied about that, yes, but it had been to protect his sweetheart and to keep her out of this. He had been home in bed a little while when he heard Rosie Cortimiglia's shrieks. He had followed his father to the Cortimiglias'. His father had been trying to help. His mother had bathed Charles Cortimiglia's face.

Sheriff L. H. Marrero testified that Rosie Cortimiglia had accused the Jordanos at once. There had been no hesitation on her part to do so, he said, no doubt in her mind. She had been positive.

On the fifth day the jury had the case in their hands. They were in consultation forty-five minutes. The Jordanos were found guilty. The courtroom resounded with angry shouts of protest.

A few days later sentence was passed. Frank Jordano was sentenced to be hanged. Iorlando Jordano was sentenced to life imprisonment.

The Axman went back to work on August 10.

Early that morning a New Orleans grocer, Steve Boca, tottered out of his home in Elysian Fields Avenue and staggered down the alley next door to the entrance of the room where his friend Frank Genusa slept. When Genusa opened the door he caught Boca in his arms. The man's skull was split and he was drenched with blood. A Charity Hospital ambulance was called.

Boca recovered but he could tell nothing. He had awakened, seen the form over his bed and the blow coming. When he was conscious once more he had gone to Genusa for refuge. He could give no description of his attacker.

Police found all the usual signs of the Axman's visit: the door panel was removed; the ax was in the kitchen; there had been no theft. Using a method that seemed usual with them, they then arrested Genusa. Boca himself defended him and he was released after a few days.

It was announced in the papers that William F. Byrnes was taking the Jordano case to the Supreme Court. It was said that most of the citizens of Gretna believed the father and son innocent, considered their conviction a miscarriage of justice. Rosie Cortimiglia was reported in hiding in New Orleans.

On September 2 William Carlson, a New Orleans druggist, heard a noise at his back door while he was reading late in the night. He got his revolver, called several times, then fired through the door. When he went outside no one was visible, but police rushing to the scene found what they believed were the marks of a chisel on one of the panels of the door.

On September 3, Sarah Laumann, a girl of nineteen, who lived alone, was found by neighbors who broke into her house when she failed to answer her bell. She was unconscious in her bed, several teeth knocked out, her head injured. A bloody ax was found beneath an open window. This time the Axman had not used a door panel for entry. Was this another of his victims? It was thought so. Miss Laumann had a brain concussion, but recovered. She could recall nothing. Evidently the attack had taken place while she slept.

There were no more Axman appearances until October 27. Early that morning Mrs. Mike Pepitone, wife of a grocer, awoke to hear sounds of a struggle in the room next to her own, where her husband slept. She reached the door between the rooms just in time to see a man disappear through another exit to her husband's room. Mike Pepitone lay on his bed covered with blood. Blood splattered the wall and a picture of the Virgin above the bed. Mrs. Pepitone shrieked and her six small children were awakened by their mother's screams. When the police arrived they found the signatures—the chiseled door panel was there and the ax lay on the back porch. Pepitone was dead. His wife could tell police little or nothing. She had seen the man, but her description was no less general than others they had received. It seemed as hopeless a case as the rest.

By now they had a feeling that there was nothing to do but wait for the Axman to strike again. Would it go on forever?

But it did not go on forever. No one knew it then, but it was over. Mike Pepitone was the last victim. Calls continued to reach the police from frightened citizens night after night, but all turned out to be scares and nothing more.

Throughout the months that passed and became a year a number of arrests were made, but in vain. New Orleans began to relax again and discussion of the Axman cases became infrequent. Only the Jordanos languished in the Gretna jail, awaiting the new trial their attorney had promised them—or the hanging of Frank.

Then, on December 7, 1920, Rosie Cortimiglia appeared in the city room of the *Times-Picayune* and asked to speak to a reporter. Later accounts of her visit were highly dramatic. Rosie was utterly changed. Thin and ill, clothed in black, her face almost unrecognizable as that of the pretty young woman of a year before, she fell to her knees before the reporter assigned to interview her, screaming, "I lied! I lied! God forgive me, I lied!"

Everyone in the offices gathered about. This was it, great, sensational copy.

Rosie remained on her knees, tears streaming down her cheeks.

"I lied," she said. "It was not the Jordanos who killed my baby. I did not know the man who attacked us."

Helped to her feet and then to a chair, Rosie leaned forward, her hands clutching her now scarred and pitted cheeks.

"Look at me!" she cried. "I have had smallpox. I have suffered for my lie. I hated the Jordanos,. but they did not kill Mary. St. Joseph told me I must tell the truth no matter what it cost me. You mustn't let them hang Frank!"

Rosie was taken to the Gretna jail at once. On the way she babbled incessantly of her suffering and that she had lied. She said Sheriff Marrero had forced the accusation of the Jordanos from her. Then she said she had made it simply out of hatred for the Jordanos.

In Frank Jordano's cell she threw herself to the floor and kissed his feet, crying, "Forgive me! Forgive me! You are innocent!"

Raising her head, she said, "God has punished me more than you. Look at my face! I have lost everything—my baby is dead, my husband has left me, I have had smallpox. God has punished me until I have offered more than you!"

The Jordanas were soon free. There had been no real evidence against them but the testimony of Rosie Cortimiglia, and so there was no reason to hold them longer.

Frank Jordano visited the offices of the *Times-Picayune* on the day of his release. He said he would marry his sweetheart at once. He had always known God would not let him die for a crime of which he was innocent. He stood at a window of an office in the newspaper building and looked out into Lafayette Square just across the street, where the sun was bright on the greens. "Ain't it fine!" he said. "It all looks fine!"

But nothing had been solved about the Axman crimes. It was almost as if the cruel attacks had been committed by a supernatural being, by a "fell demon from the hottest hell," as the letter purporting to be from the Axman had put it. Many had been charged and all had been freed. No proof of the criminal's identity existed. With the freeing of the Jordanos the Axman returned to the conversation of Orleanians and, briefly, to the editorial pages of the newspapers. Who was the Axman? Had there been one Axman or several—or many? Had each attack been the work of a different person? Or all of one?

Then, almost simultaneously with the confession of Rosie Cortimiglia, New Orleans police learned of a strange occurrence in Los Angeles. At first the news seemed almost unbelievable. Later they seem to have been anxious to believe it.

On December 2, 1920, an Orleanian named Joseph Mumfre was walking down a Los Angeles business street in the early afternoon. A "woman in black and heavily veiled" stepped from the doorway of a building, a revolver in her hand, and emptied the gun into Mumfre. He fell dead on the sunny sidewalk and the woman stood over him, making no attempt to escape or even to move.

Taken to the police station, the woman in black said at first that her name was Mrs. Esther Albano and refused to say why she had shot Mumfre. Days later she changed her mind and told Los Angeles detectives that she was Mrs. Mike Pepitone, the widow of the last victim of the New Orleans Axman.

"He was the Axman," she said. "I saw him running from my husband's room. I believe he killed all those people."

Immediately New Orleans police were drawn into the case. They knew a lot about Mumfre. He had a criminal record and had spent much time in prison. Dates were checked carefully. He had been released from a prison term in 1911, just before the slaughter of the Schiambras, of Cruti, and of Rosetti. Then he had gone back to jail and had been freed only a few weeks before the Maggio attack began the latest series of such crimes. In the lull between the end of August 1918 and March 1919 he had once more been in jail on a burglary charge; this was the span of time between the attack on Mrs. Lowe and the others of that period and the next outbreak that began with the Cortimiglia family. It was known that Mumfre had left New Orleans just after the slaying of Mike Pepitone.

That much fitted. It was almost too perfect. Yet there was no proof that Mumfre was the Axman. As the newspapers pointed out the dates might be mere coincidence. It was thought he was the man who had attacked Mike Pepitone. All else remained a matter of conjecture.

Mrs. Pepitone was tried in a Los Angeles court in April. She pleaded guilty and the proceedings were brief. Her attorney's plea was justifiable homicide. This did not hold, but there was much sympathy in her favor. She received a sentence of ten years, but in little more than three she was freed, and subsequently vanished from sight.

Were the Axman mysteries solved?

Most Orleanians did not think so and do not think so yet. Of course no one will ever know now if Mumfre was guilty of all the crimes, of some of them, or only of the murder of Mike Pepitone. Probably the most general consensus of opinion in New Orleans, both among the police and the citizens, always remained that there was not one Axman at all, but at least several.

Was the Mafia responsible?

Mumfre was not known to be a member of any such organization, but that in itself meant nothing. Membership was always
secret. Yet, as Detective Dantonio said, the crimes never fitted the
Mafia pattern. The Mafia did not attack anyone but Italians and
they never murdered women. Besides it was thought the Mafia had
passed from New Orleans forever with the apprehension of the
kidnapers of little Walter Lamana.

If the Mafia did still exist and the Italians who were attacked
were its victims, what of Mrs. Lowe, Mrs. Schneider, Sarah Laumann, and the others who were not Italians yet had also been the
Axman's prey?

It is true that in all these cases the exact pattern of the Axman's
technique was not followed. Often one or more of his habits were
omitted. He chose a different means of entry, for instance. Did this
prove the assailant was not the same? Did it then mean that when
the steps were followed carefully—when the door panel was chiseled
out, the ax borrowed from the victim himself and left behind, and
nothing was stolen—that the same murderer had called?

Was the following of that pattern indicative of the fact that the
killer was a homicidal maniac, the "Doctor Jekyll and Mr. Hyde"
of Detective Dantonio's theorizing? Adherence to such a pattern
is thought to suggest the insane killer, who kills for pleasure and no
other motive.

It must also be remembered that most of the victims were alike—
Italian grocers. Did someone hate Italian grocers? Did someone
want to kill all the Italian grocers in New Orleans—perhaps in the
world? If that is so, we come full circle again. What of the others
who were not Italian grocers?

Confusion did much harm in all the cases. Then there were the
false accusations—of Harriet Lowe against Besumer, of Rosie Cortimiglia against the Jordanos. There were lots of lies, without a
doubt. There was fear. Probably some of the victims and their relatives did not tell all they knew, either for fear that the Mafia still
existed and that they might be further punished, or because they

knew the Mafia did exist and that one of its members would extort reprisals from someone in their family if they talked.

All we know now is that the Axman did vanish from New Orleans about the time Joseph Mumfre left the city and that he never returned after Mumfre was killed. It is extremely doubtful that anyone will ever know more. The Axman came and struck and went away. The citizens of New Orleans can only hope that they never hear the sound of the chisel at work on the door panel again.

"I'M FIT AS A FIDDLE AND READY TO HANG"

Kenneth Neu left the girl at the corner of Canal and Baronne streets. He turned on the personality, as he would have expressed it. He gave her a big smile. "I'll pick you up at your sister's tonight," he said. "Be packed and ready. We'll have a big time in the big town." That was the way he always talked. Perhaps at that moment there was a song running through his head. There was always a song.

The girl, Eunice Hotte, a waitress, hesitated. "Are you sure you'll have the money, Kenneth?"

"I'll have it," he promised. "I told you I was going to meet this man from the steamship company."

He had told her the story during the nights they had spent together. He was to meet a man from a steamship company on one of whose ships he had worked as a seaman. He had said he had had an accident and the company owed him compensation money. He was to meet this man today.

"Don't you want to go to New York?" he asked Eunice now. "Don't you want to see Broadway?"

Eunice did. It was the dream of her life. She remembered all Kenneth had told her about the night clubs, the shows, the bright lights. Kenneth had told her, too, that he knew all the big shots around the night clubs, and that he had sung in some of the best ones. Eunice believed this as she believed everything Kenneth said. She had known him only three days, but she was in love, and Kenneth had said he loved her, too. "I'm crazy to go to New York," she told him.

Neu watched her walk over to the middle of Canal Street to take her streetcar, then he strolled along the sidewalk. He was worried. He had to get money somewhere. There was no man from any steamship line waiting to meet him. There was no money coming to him from any source. Yet it was characteristic of him to promise Eunice Hotte they would leave for New York tonight. He had to get the money. He would get it. He was not without practice in managing that sort of thing.

It was not yet eight o'clock, Sunday morning, September 17, 1933, and the New Orleans streets were empty, except for some early churchgoers. Neu kept walking out Canal Street until he came to a cheap restaurant. Here he turned in, ordered coffee and a roll, and paid for it out of his last dollar bill. He joked with the waitress just the way he had when he had first seen Eunice in the restaurant where she worked, and the waitress smiled. Neu was very handsome, with wavy brown hair, deep blue eyes, and brilliant white teeth. When he left the restaurant he walked out to the Jung Hotel. He strolled through the lobby and bought a package of cigarettes at the cigar stand. He lighted one and looked around.

An elderly man, well dressed and prosperous in appearance, was sitting on one of the sofas in the lobby reading the Sunday newspaper. Neu stepped on his cigarette, took a fresh one from the pack, and went over and sat beside the man on the sofa. He asked for a light. He had selected his victim.

Soon Neu and the man were conversing pleasantly. The gentleman said he was Sheffield Clark, Sr. He was the president of a hardware company in Nashville, Tennessee. He came to New Orleans often. Neu introduced himself as "Bill Adams." But the conversation did not last long. To Neu's disappointment Mr. Clark said he had an appointment. He had to get "something" from his room and go out. He took out his room key and swung it idly. Neu looked at the key and recorded the number in his memory. The men shook hands and Mr. Clark vanished toward the elevators.

Back out on Canal Street Neu walked in the direction of the river. He had hoped Mr. Clark would invite him up to his room as men often did when he met them in hotel lobbies. But he still felt

confident that Mr. Clark was not lost to him. Neu continued out
Canal Street until he found a pawn shop that was open on Sunday
mornings. He took off the wristwatch he wore and pawned it,
parting with it without too much regret, for it had not been his
originally and he had been wearing it only two weeks. Out of the
money he received he bought a blackjack and put it in a back
pocket.

Neu re-entered the Jung lobby at ten o'clock that night. He took
an elevator and went straight up to the floor where Mr. Clark had
his room. He found the room and knocked on the door. Mr. Clark
opened it. He was in his underwear and socks, and he looked
astonished. Neu stepped into the room jauntily, his smile big and
gleaming, and told Mr. Clark he had to talk with him. Mr. Clark
replied that he was about to retire and had to get some rest, that he
would see Neu some other time. Neu sat down on the edge of the
bed. "You'll talk to me now," he said.

Neu wasted no time in getting to the point. "I have to have
some money," he said. Then, in a few plain words, he told Mr.
Clark what he would do if he did not get the money. He would
make a fuss, and then certain accusations.

Mr. Clark was outraged. Probably he had never heard anything
like it in his life. He was sixty-three, dignified, very respectable.

"But you'll give me the money," Neu said. "You see, I have to
have money."

"I'll show you how much money I'll give you!" said Mr. Clark,
and went over to the telephone.

But he never got the receiver off the hook. Neu sprang from the
bed, the blackjack already in his hand. He crashed it down on Mr.
Clark's skull, and the man fell to the floor. Neu struck again and
again. Then he rolled Mr. Clark over and fastened his hands about
his throat and crushed his strong fingers into the elderly man's
windpipe.

When he was satisfied Mr. Clark was dead, Neu picked up the
body and put it on the bed. He arranged the head on a pillow so
the crushed skull wouldn't show and covered Mr. Clark to his

neck. Then he went into the bathroom and washed up, for he was splattered with blood.

He took his time going through Mr. Clark's effects. In the dead man's wallet he found over $300 and a ticket from the adjoining parking lot where Mr. Clark had his car. He found the car keys. Then he packed one of Mr. Clark's bags, selecting what he wanted, including a pair of shoes. He needed a new pair of shoes. Mr. Clark's fit.

It was ten-twenty-nine when he went down in the elevator. He winked at the elevator operator, a pretty girl, and made a teasing remark as she let him out into the lobby. Then he made a quick exit through a rear entrance of the hotel.

The attendant in the parking lot did not want to let him have the car at first. He looked at Neu suspiciously for a moment, as he knew Mr. Clark well, but when Neu said he was Mr. Clark's son and explained "Dad" had sent him for the car, the attendant released it to him. He told Neu, too, that he had found several new knives in the lot and that he was sure they were some of the samples his "dad" carried. Neu told him to hold them until the next day. Then Neu rolled the car out of the lot and went to get Eunice.

A maid entered Mr. Clark's room twice Monday morning, saw the form in the bed, thought he was sleeping, and went away. At ten-forty that night another maid, Mrs. Olivia Mockbee, went into the room and turned on the lights. She thought Mr. Clark looked strange. She went over to the bed and pulled back the covers. She saw the dry blood, the swollen, distorted face. She summoned the housekeeper and hotel detectives.

Neu and Eunice Hotte drove almost without stopping from about midnight Sunday, when they left New Orleans, until almost midnight Monday, when they reached Charleston. Early the next morning Neu was up. Before Eunice joined him he removed the license plates from the car and put on a cardboard sign, crudely lettered, which read "New Car in Transit." Then he and Eunice were off again. Tuesday night they spent at a hotel in Richmond. The following evening they were in New Jersey. Roaring across the Pulaski Memorial Skyway toward the entrance of the Holland Tunnel that would take them into New York, where Eunice was to see all the lights of Broadway, of which she had dreamed, the car was halted by the Jersey City police. "What did that sign mean?" they wanted to know. Where was Neu's license? They would have to come along for questioning. Eunice was not to see her bright lights.

At the police station their stories made no sense. Neu could not explain the sign, except to say that he had intended to buy a license in New York. Eunice said, truthfully, that Neu had told her he had bought the car off a used car lot from the money he had received Sunday from "the man from the steamship company." There was now a third person with them too, a young man in a sailor suit, whom Neu had picked up in New Jersey as a hitchhiker. It was discovered the young man was A.W.O.L. from the Navy. All three were locked up for the night.

The next day the police made more extensive investigations. Checking their files they came upon an astonishing fact. Just a little over two weeks before a wealthy owner of a string of moving picture theaters in Paterson, New Jersey, had been found murdered. He had been beaten over the head with a heavy object and strangled. He had last been seen in the company of a young man of about twenty-five, whose description fitted to perfection one that might be given of Neu. Detectives had Neu brought in. "Did you ever know a man named Lawrence Shead?" they asked him.

Neu denied it only for a moment. He gave way easily. He even grinned. "Sure," he said. "I killed him." Then he said, "This is his suit I'm wearing now."

On September 2 Neu had been walking around in the Times Square area of New York. He was tired and broke. Only that day he had been given an audition in a shabby night club, but he had not been given the job he wanted. Not watching where he was going he bumped heavily into a middle-aged man. He apologized and the man invited him to have a drink. Neu went along. During their conversation Neu told his troubles, and the man identified himself as Lawrence Shead. He said he had some theaters in Paterson, New Jersey, and that he might have a job for Neu. Why didn't Neu come home with him now? Neu went along, as Shead kept assuring him he used some vaudeville acts and he was sure he could use him. Late that afternoon Neu sang for Shead from the stage of an empty theater and Shead told him he was good. They then went to dinner and to Shead's apartment, where Neu spent the night on a sofa.

The next day they began drinking again. Neu said he saw Shead put three times as much whisky into Neu's drink as into his own. He asked Shead not to do that. He said he wanted a definite answer about the job. Shead told him they would "see about that later," and went on pouring whisky. Again Neu refused to drink that strong a drink.

"Shead, stop it," he said, becoming suspicious. He was a very worldly young man.

"I want you to feel good," Shead said. "We're going to have some real fun."

Then, according to Neu, Shead came over and put his arms around him. Neu hit him, and the two men began to fight. They knocked over furniture, Shead trying to grab Neu's arms, Neu slugging away in a rage. Finally he saw an electric iron on a shelf. He picked it up and crashed it down on Shead's skull. He hit him again and again, then, bending over him, he seized Shead's throat and strangled him. Apparently he was strangling what was already a corpse.

He went into Shead's bathroom and took a shower. He put on one of Shead's suits, his watch, and found the dead man's wallet. A few days later he was in New Orleans.

Then Neu gave the New Jersey police more than they had expected. "I killed another man in New Orleans Sunday night," he said, and described his murder of Clark. "I'm sorry I killed Mr. Clark," he concluded. "He seemed like a nice old man. But I was desperate for money."

When the detectives recovered from this shock Neu cleared Eunice Hotte and the sailor. He told them he had never known Eunice until last week. He had fed her a good line and she had no knowledge even now of either crime. The sailor he had picked up only a little while before they had been arrested.

In due time Neu's companions were released. Eunice was repentant. She said she would never have anything to do with a stranger again. She thought she would go to Texas for a while. The sailor was turned over to naval authorities.

Notified of Neu's apprehension and confession by the Jersey City police, the New Orleans Police Department asked at once that Neu be turned over to them to stand trial for the murder of Clark. At first the Jersey City authorities refused on the grounds that Neu must first stand trial for the Shead killing, but after two weeks of debating Jersey City decided to let New Orleans have him. It was feared that Neu might win the sympathy of a Jersey City jury because of Shead's alleged homosexual advances.

New Orleans Police Superintendent George Reyer and Chief of Detectives John Grosch themselves went to Jersey City and brought Neu back on a train. He entertained them during the trip by singing to them and relating bits of his life's history.

His full name, he said, was Louis Kenneth Neu, but he never used the Louis. He was from Savannah, Georgia, where he still had a father and other relatives. He was twenty-five years old, and he had once been married. He had been a night club singer, a soldier, and a seaman. He had traveled all over the world, and had been in New Orleans many times. His real ambition was to be a top flight night club singer. He had worked in New Orleans clubs, but only second rate ones. What he liked most, he said, were women. He had always had lots of women. All over the world women had fallen for him. He had been discharged from the army because a colonel's wife had fallen for him, although they had tried to say it was something else, that he was suffering from a psychosis. People were always doing things like that to him. It was like the time his family had locked him up in the Georgia State Mental Sanitarium. He had walked right out of that place. He couldn't stand being confined. He didn't know what he would do now that he was going to jail. He had to be outside where he could get women. He had always found getting them easy. He just turned on the old personality, and "Bam!" he could have his pick. Also, he had to sing and have an audience to listen. He could dance, too, tap, and clog. Would they like to see a few steps?

He turned on the old personality from the moment he was locked up in jail. He used it on the guards, on the other prisoners, on all visitors, including the Sisters of Mercy and Charity, the Catholic nuns who worked among the prisoners. He sang to everyone, and to himself. He was always singing, always smiling, always joking. The only thing he seemed to dislike was being alone. He encouraged company as much as he could. He wrote to newspapermen and offered them interviews. But always, when there was nothing else to do, he sang.

Police now went to work, checking the stories he told and his background. Except for gilded edges of elaboration most of what he had said was true. He had worked as a seaman on ships. He had been in the army and had been discharged as a psychotic. He had worked as a singer in night clubs. He had once spent four months in the Georgia State Mental Sanitarium. His father had placed him there, after he had been in trouble. The trouble had consisted of knocking out a taxi driver with a blackjack and stealing his cab. This had happened in Savannah, and Neu's father seems to have been able to convince the Savannah police that his son was insane. When asked about this Neu boasted that he had political pull in Georgia. "If I were there I'd be out of jail now," he bragged. "But I guess they'd have me back in the nut house. I'd rather be here!"

It was discovered, too, that he was well known around New Orleans night clubs. He always made himself known to band leaders, entertainers, and anyone else before whom he could put on an act. From time to time he had worked temporarily in a few of the clubs, but whether employed or not whenever he visited a night club he tried to talk the orchestra leader into letting him sing with the band. Sometimes this seems to have been an effort to get a job; other times it was simply part of his extreme exhibitionism.

This last trip he had arrived in New Orleans on the Thursday prior to the Sunday night he murdered Clark. He had been living at the DeSoto Hotel, where he had told employees he was an aviation instructor in the employ of the Chinese Army. Thursday, Friday, and Saturday nights he had toured the night clubs, singing in all of them. On Friday and Saturday he had picked up Eunice Hotte at midnight when she got off from work. He knew other women in New Orleans, most of them waitresses or night club employees, whom he had met on other trips. At least two were found who considered themselves engaged to him.

The trial opened on December 12, 1933. Neu's attorney, Clarence Dowling, a noted criminal lawyer in the city, tried to have Neu adjudged insane and avoid a trial, but after a thirty-three-day examination by the State's alienists, Dr. Joseph A. O'Hara and Dr. Edmund McC. Connely, Neu was declared legally sane. Later Dowling called in Dr. H. Randolph Unsworth and Dr. Foster M. Johns for another examination of Neu for the defense. Then Dowling entered a plea of insanity, and throughout the questioning of prospective jurors he asked constantly if the person being examined held any prejudice against such a plea.

When the jury was chosen Assistant District Attorney Bernard J. Cocke began reading Neu's signed confession into the record. Dowling objected on the grounds that Neu was insane at the time he had made the confession, but Judge A. D. Henriques overruled his objection, and the reading went on.

Neu sat through it all with his usual air of nonchalance, smiling and to all appearances having a very good time. All the newspapers commented on this the next day, always describing him as handsome. The *Times-Picayune* noted on December 13 that for his appearance in court he was wearing Shead's suit and Clark's shoes! On a table was other physical evidence, most of it property that had belonged to Sheffield Clark, Sr. In the court was Clark's son, Sheffield Clark, Jr. Also present was an aunt of Neu's, Mrs. Amy Burney. She gave a statement to newspaper reporters that Neu's father was ill and unable to make the trip from Savannah to New Orleans.

Dr. George H. Hauser was the first witness summoned by the

State. He told of examining Clark's body and that death had been caused by strangulation, hemorrhage, shock, and a fracture of the skull. He used District Attorney Stanley's head to illustrate the wounds on the deceased's head. Neu giggled at this.

After Dr. Hauser a number of Jung Hotel employees were called. Alcee Chaix, a room clerk, said he had known Mr. Clark for three years, and had registered him on Friday, September 15. Orvelia Barre and Thelma Journey, maids, told of entering the room to clean, seeing Clark in bed and leaving because they had thought he was still sleeping. Mrs. Olivia Mockbee then told of finding Clark dead Monday night. W. S. Barce, a house detective, described finding blood in the bathroom wash basin, after he had been summoned by Mrs. Mockbee, and the position of the body in the bed. Leatrice Woods, an elevator operator, said she had taken Neu downstairs at ten-twenty-nine that Sunday night and that he had joked with her and seemed in good humor.

When Dr. O'Hara and Dr. Connely took the stand in turn both stated that in their opinion Kenneth Neu was legally sane. Dr. O'Hara said if he were in charge of a mental sanitarium in which Neu was an inmate he would release him. Dowling asked Dr. O'Hara if his testimony was influenced by his political opinions and the doctor replied hotly that it was certainly not. Judge Henriques said the question had been out of order.

Dr. Connely testified that he believed Neu's behavior since his arrest was only an attempt to put up a cocky front, after being asked by Dowling if he considered Neu's attitude that of a sane man charged with murder. He said he wasn't convinced the real reason Neu was discharged from the Army was because he was found psychotic. "It is strange," he remarked, "that he would be discharged for that reason after being held for observation only two months and a half."

"Didn't Neu tell you there was another reason?" asked District Attorney Stanley.

"He told me he was in trouble with an army officer's wife," Dr. Connely said, "and that a court-martial would have embarrassed her and her husband."

"Do you think he was sane on September 17?" asked the district attorney.

"I believe he was," said Dr. Connely.

"Do you think he knew it was wrong to kill a person?"

"I think that he did know it was wrong," said Dr. Connely. "In fact he told me so himself while I was examining him."

When they were called, DeSoto Hotel employees identified Neu and told of his representing himself as working for the Chinese government. A maid, Lizzie McVetch, told of finding a blue shirt marked "S. Clark, Sr.," a polka dot tie, and a pair of cuff links in Neu's room after he checked out about eleven o'clock Sunday night. Robert Sims, who worked in the Jung Hotel parking lot, described Neu's calling for Clark's car and identifying himself as the murdered man's son.

Eunice Hotte told the court that Neu had seemed "perfectly normal" during the ride to New Jersey, except for the fact that he had seemed in a great hurry to get to New York. "He was singing most of the time and seemed to be enjoying himself," she said.

Police Superintendent Reyer and Chief of Detective Grosch described the trip back to New Orleans with Neu as their prisoner. Hermann Deutsch, a newspaper reporter, who had boarded the train before it reached New Orleans said that Neu seemed to realize the seriousness of the charges against him at that time. Meigs O. Frost, another reporter who had interviewed Neu, said that Neu had done much boasting to him about having women all over the world.

The defense called Mrs. Amy Burney, Neu's aunt. She said that Neu had always been unstable. His mother had died when he was six, and when his father had remarried he had been very upset. He had resented and hated his stepmother. At eight he had been incorrigible. At thirteen he had threatened to horsewhip his grandmother, with whom he was then living. At fifteen he had tried to beat up a man teacher under whom he was a student. He had left home at sixteen and gone to sea. In 1926 she said he had joined the United States Army four times, under different names, and each time deserted, finally being discharged as a psychotic. After the incident with the taxi driver his father had committed him to the mental sanitarium, but he had simply walked out and come home. Even then he had complained that he felt as if "wheels were going around in his head." Mrs. Burney added that he had been an instrument baby and that his mother had suffered from a curvature of the spine.

By now it was Friday, December 15, the fourth day of the trial. Through it all Neu's conduct and attitude had not altered a bit. Going and coming to and from the court he sang, usually Irish or popular ballads. A favorite was "Sweet Rosie O'Grady." During intermissions he frequently showed those close to him a few dance steps, tapping and clogging for the amusement or to the horror of those present. He tried constantly to joke with Clarence Dowling and with Charles A. Danna, another attorney, who was assisting Mr. Dowling in the case.

On that Friday the defense called Dr. H. Randolph Unsworth, the director of the St. Vincent de Paul Sanitarium for Mental Diseases in New Orleans, as it was then called, and Dr. Foster M. Johns to the witness stand. Dr. Unsworth stated flatly that in his opinion "Neu is now insane, was insane at the time of the murder, and has always been insane." When his turn came Dr. Johns stated that he agreed with Dr. Unsworth.

Under cross-examination Dr. Unsworth revealed that he had taken a sample of fluid from Neu's spine. Neu, he said, had cerebro-syphilis. This was the only moment in court when Neu showed emotion. For almost the first time the smile faded from his face and he went pale. Then he recovered himself and forced the smile back into place. Dr. Unsworth said he believed there was no doubt that Neu's brain had already suffered a certain amount of deterioration, a process that would continue and increase. Neu covered his eyes with a hand.

Dr. Unsworth antagonized Judge Henriques. He kept making side remarks to the jury, once pointing out to them that neither Dr. O'Hara nor Dr. Connely had taken a spinal test from Neu. He also said that after he had performed the spinal puncture he had asked Neu how he felt. Neu had said, "Doctor, I feel just like I did when

I killed Mr. Clark. I could kill you right now." After more remarks
to the jury, Judge Henriques, becoming angrier, said, "Dr.
Unsworth, you have the worst court manners I have ever seen in
my life." Dr. Unsworth left the stand and then Judge Henriques
ordered the jury to tear up notes they had been taking.

Dr. Johns added the information that Neu's face and chest had
become inflamed after the spinal test which indicated he was not
normal. He said, too, that possibly Neu's brain had been injured
at birth and that he had been further influenced psychologically by
the early death of his mother and his father's remarriage.

Assistant District Attorney Cocke opened the argument for the
State. He told the jury that all Neu's actions were those of a sane
person, and that Dr. O'Hara and Dr. Connely had found him perfectly sane. They must remember that he had been under the
observation of these doctors for thirty-three days. Dr. Unsworth and
Dr. Johns had spent only a short time with the accused, so how
could the value of the defense's psychiatrists be accurate as compared to that of the State's? He said that Dr. O'Hara and Dr.
Connely were well-known and distinguished experts in their field
and would certainly never send an insane man to the gallows.
Neither would the representatives of the State.

Mr. Cocke described what he considered Neu's motives. At least
in the case of Clark it was simply robbery. Perhaps Shead had
made amorous advances to Kenneth Neu, perhaps not, but if Shead
had done that it might be reasoned that Neu had lost his temper,
the two men had begun fighting and Neu had killed him. But
nothing of that sort had ever been brought into his killing of Clark.
He had murdered Mr. Clark with malice and after careful planning.
It was certainly as premeditated a murder as had ever been committed. He had picked Mr. Clark out in the lobby of the hotel, he
had noticed his room number, he had gone out and bought a blackjack. Then he had gone back to Mr. Clark's room and tried to
blackmail him for money in as crude a manner as could be
imagined. When Mr. Clark reached for the telephone he had
struck him, knowing that if he were arrested it would mean apprehension for the murder of Lawrence Shead. And he had not been

content with knocking him out and robbing him; he had proceeded to kill him. It had been brutal and cruel, but cold and calculated. It was the act not of a lunatic, but of a sane, ruthless man, who had no regard for human life and no thought for anyone except himself. Mr. Cocke said also that Neu's army discharge meant nothing. Perhaps Neu had feigned a psychosis. He was capable of doing that and clever enough to do it. At any rate his discharge papers showed that he was well when he was released and that no further treatment was necessary. As to the months he spent in the Georgia institution had not Neu himself boasted he had political pull and was it not natural enough for his father to have done everything to place him there rather than see him go to prison for the attack on the taxi driver?

When he addressed the jury Clarence Dowling said that Neu was insane. Dr. Unsworth and Dr. Johns had proved that Neu had syphilis of the brain. A victim of paresis was a hopeless lunatic. As a matter of fact, Neu had not even long to live. Was it just or human to send a man in his condition to the gallows? The place for him was an institution where he might live out what remained of his life. The defense had never denied that Neu had killed Mr. Clark. They were only trying to prove that it had been the act of an insane man. Neu had confessed at once. The very fact that he had so easily confessed to the Jersey City police was proof that he was not sane. None of his acts had been rational. He had made mistakes that no sane man could make. He had gone openly to the parking lot and presented the check for the car. He had left the shirt, tie, and cuff links that had belonged to Clark in his room at the DeSoto Hotel, then he had driven right back to New Jersey, where he had killed Lawrence Shead only two weeks before. True, he was going to New York, but would not a sane man have chosen some place else to go rather than risk crossing the state wherein he might be arrested at any moment, especially driving a car without license plates? No, Neu had done "everything to upset the protection his cunning mind had built for him in the hotel room where he had murdered Clark."

Mr. Dowling lashed out at Dr. O'Hara and Dr. Connely. Why

had they not taken a spinal test as had Dr. Unsworth and Dr. Johns? They had slipped up and were now willing to send Neu to the gallows to save their professional reputations.

The defense had offered evidence that Neu had always been unstable. He had been affected by his father's remarriage. He had not been a normal child. The army had recognized his condition and discharged him. His own story of the discharge being for other reasons was simply another fabrication of his disordered mind. Then his father, recognizing his condition, had committed him to an institution.

Had his conduct during the trial been normal? Would a sane man, realizing his desperate situation, act that way? No, said Mr. Dowling, Neu was not a sane man.

District Attorney Stanley closed for the State. He reminded the jury that Neu's aunt had never said she considered him insane. Her account of the forced delivery, his mother's curvature of the spine had no bearing on the case and no effect upon Neu's mental condition. His childish tantrums, his hatred of his stepmother were normal enough. His misbehavior when he was older did not indicate insanity. Were all bad boys insane? He was simply sinking deeper into an evil life, becoming a criminal. As to the matter of the spinal puncture, said the district attorney, Dr. O'Hara and Dr. Connely would have taken one had they thought it necessary. Far too much had been made of that. Neu might have syphilis, but that did not mean he was not responsible for his actions. Neu was a killer, a murderer, and a thief.

The jury was out five hours. During that time Neu sat joking with his attorneys, winking at people in the courtroom, grinning often, seeming perfectly at ease.

When the jury filed back into the room, Neu rose. The foreman gave the verdict. Guilty!

Neu bowed, took a stance as if he were about to render a song in front of a night club orchestra and made a little speech. "Gentlemen of the jury," he said, "you have my best wishes."

Going back to the Parish Prison he sang "Sweet Rosie O'Grady" at the top of his voice. When his cell door clanged behind him he did a fast tap dance.

The trial was over, but Clarence Dowling announced he would take the case to the Louisiana Supreme Court and, if necessary, to the Federal Supreme Court. For Neu it was only the beginning of the show.

He clowned all through the next few weeks. When Dowling failed to get a new trial and Neu was brought before Judge Henriques for sentencing on January 9, 1934 he was as flippant as during the trial. He heard himself sentenced to hang at a date to be set later by Governor O. K. Allen, he flipped a half dollar in the air and caught it neatly. "Good luck to you, Judge," he said, with a grin, "and good-by." Leaving the court with deputies, he flipped the coin again. "My lucky piece," he said. "Look at those nerves, boys! Look at those nerves!" To a reporter he said, "Come see me any time you like. You'll always be very welcome."

There were people who fought for him, and most of them were women. Appeals for a supreme court hearing and to the governor came from clubs and from individuals, but the Supreme Court refused to review the case and Governor Allen remained silent.

As the months went by Neu sang the time away in his cell. Then the woman came into his life. There had always been women. There was to be one even while he was in prison.

Her identity was not to be known for years to come. Whoever knew it then kept it secret, including Neu. She was a friend of the Sisters of Mercy who worked among the prisoners and they brought her to talk to Neu. She was young and beautiful and soon she was coming whenever he was allowed a visitor. In the diary he now began to keep he called her nothing but "my mystery woman," or "my beautiful, mysterious love." By the end of the summer of 1934, the fight for his life still going on, the date of execution still not set, he was writing, "She means all to me." By autumn she had converted him to the Roman Catholic faith. He was baptized in the prison chapel and the mystery woman served as his godmother. "Our love is on a high spiritual plane," he told reporters. "You wouldn't understand."

Of course the New Orleans newspapers made much of Kenneth

Neu's "mystery woman." She was described as being young and beautiful, a ravishing brunette. It was said that only the nuns, the prison chaplain, Father James Ryan, and Neu could tell her identity and none of them would. She had special privileges now and came and went as she pleased to visit Neu. She brought him flowers and reading matter, mostly of a religious nature, and spent long hours talking to him in his cell.

Neu had now become very religious. He attended mass every morning, prayed for long periods with the nuns, Father Ryan, and with his "mystery woman." He became so devout and strict that he chided other prisoners or guards if they swore in his presence. Fingering through a man's magazine he came upon what he called a "dirty picture," and he ripped it out with indignation and disgust.

However, none of this made his spirits less buoyant. He sang as much as ever and amused himself practicing dance steps. He took pains with his appearance, was always neat and clean, and combed his brown hair carefully. At least once while in prison he had his teeth fixed. He had always been very proud of his teeth.

He sang to the "mystery woman," most frequently "Love in Bloom," which they called "their song." At night he sang with his radio, a gift from his most frequent visitor, and he often wrote to radio stations requesting they play selections he liked. He began composing little songs of his own, all of them reeking with slush and sentiment, which he would try out on everybody within reach. But except for the noise he made he was a model prisoner.

When the date of his coming execution, February 1, 1935, was announced to him, he accepted it as he had all the other events since his arrest. He shrugged, grinned, and flipped his lucky coin. In his cell he composed a song entitled "I'm Fit as a Fiddle and Ready to Hang." Verses dedicated to the hangman went:

> Oh, you nasty man, hanging me
> Just 'cause you can.
> But I don't give a good-by damn,
> Oh, you nasty, nasty man.

What he really felt no one knows. Some of the people who visited him thought he felt nothing, even that he did enjoy all the attention he received, that he was so completely what we now call a moral imbecile that his own approaching death touched him no more than had his killing of Clark and Shead. Another opinion was that after being told by Dr. Unsworth that he had an incurable form of syphilis he welcomed death, perhaps even such a way of dying as hanging, and that this of course was supplemented by his conversion to Catholicism, which he thought assured him absolution of his sins, for his conversion was no doubt sincere and serious. A third opinion, one held by some of the newspapermen, was that his act was all bravado and bluff. Whatever it was it made good copy, although now and then some reporters would sicken of it. One wrote in the *Times-Picayune* that his reaction was of wanting to say to Neu, "Please! Please turn off the personality and be yourself!"

But he never turned off the personality. He was always the ham actor, the second rate night club entertainer, tapping and singing and making his speeches, grinning and bowing and making "corny" statements. If the ego ever faltered it never did in the presence of anyone else.

Toward the end the newspapers became less kind. He was referred to as a "nasal crooner." Once or twice the affair of the "mystery woman" was made to sound cheap and somewhat less than a beautiful relationship destined to be recorded as one of the great love stories of the world. In December Neu requested that no more reporters be allowed near his cell. He would give two interviews on the eve of his execution, he promised, but until then he wanted the press kept out. He had not liked the kind of publicity he had been receiving lately. From then on he saw almost no one except Father Ryan, the Sisters of Mercy and Charity, and his "mystery woman."

Just after the beginning of 1935 a woman's club made a final appeal to Governor O. K. Allen. There was no response. The governor of Louisiana was a pretty busy man in those days. Huey P. Long was in the United States Senate, but he kept Allen hopping. Too, the United States was in the depths of the Depression. Sirloin steak was selling for nineteen cents a pound, but there were no jobs for the millions of unemployed, although the new president, Franklin D. Roosevelt, had begun taking measures to alleviate the situation. New Orleans had been promised federal housing projects and some relief employment. So Neu received no attention from the governor, but if this made any difference to him, or if he had ever held any hope of a stay of execution, as usual it didn't show in his attitude.

His "mystery woman" visited him for the last time on January 31. She brought him a dozen bright red American Beauty roses and a pure white gardenia. Neu promised to carry the gardenia to the gallows. He sang "Love in Bloom" to her, for the last time.

In the morning he had gone to confession and to communion. Later he gave the two final interviews to the newspapers as he had promised. To one, Scoop Kennedy, he revealed that Barney Rapp, an orchestra leader now playing in a Cincinnati night club, but formerly of Club Forest near New Orleans, had promised to dedicate a song to him over a radio network that night. Rapp had sent him a telegram, too, which said simply, "God bless you."

Still later in the afternoon he autographed photographs of himself to give or have mailed to friends. When the time came he turned on his radio to listen to Rapp's broadcast. Speaking from the Cincinnati night club, Rapp said, "These songs are dedicated to a dear friend of mine in New Orleans." The orchestra rendered "Love in Bloom" and "June Moon." Neu sang with the orchestra, using all his preferred gestures and expressions. A little later he said he was hungry again, and a deputy brought him a chicken sandwich and a soft drink. When he had eaten he told those present, "I have to sleep tonight, boys. I want a good night's sleep. I'll see you in the morning."

The execution was scheduled for noon the next day. In the morning he received Holy Communion again and made the Way of the Cross with some of the nuns. Later he prayed for a long time in his cell with Father Ryan. That morning the *Morning*

Tribune ran a headline that stated: "NEU AND HANGMAN BOTH HAPPY AS HOUR OF EXECUTION APPROACHES."

The hangman, Henry Meyer, according to this story, had said he was happy because he had recently recovered from a heart attack, during which he had worried that he might miss the Neu hanging. Neu said he was happy because he had made his peace with God.

A little before noon Neu gave his diary to one of the nuns. "Give it to her," he said, meaning the "mystery woman." He shook hands with everyone who came to his cell and thanked them for their kindnesses. "Don't forget me," he always said.

He walked out to and mounted the steps of the gallows without any assistance, carrying the gardenia, smiling as ever. When he reached the platform he sang a verse of "Love in Bloom" one more time, and everyone knew it was for his last girl. Then he did a few tap and clog steps on the loudly reverberating steel trap. He made little jokes. Not seeing Meyer, he asked, "Where is that fellow? He can't keep me waiting all day." When Meyer came over, the black cap in his hands, Neu asked, "Has that thing been laundered since the last time you used it?" Then he looked at the crucifix Father Ryan held aloft for his gaze, and said, "That's the last thing I'll ever see, Father, isn't it?" The priest said, "The last thing, Kenneth." Meyer lifted the black cap, and Neu said, "Don't muss my hair." Meyer drew the black cap down, began adjusting the rope about the muscular young throat.

His neck was broken and laymen would have said he died instantly. Yet the doctor reported later that such was his vitality that there was still life in his body twenty minutes after the trap was sprung. Unnerved by Neu's "performance," Meyer resigned after hanging him.

No one but Father Ryan, the nuns, some prison employees, newspapermen, and the "mystery woman" attended his funeral in a Canal Street funeral parlor. The "mystery woman" had provided a proper funeral. His body was well dressed and he had three bouquets of flowers, but for all the undertaker's work, reporters said next day that the face of the man in the casket was no longer so handsome, but still showed signs of the work done by the noose.

From the funeral parlor he was taken to the Sacred Heart Church.
Here about one hundred and fifty curious Orleanians waited, staring
at the casket and at the girl who walked with the nuns. One paper
now called her "the girl in grey." Finally, the funeral reached St.
Patrick Cemetery No. 3, where Neu was lowered into a plot marked
"St. Alphonsus Orphanage," a grave which was the property of the
sisters who had been among Neu's last friends. As the "mystery
woman" left the cemetery one of the prison deputies came up to
her and gave her the gardenia Neu had carried to the gallows.
Another handed her a red rose from the grave. She walked out of
the graveyard between two nuns, her head lowered, and the three
entered a black limousine and drove away. A little later a headstone
appeared on the grave which read simply:

KENNETH NEU

Died Feb. 1, 1935

R. I. P.

The "mystery woman" had placed it there.

But even death did not keep Kenneth Neu's name out of the
New Orleans newspapers. Shortly after the funeral it was reported
that flowers were appearing on his grave regularly. Of course it was
guessed that they were placed there by the "mystery woman." Soon
she was reported seen by numerous persons, entering and leaving
the cemetery, kneeling at the grave in prayer, "a slim figure in
black," a reporter wrote. Now and then she was reported as being
heavily veiled; at other times it was said that she kept her head
down, her face concealed from view, and hurried from the cemetery
and entered an automobile that rushed her away before anyone
could observe her features. As the years passed and the flowers continued to be placed on the grave she became the New Orleans
equivalent of the "woman in black" who placed flowers on the
resting place of Valentino in Hollywood and newspapers compared
the two stories.

Now and then, too, some writer, in the telling and retelling of
the story of the girl, speculated on whether or not Kenneth Neu

should have hanged. Had he really been insane? Could a sane man have behaved in his fashion, have played the clown so relentlessly? Or had he acted that way because of a hope that he would finally be thought insane? In any case, it did Neu no good now.

Kenneth Neu had been dead fifteen years before the identity of his "mystery woman" was made public. On June 24, 1950, she was in newspaper headlines again, and for the last time.

The night before a couple running an apartment house in Esplanade Avenue broke into the apartment of one of their tenants, Aline Hull, and found her dead in her bed. Nearby was a suicide note. After his examination, the coroner reported she had died of an overdose of sleeping tablets. Now what newspapermen had obviously known for some time appeared in their accounts of the tragedy.

Aline Hull had been Kenneth Neu's last love. In 1950 she was forty-two years old, according to recent photographs still youthful and attractive in appearance. All newspaper stories of her suicide revealed it was she who had been Neu's constant visitor fifteen years before, that she had paid for his funeral, placed the headstone on his grave, and thereafter had never forgotten to decorate it with flowers.

According to these stories she had had a varied and colorful career. She had made two fortunes before she was twenty. The New Orleans *Item* said one had been made in gambling, that she had been "a vivid and flashing beauty in the gambling casinos near New Orleans in the early 1930's." This must have been wrong for she must have been about Neu's age when she met him in prison, so her gambling career, if any, must have been almost a decade earlier. It was said also that she had made a second fortune in the restaurant business. At eighteen she had married and her husband had been killed in an automobile accident. After that, possibly in her grief, she had become very religious and charitable. She had given all her money away. It was known that during the years of the Depression she supported numerous families. Recalled, too, was that in 1938 she had paid for the funeral of a mother and baby who had died in Charity Hospital so that they would not be put in a pauper's grave. It was even said that she had once been engaged to a prominent and rich New Orleans politician. During the 1940's, the years of World War II, she had worked in war plants. For some time now she had been broke.

There was some speculation as to whether or not she would be buried beside Neu. She was not. She was buried with her family in another cemetery.

But in her bedroom they found a prayerbook and in it was a pressed gardenia, brown, dry, and crumbling with age. With it was a clipping of some verses from A. E. Houseman's *A Shropshire Lad*, part of which reads:

> There sleeps in Shrewsbury jail tonight,
>   Or wakes, as may betide,
> A better lad, if things went right,
>   Than most that sleep outside.

> And naked to the hangman's noose
>   The morning clocks will ring
> A neck God made for other use,
>   Than strangling in a string.

BIBLIOGRAPHY

Asbury, Herbert. *The French Quarter*. New York, 1936.
Buell, J. W. *Metropolitan Life Unveiled, or the Mysteries and Miseries of America's Great Cities*. San Francisco, 1882.
Byrnes, Thomas. *Professional Criminals of America*. New York, 1886.
Cable, George W. *The Creoles of Louisiana*. New York, 1884.
———. *Strange True Stories of Louisiana*. New York, 1889.
Carter, Hodding. *Lower Mississippi*. New York, 1942.
Castellanos, Henry C. *New Orleans As It Was*. New Orleans, 1895.
Coates, Robert C. *The Outlaw Years*. New York, 1930.
Devol, George H. *Forty Years a Gambler on the Mississippi*. New York, 1926.
Gayarré, Charles. *History of Louisiana*. Three volumes. New York, 1854. *History of the New Orleans Police Department*. Anonymous. New Orleans, 1900.
Jewell. Edwin S. *Jewell's Crescent City*. New Orleans, 1873.
Kendall, John S. *History of New Orleans*. Three volumes. Chicago, 1922.
King, Grace. *New Orleans, the Place and the People*. New York, 1895.
Lafargue, André. *A Reign of Twenty Days; Louisiana Historical Quarterly* (July, 1925).
Mafia Lynching, The. *The New Review* (May, 1892).
Pearson, Edmund. *Studies in Murder*. New York, 1924.
Rightor, Henry. *Standard History of New Orleans*. Chicago, 1900.
Ripley, Eliza. *Social Life in Old New Orleans*. New York, 1912.
Saxon, Lyle. *Fabulous New Orleans*. New York, 1928.
———. *Lafitte the Pirate*. New York, 1930.
Saxon, Lyle, Edward Dreyer, and Robert Tallant. *Gumbo Ya-Ya*. Boston, 1945.
Twain, Mark. *Life on the Mississippi*. New York, 1903.
The files of the following New Orleans newspapers and periodicals: *The Bee*, the *Courier*, the *Daily Delta*, the *True Delta*, the *Times*, the *Daily Picayune*, the *Mascot*, *The Daily States*, the *New Orleans Item*, the *Times-Democrat*, the *Morning Tribune*, and the *Times-Picayune*.

CPSIA information can be obtained at www.ICGtesting.com
Printed in the USA
LVOW122139220812

295541LV00001B/4/P